# RESURRECTION RECONSIDERED

# Resurrection Reconsidered

## Thomas and John in Controversy

Gregory J. Riley

FORTRESS PRESS · MINNEAPOLIS

RESURRECTION RECONSIDERED
Thomas and John in Controversy

Cover design: Ann Elliot Artz, Studio Artz

Cover art: Doubting Thomas. S. Domingo de Silos.
    Stone carving, eleventh century.

Interior design and composition: Kelby Bowers, Compublishing, Cincinnati, Ohio

Library of Congress Cataloging-in-Publication Data

Riley, Gregory John, 1947–
    Resurrection reconsidered : Thomas and John in Controversy/
Gregory John Riley.
        p.    cm.
    Includes bibliographical references and indexes.
    ISBN 0-8006-2846-2 (alk. paper)
        1. Gospel of Thomas—Criticism, interpretation, etc. 2. Bible.
N.T. John—Criticism, interpretation, etc. 3. Resurrection—
History of doctrine—Early church. ca. 30–600. I. Title.
BS2860.T52R55    1995
229'.8—dc20
                                                    94-39490
                                                        CIP

The Paper used in this publication meets the minimum requirements of American National Standard for Information Sciences — Permanence of Paper for Printed Library Materials, ANSI Z329.48-1984. ∞™

Manufactured in the U.S.A.                                    AF 1-2846

99    98    97    96    95    1    2    3    4    5    6    7    8    9    10

# Contents

# *Acknowledgments*

Several scholars and friends have read this book and offered kind and intelligent critique. I would like to thank especially Helmut Koester, Demetrios Trakatellis and Gregory Nagy, all of Harvard University, Bernadette Brooten of Brandeis University, and Birger Pearson of University of California at Santa Barbara, for careful reading and comments both perceptive and constructive. Others, friends and fellow travelers, have shared stimulating conversation over aspects of the concepts and arguments, and in ways unknown to themselves given encouragement and direction, among whom are Paul Morrissette, Kimberly Patton, Bruce Beck, Kerry and Linda Kunst, and especially, over some years, Susan and Mark Riley.

# Abbreviations

| | |
|---|---|
| *1 Apol.* | Justin Martyr, *1 Apology* |
| 1QH | *Thanksgiving Hymns* from Qumran Cave 1 |
| *Ad Autol.* | Theophilus, *Ad Autolycum* |
| *Ad Phil.* | Polycarp, *Letter to Philippians* |
| *Adv. Haer.* | Irenæus, *Against Heresies (Adversus Haereses)* |
| *Adv. Marc.* | Tertullian, *Against Marcion (Adversus Marcionem)* |
| *AJA* | *American Journal of Archaeology* |
| *Apost. Const.* | *Apostolic Constitutions* |
| *ATh* | *Acts of Thomas* |
| *BA* | *Biblical Archaeologist* |
| BibOr | Biblica et Orientalia |
| *BJ* | Josephus, *Bellum Judaicum (The Jewish War)* |
| *BJRL* | *Bulletin of the John Rylands University Library of Manchester* |
| BJS | Brown Judaic Studies |
| *BTB* | *Biblical Theological Bulletin* |
| *BTh* | *Book of Thomas* |
| *CBQ* | *Catholic Biblical Quarterly* |
| *CIL* | *Corpus inscriptionem Latinarum* |
| *Comm. in Jn.* | Origen, *In Johannem Commentarius* |
| *Contra Ar.* | Athanasius, *Contra Arius* |
| *Contra Iud.* | Cyprian, *Treatise 12: Contra Iudaeum* |
| *CSCA* | *California Studies in Classical Antiquity* |
| *De Exhort. Cast.* | Tertullian, *De Exhortatione Castitatis* |
| *De Monog.* | Tertullian, *De Monogamia* |
| *De Princ.* | Origen, *De Principiis* |
| *De Res.* | *De Resurrectione* (Athenagoras or Justin Martyr) |
| *De Res. Carnis* | Tertullian, *De Resurrectione Carnis* |
| *De Res. Mort.* | Tertullian, *De Resurrectione Mortuorum* |
| *Dial. Try.* | Justin Martyr, *Dialogue with Trypho* |
| *Eccl.* | Aristophanes, *Ecclesiazuae* |
| *Enn.* | Plotinus, *Enneades* |
| *Epist.* | *Epistulae* (various writers) |
| *Epist. Apost.* | *Epistula Apostolorum* |
| *Ep. Johannis* | Augustine, *Tractatus X in Epistula Joannis* |

| | |
|---|---|
| FB | Forschung zur Bibel |
| *GPt* | *Gospel of Peter* |
| *GRBS* | *Greek, Roman, and Byzantine Studies* |
| *GTh* | *Gospel of Thomas* |
| HDR | Harvard Dissertations in Religion |
| *HE* | Eusebius, *History of the Church (Historica Ecclesiastica)* |
| *Hom. Joh.* | John Chrysostom, *Homily on John* |
| *HR* | *History of Religions* |
| *HSCP* | *Harvard Studies in Classical Philology* |
| HSM | Harvard Semitic Monographs |
| *HTR* | *Harvard Theological Review* |
| ICC | International Critical Commentary |
| *IEJ* | *Israel Exploration Journal* |
| *IG* | *Inscriptiones Graecae* |
| *Il.* | Homer, *Iliad* |
| *Int* | *Interpretation* |
| IRT | Issues in Religion and Theology |
| *IT* | Euripides, *Iphigenia Taurica* |
| *JBL* | *Journal of Biblical Literature* |
| *JHS* | *Journal of Hellenic Studies* |
| *JR* | *Journal of Religion* |
| *JSNT* | *Journal for the Study of the New Testament* |
| *JTS* | *Journal of Theological Studies* |
| *Leg. All.* | Philo, *Legum Allegoriae* |
| *Legatio* | Athenagoras, *Legatio pro Christianis* |
| *Met.* | *Metamorphoses* (Apuleius or Ovid) |
| *Mus.* | *Muséon* |
| NHC | Nag Hammadi Codex |
| NHS | Nag Hammadi Studies |
| *NovT* | *Novum Testamentum* |
| NovTSup | Novum Testamentum, Supplements |
| *NTS* | *New Testament Studies* |
| *Od.* | Homer, *Odyssey* |
| *Opif. Mun.* | Philo, *De Opificio Mundi* |

| | |
|---|---|
| P. Oxy. | Oxyrhynchus Papyri |
| *Pyth.* | Pindar, *The Pythian Odes* |
| *Q Gen* | Philo, *Quaestiones et solutiones in Genesium* |
| *Refutatio* | Hippolytus, *Refutatio omnium Haeresium* |
| *Rep.* | Plato, *Republic* |
| *RTP* | *Revue de théologie et de philosophie* |
| *Sanh.* | *Sanhedrin* |
| SBLDS | Society of Biblical Literature Dissertation Series |
| SBT | Studies in Biblical Theology |
| *SJT* | *Scottish Journal of Theology* |
| *SecCent* | *Second Century* |
| *Smyr.* | Ignatius, *Letter to the Smyrnaens* |
| SNTSMS | Society for New Testament Studies Monograph Series |
| *SE* | *Studia Evangelica* |
| *Strom.* | Clement of Alexandria, *Stromateis* |
| Syr. | Syriac |
| *TDNT* | *Theological Dictionary of the New Testament* |
| *TGl* | *Theologie und Glaube* |
| *Tral.* | Ignatius, *Letter to the Trallians* |
| *TS* | *Theological Studies* |
| TU | Texte und Untersuchungen zur Geschichte der altchristlichen Literatur |
| *Tusc. Disp.* | Cicero, *Tusculan Disputations* |
| *TZ* | *Theologische Zeitschrift* |
| *TZeb* | *Testament of Zebulon* |
| *VC* | *Vigliae christianae* |
| Vulg. | Vulgate |
| ZNW | Zeitschrift für die Neutestamentliche Wissenschaft |

# Introduction

Early Christian missionaries proclaimed the resurrection of Jesus throughout the Roman world not only as the founding event of their own faith but also as the central event in human history. Yet the claim that anyone might rise bodily from the dead was met in the Hellenic world by utter disbelief; it shocked the listeners into ridicule. We are told that the Athenians sneered at the apostle Paul; the philosopher Celsus thought the idea was disgusting and impossible. Even more remarkable, however, was that for the first four hundred years of the movement many Christians, often the most educated and often in the majority, agreed with the opponents. Jerome complained as late as the fifth century that the Eastern Church had written the great ecumenical creed of Constantinople in such a way as to be able to continue to deny resurrection of the flesh. This opinion, that neither Jesus nor anyone else could rise from the dead in the flesh, had ancient roots in Greco-Roman culture and in earliest Christianity. Representative of such a view was the brand of apostolic Christianity which arose around the figure of the disciple Thomas and is found in the earliest document which bears his name, the *Gospel of Thomas*.

The *Gospel of Thomas* was born, as was Christianity itself, in the midst of controversy. It is in conscious debate with aspects of the religious world of the New Testament writings, and some of its concepts, teachings, and associated traditions are themselves countered in Paul, the Gospels, and elsewhere. The New Testament writings, for example, while displaying remarkable diversity among themselves, proclaim in general the crucifixion and resurrection of Christ, warn of the apocalyptic end of this world in vivid imagery, and recommend faith, obedience, and ritual as the central spiritual modes. Much of this material is never mentioned in *Thomas*, let alone prescribed. In this the *Gospel of Thomas* is hardly unique: each of the other Gospels, and especially Paul, has its own perspective

1

and polemic, tacit or explicit. One may but mention Paul's advocacy of salvation by faith apart from works of the Law, and the counter-position of the epistle of James, that a person is justified by works, and not by faith alone.[1] As this one example illustrates, and many others could be cited, a situation of mutual disagreement and dissension was already present among the first Christian communities for which we have evidence.

This study centers on a protracted debate within early Christianity concerning a foundational aspect of the *Gospel of Thomas* and its related literature: the concept of the body and resurrection. It traces the background of this idea in the Semitic and Greco-Roman world, and its expression in the Thomas literature as a whole: the *Gospel of Thomas*, *Book of Thomas*, and *Acts of Thomas*. But the inspiration for the study, and its main focus, is the controversy between the two closely related Christian communities of Thomas and John, between the *Gospel of Thomas* and the Gospel of John, on the issue of resurrection, expressed in John most clearly in the story of Doubting Thomas.

By far the majority of work on the *Gospel of Thomas* compares it with the Synoptic Gospels; relatively little has centered on its relationship to the Gospel of John. One notable exception is an influential article by R. E. Brown, "The Gospel of Thomas and St John's Gospel."[2] In this work, Brown assumes for no stated reason that the *Gospel of Thomas* is a work later than the Gospel of John,[3] and then proceeds to "demonstrate" its dependence on John. Yet so great are the difficulties in finding dependence that he concludes that there were at least two, and perhaps several, intermediaries between John and the *Gospel of Thomas*[4] This desperate solution stems from the

---

1. Romans 3:28 *inter alia* and James 2:24.

2. R. E. Brown, "The Gospel of Thomas and St John's Gospel," in *NTS* 9 (1962) 155–177.

3. "Presuming that *GTh* is the later work, . . . ": R. E. Brown, "The Gospel of Thomas and St John's Gospel," 157.

4. R. E. Brown, "The Gospel of Thomas and St John's Gospel," 177. He describes the problem at the outset, that "it is not always possible to determine whether John was a direct or only an indirect source for *GTh*, because there is a possibility that

fact "that there is not a single verbatim citation of John" in the entire *Gospel of Thomas*[5] Such a reality itself should give one pause. "Dependency" of Thomas on John not only is not demonstrable, it is indeed nothing more than a presupposition of some early *Thomas* scholarship to which Brown and others subscribed, which obscured the actual relationship of the texts. Instead, the two Gospels stand in a somewhat similar and parallel position relative to the traditions preserved in the Synoptics. Each expresses its own distinctive and at times opposing theology in part by manipulating this common inheritance, yet the two are much closer to each other in spirit than either is to the Synoptics. In addition, the two Gospels share material that is not found in these other texts, or interpret material in a common manner but distinct from the Synoptics. One aspect of this situation is that it is possible to see John at points as a correction not of some lost Gnosis, but of ideas actually preserved in the *Gospel of Thomas*. Likewise and to a significant extent, *Thomas* is in a reciprocal relationship with John. This reciprocity, as will be seen, is much in evidence in the pericope of Doubting Thomas.

Although Thomas never appears as more than a name on the disciple lists in the Synoptics, in John he is a significant figure. According to Schnackenburg,[6]

> The prominence of Thomas may derive from the fourth gospel's connection with Syria . . . ; the Acts of Thomas and the Gospel of Thomas probably come from there, where this apostle was particularly venerated. . . . Probably the Thomas tradition developed in Syria in two directions, one in the Johannine circle, in which he is less prominent than the other disciples and is the type of the disciple who takes a long time to

---

GTh has used an intermediary, oral or written, that was familiar with John" (157). Yet his investigation and conclusions show no *direct* influence at all. *Indirect* influence through two (or several) intermediaries can be claimed for almost any two similar texts of debatable date, in either direction of dependence.

5. R. E. Brown, "The Gospel of Thomas and St John's Gospel," 175.

6. Rudolph Schnackenburg, *The Gospel according to St John* (trans. by David Smith and G. A. Kon; New York: Crossroad, 1987) 2.327.

understand, and one in Gnostic circles, where he is regarded as the recipient of secret revelation. The Johannine portrait of the disciple is definitely the earlier stage, and the basis for the later development of the Gnostic cult.

Schnackenburg correctly recognizes that the reason for the prominence of Thomas in John's Gospel is the contact of the two communities of John and Thomas. His analysis, however, is hampered as was that of Brown by the assumption that the Syrian Thomas tradition developed in dependence upon the Gospel of John in "Gnostic circles" of a post-Johannine era. This is to overlook the basis for the development of the Thomas tradition: Thomas in Syria was the center of a community, much as was Peter or James or Paul, around whom tradition developed and in whose name literature was written; similarly the Johannine community had its own tradition and literature around the figure of John. It is far more consonant with the evidence to view Thomas Christianity in Syria as a continuum, founded in the early decades of the Christian movement, which developed in its own linguistic and cultural environment according to its own lights. The character "Thomas" in John is a literary portrayal of the dominant figure in someone else's community and is meant to convey a message to that community. The picture of Thomas in John, far from being the original source of Thomas tradition, is an attempt to influence a Thomas Christianity already in existence. The earlier stage is the living Syrian Thomas tradition that John is at pains to counter.

Thomas is found in three passages in John 11–20.[7] In chapter 11 concerning the raising of Lazarus, he is the only disciple of the Twelve named. In chapter 14, he appears with Philip questioning Jesus. If chapter 20 is seen, as it should be, as the original ending of the Gospel, then the importance of the Doubting Thomas pericope to

---

7. The name appears in John 11:16; 14:5; 20:24 (26, 27, 28); and 21:2. In all but 14:5 he is further identified as "the one called 'twin'" [Θωμᾶς ὁ λεγόμενος Δίδυμος]. Chapter 21 is left out of this discussion, as Thomas is mentioned in 21:2 as a means of linking Chapter 21 to the conclusion of Chapter 20.

the author of John, coming as it does immediately before the conclusion, is quite apparent: the issue of Thomas is the last subject dealt with by the evangelist. Chapter 11 is the resurrection of Lazarus, which closes out the public ministry of Jesus, prefiguring the crucifixion and his own resurrection. Chapter 20 contains the post-resurrection appearances of Jesus, and closes with the pericope of Doubting Thomas. Thus the Thomas passages bracket the concluding section of John, the Farewell Discourses, and Passion narrative. Two are concerned with the theme of resurrection; one is within the discourse about the way to Jesus' final heavenly destination.

The question arises as to the purpose of these passages: Why is Thomas the only disciple named, and that negatively, before the raising of Lazarus (John 11:16)? Why does Thomas not know the place ($\tau \acute{o} \pi o \varsigma$) of Jesus, nor the way to get there (John 14:5)? Why should Thomas appear as the Doubter in chapter 20, as the only negative example among the disciples? Secondary literature has in the main not addressed these questions, nor noticed that there is a Johannine message here which has remained unattended. The "historical" Thomas was, according to the Gospels, an original disciple and apostle of Jesus. The Thomas literature and tradition that arose around him was sponsored by a community in close spiritual proximity to that of John. Yet the two communities differed fundamentally on, among other doctrines, the central issues of the Doubting Thomas pericope: physical resurrection, faith, and the deity of Christ. John, as this study will show, is communicating a message through the figure of Doubting Thomas not only to his own community and subsequent generations, but also to those who followed and valued the apostle Thomas. It is worth some effort, then, to set the "problem" of this pericope, and then explore John's creative use of the character of Doubting Thomas.

# Chapter One

# Afterlife and Resurrection in the Ancient Mediterranean World
## *The Background of the Thomas Tradition*

The contrasting ideas concerning afterlife and the body in the first century in Palestine present a variegated background against which the resurrection of Jesus was proclaimed. Several interpreters have collected passages from the Bible, intertestamental Judaism, and less often Greek authors, in order to trace the history and development of the idea of resurrection among the Jews.[1] The results demonstrate more or less successfully that the doctrine of physical resurrection had precedent, and conversely that Christians had to combat certain ideas of the supposed Greek concept of "immortality of the soul,"

---

1. For example, Thomas Wilson, *St. Paul and Paganism* (Edinburgh: T. and T. Clark, 1927); Aimo T. Nikolainen, *Der Auferstehungsglaube in der Bibel und ihrer Umwelt* (Helsinki: Druckerei — A. G. der finnischen Literaturgesellschaft, 1944); Robert Martin-Achard, *From Death to Life: A Study of the Development of the Doctrine of the Resurrection in the Old Testament* (trans. by John Penney Smith; Edinburgh and London: Oliver and Boyd, 1960); S. H. Hooke, *The Resurrection of Christ as History and Experience* (London: Darton, Longman and Todd, 1967); André-Marie Dubarle, "Belief in Immortality in the Old Testament and Judaism," in Pierre Benoit and Roland Murphy, eds., *Immortality and Resurrection* (Herder and Herder, 1970) 34–45; G. Nickelsburg, *Resurrection, Immortality and Eternal Life in Intertestamental Judaism* (Harvard Theological Studies XXVI; Cambridge, Mass.: Harvard Univ. Press, 1972); Günter Stemberger, *Der Leib der Auferstehung: Studien zur Anthropologie und Eschatologie des palästinischen Judentums im neutestamentlichen Zeitalter (ca. 170 v. Cr.—100 n. Chr.)* (Rome: Biblical Institute Press, 1972); Hans Clemens Caesarius Cavallin, *Life After Death: Paul's Argument for the Resurrection of the Dead in 1 Cor 15. Part I: An Enquiry into the Jewish Background* (Lund, Sweden: CWK Gleerup, 1974); C. K. Barrett, "Immortality and Resurrection," in Charles S. Duthie, ed., *Resurrection and Immortality: A Selection from the Drew Lectures on Immortality* (London: Samuel Bagster and Sons, 1979) 68–88; Otto Kaiser and Eduard Lohse, *Death and Life* (trans. by John E. Steely; Nashville: Abingdon, 1981); Ramsay MacMullen, *Paganism in the Roman Empire* (New Haven and London: Yale Univ. Press, 1981); K. Corrigan, "Body and Soul in Ancient Religious Experience," in A. H. Armstrong, ed., *Classical Mediterranean Spirituality: Egyptian, Greek, Roman* (New York: Crossroad, 1986) 360–383.

which denied the possibility of fleshly postmortem survival, as they spread the gospel of Jesus throughout the Roman world.

It has been less often noted how late a development in early Christian history was the doctrine of the physical resurrection of Christ, and how common the "heresy" of its rejection in the Church.[2] The original Christian idea was, if not identical with, then far more in accord with "spiritual resurrection" and "Greek" ideas than with mundane restoration of corpses. In response, for example, to the Corinthian party which denied the resurrection of the body, Paul declared that Jesus had appeared to many irrefutable witnesses (1 Cor 15:3ff.), but in a transformed "spiritual body" (1 Cor 15:44). This body was a "dwelling from heaven" made by God and given in exchange for the earthly body (2 Cor 5:1-4), for "flesh and blood cannot inherit the kingdom of God" (1 Cor 15:50). Mark, the earliest canonical Gospel, contains no physical demonstration of Jesus' postmortem body. All three Synoptic Gospels preserve the saying that the resurrected believers would become like the angels (Mark 12:25 and parallels). Among non-Christian Greeks and Romans, some believed that there was no survival at all beyond the grave, while the majority opinion was clearly that of nonphysical, postmortem survival. None at all conceived of fleshly resurrection of the body.

Opinion among Jews was similar, but ill-defined and among some groups mixed with ideas of a general resurrection of differing types. The contrasting and exclusive pair, often seen in secondary literature, of "the Jewish belief in physical resurrection" as opposed to "the Greek idea of immortality of the soul" is far too simplistic to substantiate.[3] Greeks certainly did not believe in physical resurrection, but neither did many Jews; even among the Pharisees and Es-

2. The lessons learned from Walter Bauer could be applied in principle to this more limited subject: Walter Bauer, *Orthodoxy and Heresy in Earliest Christianity* (Robert Kraft and Gerhard Krodel, eds.; trans. by the Philadelphia Seminar on Christian Origins; Philadelphia: Fortress Press, 1971) 100, 147.

3. For an example of this misleading antithesis, cf. Grant R. Osborne, *The Resurrection Narratives: A Redactional Study* (Grand Rapids: Baker Book House, 1984) 219: "The Jews would never have accepted a resurrection of the spirit without the body." Also, M. E. Dahl, *The Resurrection of the Body* (SBT 36; London: SCM Press, 1962) 89. On differences among Jews, and rejection of this misleading opposition, see infra, and cf. Peter Carnley, *The Structure of Resurrection Belief*, 231: "There was

senes evidence is at best ambiguous, and very Hellenistic. One would surmise from what evidence there is that the majority of pre-Christian Jews believed in something other than the "Jewish belief in physical resurrection," and that none had yet conceived of the doctrine of the resurrection of the flesh, highly developed in the second century CE and later, which seems to determine much modern thinking.

The Church moved gradually toward a doctrine of the fleshly postmortem body of Christ, away from the "spiritual" conception. Yet throughout the early centuries of the Empire Christians continued to believe the earlier idea against the arguments to the contrary. No study to my knowledge has sufficiently explained what "life after death" meant to the ancients, especially those not well schooled in the philosophies of Greece, Rome, and Jewish Hellenism; more importantly, no study has addressed how "immortality of the soul" could account for the original resurrection and appearances, and continue to stand for many Christians in place of and against the idea of "physical resurrection" maintained by others. This point needs emphasis: "immortality of the soul" explained the resurrection of Christ for many Christians for centuries, and did so based on the same traditions and texts as those used by the "orthodox" who advocated resurrection of the flesh. One such early community was that which arose around the disciple Thomas.

If so, then the spiritual risen Jesus was far more substantial than one would assume from modern secondary literature, and the view of the Thomas tradition far more reasonable and understandable. It is worth asking the ancients: What was the "stuff" of the soul after death? What was it made of, and how did it function? We shall see that all of the things claimed as proofs for the "physical" risen Christ in the Gospel accounts could be said for the "spiritual" Jesus also, and therefore that the proofs offered by Luke and John and the Fathers, for those disposed to see them in a contrary light, proved

---

by no means a clear and uniform tradition which can be used to clarify Paul's views. Paul inherited a wide spectrum of beliefs which had evolved in Hellenistic Judaism, . . . "

nothing. Thomas Christians did not accept the idea of the resurrection of the flesh, yet they were, one assumes, as faithful and intelligent as any Christians: How, and in what form, did they see the "Living Jesus"?[4] The following chapter accounts for how they and other Christians of similar opinion were able to interpret the evidence of the appearance traditions in categories which did not necessitate a belief in a fleshly risen Christ.

## Afterlife in Israel

### *Traditional Views*

Early Israelite speculation on the fate of the dead did not include the hope of physical resurrection at all. We are told that "We shall certainly die; and we are like water poured out on the ground which cannot be gathered up" (2 Sam 14:14). The dead cannot be "gathered up." Such views were in continuity with the traditions of Mesopotamia and Canaan, and similar to that in archaic Greece, that the departed could expect little more than a shadowy existence in Sheol/Hades under the earth.[5] In Psalm 88, for example, the writer despairs under what is perceived as the anger of the Lord, describing himself as one of the dead (vv. 6–7 and 11b):

> Among the dead I am cast away, like the slain who are forgotten in the grave, whom you remember no more, for they are cut off from your hand. You have put me in the pit of the [earth's] lowest parts, in the dark places,[6] in the depths. . . . Do the shades rise, to praise you?

---

4. The "Living Jesus" is the title of Jesus in the opening line of the *Gospel of Thomas* in both the Coptic and Greek versions.

5. Cf. Walther Eichrodt, *Theology of the Old Testament* (trans. by J. A. Baker; Philadelphia: Westminster Press, 1967) 2.95–96, 210–211; and Bruce Vawter, "Intimations of Immortality and the Old Testament," in *JBL* 91 (1972) 145–157.

6. Cf. Ps 63:10 where the term "lowest parts" (תַּחְתִּיּוֹת) is in parallelism with Sheol; Ps 143:3 where the term "dark places" (מַחֲשַׁכִּים) is used of the place of the dead.

In this view, the dead neither rise nor participate in any other aspect of the cult of Yahweh.[7] The attempt made by the psalmist is to "bribe" Yahweh with praises into offering help while he is yet alive, based on the belief that the dead are incapable of praise or any substantial activity: their world is one of silence. If the psalmist dies, Yahweh will be deprived of the praise he needs and desires. This argument is reiterated in Psalm 115:17: "The dead do not give praise to Yah, nor do any who go down into silence."[8] Sirach 17:27–28 reflects this belief in the virtual non-existence of the dead,[9] and therefore the continued efficacy of the "praise–bribe" in the second century BCE:[10]

> *Who will sing praises to the Most High in Hades,*
>   *as those who are alive and give thanks?*
> *From the dead, as from one who does not exist, thanksgiving has*
>   *ceased.*

The *cultus* of Yahweh ceased in the grave.[11] Existence in the underworld for the worshipper of God is as non-existence.

The means of postmortem survival recommended by the author of Sirach is twofold: that of a good name which survives in the mem-

---

7. Cf. Job 7:9 יוֹרֵד שְׁאוֹל לֹא יַעֲלֶה "he who goes down to Sheol does not come up," and Job's lament about his own impending non-return from the netherworld in 10:20–22 and 16:22.

8. Cf. also Ps 6:5 (6 Heb); Ps 30:9–10. In Isa 38:18–19, the author makes the argument that the reason why the Lord saved the life of Hezekiah was that he might give back the praise the Lord desires, since "Sheol cannot thank you, . . . the living, they thank you."

9. Cf. Yehezkel Kaufmann, *The Religion of Israel* (abridged and trans. by M. Greenberg; Chicago: Univ. of Chicago Press, 1960) 311–316, for relevant passages.

10. The Hebrew of 7:17, "the expectation of man is worms," may lead one to think that Sirach teaches the nonexistence of the person after death (cf. 14:19). But certain other passages speak of death as "rest" (30:17), and of a reward from God on the day of death (11:26 "For it is easy for the Lord on the day of death to reward a person according to his ways"; ὅτι κοῦφον ἔναντι κυρίου ἐν ἡμέρᾳ τελευτῆς ἀποδοῦναι ἀνθρώπῳ κατὰ τὰς ὁδοὺς αὐτοῦ). It is clear nevertheless that postmortem existence is not a focus for moral exhortation, as it would be if such life had substance.

11. "The dead had no further relationship with" Yahweh: Eichrodt, *Theology of the Old Testament*, 2.221. "To be sure, YHWH rules Sheol, yet there is no relation between him and the dead. . . . The realm of the dead in Israelite religion is godless": Kaufmann, *The Religion of Israel*, 314.

ory of subsequent generations, and progeny. These two avenues to immortality are also, as we shall see, two traditional goals of the ancient Greek, to leave behind a lasting name and children. So the author declares that the one devoted to "the study of the Law of the Most High" (38:34) will never pass away: "his memory will not disappear, and his name will live through all generations" (39:9), for "a good name lasts forever" (41:13; also 37:26). So also are the "godly, whose righteous deeds have not been forgotten" (44:10); they will live on in their children, who carry on their name and good reputation (44:13–14):[12]

> *Their offspring will continue forever,*
> *and their glory will never be blotted out.*
> *Their bodies are buried in peace,*
> *but their name lives on for generations.*

Thus the means to immortality is not postmortem survival or bodily resurrection, but one's lasting reputation and continuing posterity.

Yet even this is called into question by the writer of Ecclesiastes.[13] The impermanence of one's reputation after death, a matter which depends on the ephemeral nature of human memory, shows this hope to be futile. We are told (Eccl 2:16):

> *There is no perpetual remembrance for the wise man any*
> *more than for the fool.*
> *Because in the days to come, everything will be forgotten,*
> *and as the wise man dies, so does the fool.*

The idea that one should hope for immortality in a good name is seen, as all else in Ecclesiastes, as vanity. This perhaps stems from the author's own experience and somewhat cynical observations of

---

12. Cf. also Sirach 30:4–6.

13. Cf. Howard N. Bream, "Life without Resurrection: Two Perspectives from Qoheleth," in H. N. Bream, R. D. Heim, and C. A. Moore, eds., *A Light unto My Path: Old Testament Studies in Honor of Jacob M. Myers* (Philadelphia: Temple Univ. Press, 1974) 49–65.

the author's compatriots, but it is founded on the ancient and persistent idea that no one survives death. Humans were seen in this regard to be in the same predicament as the animals. We read (Eccl 3:19–20):

> For the situation of the children of Adam and the situation of the animals is the same: just as one dies, so does the other. They all have the same breath. Indeed, there is no advantage to the human over the animal, for all is vanity. 20 They all go to the same place. They all came from the dust, and they all return to the dust.

The grave was the end of all useful life. Yet there was in the writer's world the nearly ubiquitous tradition of Sheol (9:10), the place of the shades of the dead. There the cult of Yahweh ceased and "life" was as nonexistence. Yet for those less skeptical than the author of Ecclesiastes, it was not actual nonexistence.

## Cult of the Dead

If the dead no longer served Yahweh, they were nevertheless not lost to the living. As in Mesopotamia and Canaan, *cultus* of the dead existed in Israel.[14] There is a curious uncertainty as to the powers of the dead and their ability to affect the living both in Palestine and, as we shall see, in Greece. Fear of and care for the dead body, proper burial, cult practices for the dead,[15] and necromancy[16] were all present in

---

14. See the interesting discussion of the cult of the dead in Israel by Jack N. Lightstone, *The Commerce of the Sacred: Mediation of the Divine among Jews in the Greco-Roman Diaspora* (BJS 59; Chico: Scholars Press, 1984) 57–87. Also, Mark S. Smith, *The Early History of God* (San Francisco: Harper and Row, 1990) 126–132.

15. *Inter alia nonnulla*: Deut 26:14 (feeding the tithe to the dead); Isa 8:19–20 (necromancy; also Deut 18:10–11); Isa 57:6 (making libations and grain offerings to the dead); Isa 65:4 (visitation of and incubation in tombs); Ps 106:28 (eating sacrifices to the dead); as apotropaic mourning rites: Lev 19:28 (cutting one's flesh for the dead; also Deut 14:1); Lev 21:1–5 ("defiling oneself", i.e., putting dirt on one's head or rolling in dirt [or worse], and shaving bald spots for the dead).

16. Perhaps the best known example of necromancy in the Hebrew Bible is the conversation of Saul and the dead Samuel in 1 Sam 28:3–19. The correspondence of Samuel with the prophet Teiresias of Greece, the only Greek who keeps his mental powers in Hades and retains his prophetic function, is worth noting (*Od.*

ancient Israel. Despite censure, the dead were not forgotten in the popular religion.[17] Their presence in the grave and the family[18] was somehow felt to continue, and gifts and prayers were offered at the tombs to insure blessing and gain information for the living. Some tombs were outfitted with tubes or openings through which the petitioners could insert gifts of food or especially water.[19] Such constructions were expensive, and therefore limited in social class; far more usual would have been offering by simple deposition upon or next to the grave. An example of such funeral cult is the instruction given by Tobit (4:27) before his death to his son: "Pour out your bread upon the grave of the righteous and do not give it to sinners." The son is told to *limit* his offering to the just.[20] The shadowy existence in the underworld is abetted by the living.

Such a *cultus* of offering food and water to the dead, even putting these offerings into the tomb, while the living knew full well that no body remained to consume it, presupposed some belief in substantial but bodiless existence in the afterlife. The literature of Wisdom

---

10.492–495). Cf. Cyrus H. Gordon, *The Common Background of Greek and Hebrew Civilizations* (New York: W. W. Norton, 1965) 260. Manasseh permits necromancy in 2 Kgs 21:6.

17."From the Deuteronomistic material it is clear that there was an ongoing battle in ancient Israel to resist cults of the dead, which seem to have had a lasting appeal in certain forms of 'popular religion.' The prophetic material supports such a conclusion": Theodore J. Lewis, *Cults of the Dead in Ancient Israel and Ugarit* (HSM 39; Atlanta: Scholars Press, 1989) 174.

Some talismanic use of the bones of one's parents (making spoons of the bones of one's father and mother, attributed apparently to Pharisees) is mentioned in Mishnah *Yadaim* 4.6.

18.The family was kept together even in the grave: family members were buried together. The phrase "gathered to one's fathers" as a circumlocution for death had a literal application in burial custom. Cf. Eric M. Meyers, "Secondary Burials in Palestine," in *BA* 33 (1970) 91–114, esp. 101f.

19.Cf. Lewis, *Cults of the Dead*, 179f. Cf. also the similar constructions in Greek tombs discussed below.

20.Bickerman, in reference to another limit on such offerings, takes Deut 26:14 to prohibit the giving of consecrated food only for the dead, and to allow offerings of other foods and items in this common practice: Elias J. Bickerman, *The Jews in the Greek Age* (Cambridge, Mass.: Harvard Univ. Press, 1988) 271. Not only texts, but also "Excavations have shown that there was a time when the Israelites followed the Canaanite custom of depositing food in the tomb": Roland de Vaux, *Ancient Israel* (New York: McGraw-Hill, 1965) 1.60.

sees this as near nonexistence, and later Yahwistic religion polemicizes against such cult. But in the popular mind, the dead could eat and communicate with their visitors. Such *cultus* also implied that the souls of the dead felt discomfort and lack.[21] The dead could even appear to the living, if one recalls the example of Samuel's appearance to Saul, without resurrecting, with the excarnated bones still in the grave.[22] Similar examples will be noted in Greece; the implications for differing interpretations of the post-Easter appearances of Jesus are substantial.

## Development of Ideas of Immortality and Resurrection

By the second century BCE,[23] some expressions of Jewish eschatology included a conception of resurrection after death.[24] Two of the

21. This is the basis for ideas of underworld punishments, during which the souls of the dead were made to pay for their misdeeds. The such punishments, shame and discomfort, were abetted by the living in the maltreatment of the corpse, especially by denying proper burial and exposing the corpse to carrion animals and birds: cf. 1 Kgs 13:22, Ps 79:2–3, and Rev 11:9.

22. Secondary burials (exhumation of bones and reinterment in another location) also indicate post-mortem cult and survival: Eric M. Meyers, *Jewish Ossuaries: Reburial and Rebirth* (BibOr 24; Rome: Biblical Institute Press, 1971), esp. 85ff. For possible later use of this idea in Paul, cf. Norman R. Peterson, "Pauline Baptism and 'Secondary Burial,'" in George W. E. Nickelsburg and George W. MacRae, S. J., eds. *Christians Among Jews and Gentiles* (Philadelphia: Fortress Press, 1986) 217–226.

23. Isa 26:19, and Ezekiel's vision of reconstitution of the dry bones (37:1–14) are earlier precursors to the following second century texts. Rabbinic interpretation of Hosea 6:2 and the story of Jonah definitely connected these passages also to resurrection; cf. Harvey K. McArthur, "'On the Third Day,'" in *NTS* 18 (1971–72) 81–86.

24. Why and when such an idea arose in Israel has been a vexing problem. Ringgren posits three likely antecedents: Canaanite ideas of a dying and rising fertility god; the doctrine that Yahweh was stronger than death and Sheol; and Persian influence: Helmer Ringgren, *Israelite Religion* (trans. by D. Green; Philadelphia: Fortress, 1966) 244–247, 323. For Persian ideas, cf. Geo Widengren, "Iran and Israel in Parthian Times with Special Regard to the Ethiopic *Book of Enoch*," in Birger A. Pearson, ed., *Religious Syncretism in Antiquity: Essays in Conversation with Geo Widengren* (Missoula: Scholars Press, 1975) 118–120; also Martin Hengel, *Judaism and Hellenism* (trans. by John Bowden; Philadelphia: Fortress Press, 1981) 196–202, esp. notes 574–576. Zoroastrianism clearly had a basic theology to support such a restoration at the *eschaton*, unlike that of early Israel; Hinnells traces the doctrine into the Avesta: John R. Hinnells, "Zoroastrian Savior Imagery and its Influence on the New Testament," in *Numen* 16 (1969) 168. Nikolainen (*Auferstehungsglauben*, esp. 1.198–206) builds a case that ideas on the soul's survival in Persia, Egypt,

earliest texts may serve as examples. We read in Daniel 12:2 that at
the end of time:[25]

> Many of those who sleep in the dust of the earth shall awake,
> some to everlasting life, and some to shame and everlasting
> contempt.

2 Maccabees 7 declares a similar hope. Describing the murder of
seven brothers by Antiochus IV for their refusal to forsake their an-
cestral Law, the author has the second brother exclaim to the king
with his dying breath (v. 9):

> You accursed wretch, you dismiss us from this present life, but
> the King of the universe will raise us up to an everlasting re-
> newal of life, because we have died for his laws.

Clear expression of the hope of bodily renewal is expressed by
brother number three. He offers his tongue and hands to be cut off,
and declares (v. 11):[26]

> I got these from heaven, and because of his laws I disdain them;
> and from him I hope to get them back again.

The transition, however, from a long tradition of no resurrection at
all to the idea among some of a general resurrection at the end of
time was not immediate. Certain texts speak of such a resurrection
(e.g. 2 Macc 12:39–45);[27] others seem to speak of a resurrection for

Greece (and the OT), stimulated development of like ideas of bodily survival in Israel. Barrett ("Immortality," 74) points to a growing individualism, and martyrdom among the Maccabees, necessitating an individual postmortem reward.

25. "Our writer appears to envision a resurrection of the body. The Isaianic passage on which he draws (26:19) says that the bodies of the dead will rise. Moreover,
his use of Third Isaiah suggests such a bodily resurrection": G. Nickelsburg, *Resurrection*, 23. Isa 26:19a reads, "Your dead shall live, their corpses shall rise" (NRSV).

26. Likewise brother number four (v. 14), and their mother (v. 23, 29). Cf. also 2
Macc 12:43–45; 14:46.

27. Cf. the commentary on 2 Macc and related texts by Stemberger, *Der Leib der
Auferstehung*, 5–25.

the righteous only. Certain of these latter texts are quite explicit on the point of annihilation for the wicked. Zebulon in the *Testament of the Twelve Patriarchs* (*TZeb* 10:2) declares that while he will rise again, the wicked will be destroyed for all generations. The Psalms of Solomon 3:10–12 speaks of the sinner as follows:[28]

> *He falls, since his fall is grievous, and he does not rise up.*
> 11 *The destruction of the sinner is eternal,*
> *And he will not be remembered, whenever God oversees the just.*
> 12 *Such is the fate of the sinners for ever.*
> *But those who fear the Lord shall rise up unto eternal life,*
> *And their life shall be in the light of the Lord and shall not ever fail.*

"Whenever God oversees the just" (11b) refers to the final judgment, at which time the righteous rise up and the sinners are simply forgotten. This position appears to be a melding of the idea of Sheol (for the wicked) and the newer conception of a judgment at the end of time and its attendant reward for the righteous.

### Qumran and Essenes

The Qumran community seems likewise to have inherited and held various and composite opinions on afterlife and resurrection of the body. We read in 1QH 11:11–12 a poet's prayer, that one who receives God's grace

> . . . may be one [with] the children of your truth, and (partake) in the lot of your holy ones; that the worm eaten dead may be raised from the dust. . . .

---

28. These texts are dated to the second and first centuries BCE by H. C. Kee in his introduction to "The Testaments of the Twelve Patriarchs," in J. H. Charlesworth, *The Old Testament Pseudepigrapha* (Garden City, N.Y.: Doubleday, 1985) 1.777–778, and R. B. Wright in his introduction to the "Psalms of Solomon," ibid., 2.639.

Similar is 1QH 6:34: "O you who lie in the dust, raise up a banner; and you worm-eaten dead, lift up an ensign." These passages are not unequivocal.[29] According to Vermes, they "may connote bodily resurrection. On the other hand, the poet's language may just be allegorical. Immortality as distinct from resurrection is better attested."[30] Evidence from the scrolls is ambiguous and mixed, reflecting the influence of the ancient Israelite tradition of Sheol, the post-Exilic view of eschatology, and the Hellenistic concept of the immortality of the soul.[31]

Corresponding attestation of contradictory or ambiguous views of the afterlife among the Essenes is found in a parallel between Josephus and Hippolytus. Josephus, in describing the Essene position on the postmortem state, writes (*BJ* 2.154–155):

> For in fact this opinion is held among them, that bodies are corruptible and their material substance is not permanent, but that souls are immortal and remain forever, and are entangled in bodies as though in prisons, after coming [down] from the finest aether. . . . having the same opinion as the children of the Greeks. . . .

In the continuation of the passage, he constructs his views of the Essenes on the basis of the Hellenistic conception of the afterlife (156: "The Greeks seem to me to be of the same mind"), even calling up Sisyphus and his compatriots from Hades as illustrations of the Es-

29. According to Hengel (*Judaism and Hellenism*, 199), these are the only two passages on bodily resurrection from Qumran; their belief was more Hellenistic immortality, or perhaps that of a finely material, postmortem soul as in Stoicism: " . . . the Essene doctrine still lacks that [material] crudeness which we later find among the Pharisees" (200). But this should read, "among some Pharisees"; see the following section on the Pharisees.

30. Cf. Geza Vermes, *The Dead Sea Scrolls: Qumran in Perspective* (rev. ed.; Philadelphia: Fortress Press, 1981) 187.

31. So John Pryke ["much nearer to the 'immortality of the soul' than to the 'resurrection of the flesh'"], in "Eschatology in the Dead Sea Scrolls," in Matthew Black, ed., *The Scrolls and Christianity* (SPCK Theological Collection 11; London: SPCK, 1969) 57; and Matthew Black ["no unambiguously clear evidence" of physical resurrection], in "The Dead Sea Scrolls and Christian Origins," in idem, ed., *The Scrolls and Christianity*, 106.

sene doctrine of underworld punishment. Hippolytus (*Refutatio* 9.22), however, in his treatment of the same issue, perhaps using the same source as did Josephus, declares that the Essenes believed that "the flesh will also rise and be immortal, as the soul is already immortal. . . ." It is possible that Josephus omitted this (embarrassing) point from his account directed to Greco-Roman readers.[32] Hippolytus, in turn, may have inserted resurrection of the flesh here to further ground Christian doctrine in earlier Judaism. "Hippolytus may equally well, however, be faithful to his source, and the ancient Essenes may have taught both."[33] Thus the Essenes may have been unclear or divided as to their opinions on bodily postmortem survival.

## Pharisees

Hellenic ideas are also prominent in Josephus' treatment of the Pharisees. Josephus ascribes to this sect a view of the afterlife which must have sounded like the Platonic doctrine of transmigration of souls to his Roman readers (*BJ* 2.163):[34]

> The Pharisees [say] that every soul is immortal, but that only that of the good goes into a different body; but those of the wicked are chastised with eternal punishment.

In another such passage, Josephus himself addresses his fellow soldiers in similar fashion (*BJ* 3.372, 374):

> The bodies of all are mortal and constructed of perishable matter, but the soul is deathless forever and a portion of God dwelling within our bodies. . . . And the souls [of the brave] remain clean and obedient, receiving as their lot a heavenly

32. Simon takes the side of Hippolytus against Josephus, who clothes the Essenes "in Greek garb (or more precisely, in Pythagorean garb)": Marcel Simon, *Jewish Sects at the Time of Jesus* (trans. by James H. Farley; Philadelphia: Fortress Press, 1967) 79.

33. Matthew Black, "The Essenes in Hippolytus and Josephus," in W. D. Davies and D. Daube, eds., *The Background of the New Testament and Its Eschatology* (Cambridge: Cambridge Univ. Press, 1964) 172–175.

34. Cf. F. F. Bruce, "Paul on Immortality," in *SJT* 24 (1971) 458.

place most holy, from which at the turning of the ages they again indwell pure bodies.

These ideas were Josephus' own beliefs. The soul was immortal, a portion of the divine nature, indwelling the perishable body. Yet at the end of the ages the souls will again indwell bodies, "pure" and therefore apparently immortal and no longer constructed of perishable matter. It is possible that he has attributed his own (Hellenistic) opinion to the Pharisees, whom he clearly admires.[35] But it is more in accord with the evidence that he held a valid Pharisaic position, and that opinions were mixed and in transition: "The Pharisees believed both in the immortality of the soul and also in the resurrection."[36]

There was thus room for accord between two soon-to-be inimical groups, with as yet ill defined opinions on resurrection: the early Christians and the party of the Pharisees.[37] Their affirmation of this doctrine is demonstrated by the exclamation ascribed to Paul in Acts 23:6:

Brethren, I am a Pharisee, a son of Pharisees. I am on trial for the hope and resurrection of the dead.

The doctrine of resurrection remained unequivocal common ground between the Pharisees and the early Christians, against its

35. Cf. James D. Tabor, "'Returning to the Divinity': Josephus' Portrayal of the Disappearances of Enoch, Elijah, and Moses," in *JBL* 108 (1989) 225–238, esp. 230ff. Greco-Roman ideas were the models for the "Pharisaic Revolution," the rise of the Pharisaic movement, according to Ellis Rivkin, *A Hidden Revolution* (Nashville: Abingdon, 1978) 242–243.

36. Sjöberg works out this apparent contradiction by adding that "The two ideas were understood in such a way as not to be mutually exclusive. The link between them is the idea of the intermediate state of the soul after death and before the resurrection": Eric Sjöberg, "πνεῦμα, πνευματικός: C. III. רוח in Palestinian Judaism," in Gerhard Friedrich, ed., *Theological Dictionary of the New Testament* (trans. and ed. by Geoffrey W. Bromiley; Grand Rapids: Eerdmans, 1968) 6.379.

37. Evidence for this in the early period is dependent in the main on Josephus and the NT, which do not coincide completely. Josephus, for example, sees the Pharisees as Jewish Stoics (*Life* 12). Cf. Rivkin, *Revolution*, 75; also R. Travers Herford, *The Pharisees* (Boston: Beacon Press, 1962) 169–175.

denial by the Sadducees[38] and others. Yet "the doctrine of the resurrection which was current amongst the cultured Pharisees in the century immediately preceding the Christian era was of a truly spiritual nature."[39] The conception appears, in fact, to have been a melding of the idea of a future resurrection and the immortality of the divine soul: the soul is immortal and will after death abide in heaven apart from the flesh; yet in some future age it will again be clothed in a spiritual body, perhaps like that of the angels (cf. Luke 20:34-36). In this context, the argument of Paul for a postmortem heavenly state of the soul without the body ("absent from the body and at home with the Lord": 2 Cor 5:8), and the eventual acquisition of a "spiritual body" by the risen individual at the end of the age (1 Cor 15:44, 51-52) must be seen as a possible, even typical, Pharisaic doctrine.

## *Israel: Summary*

How does one respond to the ambiguity of our only early sources on the type of resurrection belief held by the Pharisees, the Essenes, and the early Christians? During this period, acceptance or rejection of the doctrine of "the world to come" itself was far more important than the particular type of postmortem survival envisioned.[40] The argument in the New Testament Gospels on this subject is against

38. The Sadducees continued to hold the older conception of pre-Exilic Israel. Cf. the NT evidence: Matt 22:23; Mark 12:18; Luke 20:27; Acts 23:8; and Emil Schürer, *The History of the Jewish People in the Age of Jesus Christ* (new Eng. ed., revised and ed. by G. Vermes, Fergus Millar and Matthew Black; Edinburgh: T. and T. Clark, 1979) 2.391-392. For a sociological explanation for the appearance among Pharisees of this doctrine, cf. Louis Finkelstein, *The Pharisees: the Sociological Background of Their Faith* (Philadelphia: Jewish Publication Society, 1938) 145-159.

39. R. H. Charles, *Eschatology: The Doctrine of a Future Life in Israel, Judaism, and Christianity. A Critical History* (New York: Schocken, 1970) 295.

40. The Mishnah (*Sanh* 10:1) excludes from the world to come "he that says there is no resurrection of the dead [תחיית המתים] laid down in the Law." But the doctrine could not be derived directly from the Pentateuch; it was found there by creative interpreters (so also argues Rivkin, *Revolution*, 230: "the Mishnah does not hesitate to hang this dogma on a scriptural 'hair'"). Jesus argued against Sadducees for postmortem survival from the mere phrase "the God of Abraham, Isaac and Jacob" (Mark 12:26). Thus the possibility of an afterlife at all had first to be established.

the Sadducees, against those who denied the future life entirely. Josephus held very Greek ideas about the afterlife, but considered himself a Pharisee. The ambiguity in the sources, one must conclude, reflects the actual diversity of opinion among these groups themselves.[41] According to Cavallin,[42]

> There is obviously no single doctrine about life after death in the period under consideration; there is rather a great variety and pluralism of ideas both about the end of world history and about death and about that which follows the death of the individual person. . . .

> The establishment of the belief in the resurrection of the dead as a dogma in Rabbinic Judaism represents the final result of a development which started with unclear and tentative formulations in the early inter-testamental literature.

If so, then the eventual diversity among early Jewish Christian groups on the same issue is much easier to understand: ideas were not yet clearly standardized, and more than one view could be found among those groups that contributed to the makeup of the early Church. A facile view of "the Jewish doctrine of resurrection" as against "the Greek view of immortality of the soul" obscures this complexity in Palestine itself. The resurrection of Jesus, while affirmed by all Jewish Christians, could mean different things to different Jewish Christian groups.

Meanwhile, during the entire period in which this development of thought was taking place regarding resurrection and the afterlife, the dead were still being visited, consulted, and fed at their grave sites; they for their part were still answering the prayers of, and conferring

---

41. Cf. Bousset, *Kyrios Christos*, 105: " . . . conceptions and imaginations in this area were still in an extremely lively and fluid state." Also Hinnells, "Zoroastrian Savior Imagery," 176: "The evidence suggests, therefore, that at the time of Christ there was no uniform interpretation of the resurrection doctrine even among those who held the belief."

42. Cavallin, *Life After Death*, 199 and 201.

blessings upon, the living. The cult of saints so well familiar from the later Christian period had very ancient roots, and continued uninterrupted from pre-Biblical times through the first century, indeed even to the present. The religious leaders were censured who "built the tombs of the prophets and adorned the monuments of the righteous."[43] As among the Greeks, the special dead in Israel received frequent pilgrimages.[44] Their tombs were shrines and holy places, as are certain tombs of Biblical figures and venerated rabbis even today. Such *cultus* was continued by the early (and later) Christians, who visited the tombs of their special dead in turn.[45] The speculations and controversies among ancient religious writers concerning the dead and their eventual fate at the *eschaton*, and the censure by powerful prophets and teachers, had little effect on the religious observances performed by humble people living their daily lives. And it was in the ordinary time of daily life, among the humble of the land, that the resurrection of Jesus occurred.

## Greek and Roman Views of Postmortem Existence

### Homer

Greek conception of the afterlife never did include the encumbrances of the body. For Homer resurrection of the body was impossible.[46] In *Iliad* 24, for example, Achilles attempts to comfort Priam

43. Matt 23:29; Luke 11:47. Cf. David Ussishkin, "The Necropolis from the Time of the Kingdom of Judah at Silwan, Jerusalem," in *BA* 33 (1970) 34–46; Joachim Jeremias, *Jerusalem in the Time of Jesus: An Investigation into Economic and Social Conditions during the New Testament Period* (trans. by F. H. and C. H. Cave; Philadelphia: Fortress Press, 1969) 15–16, and 253–254; and *Heiligengräber in Jesu Umwelt* (Göttingen, 1958).

44. Not only in Israel; on Jewish cult of the dead in the Roman catacombs, cf. J. M. C. Toynbee, *Death and Burial in the Roman World* (Ithaca: Cornell Univ. Press, 1971) 228; for Palestine, cf. Bas van Iersel, "The Resurrection of Jesus — Information or Interpretation?," in Pierre Benoit and Roland Murphy, eds., *Immortality and Resurrection* (Herder and Herder, 1970) 54–67, esp. 62.

45. Cf. Robert Houston Smith, "The Tomb of Jesus," in *BA* 30 (1967) 74–90.

46. On the word "body" in Homer, cf. Robert Renehan, "The Meaning of ΣΩΜΑ in Homer: A Study in Methodology," in *CSCA* 12 (1979) 269–282. Several heroes of myth did, while still alive, descend to Hades and return: Sisyphos, Odysseus, Herakles, Orpheus, Dionysus, Theseus, Peirithoos, and others. A list of

over the death of Priam's son, Hector, whom Achilles himself has
killed. Because of his great grief, he counsels Priam in the following
words (24.549–551):

> *Bear up, and do not unceasingly lament away your heart.*
> *For you will not accomplish anything grieving for your son,*
> *Nor will you raise him up, and sooner will you suffer another evil.*

The other "evil" is of course Priam's own death; he will die long before his grieving will accomplish the impossible, the raising of his
son. A like sentiment is expressed by the chorus in Sophocles' *Elec-
tra*, as they attempt to comfort her grief for her father, Agamemnon
(137–139):

> *But neither will you raise your father up from the lake of Hades,*
> *common to all, not by laments nor by supplications; but by moaning*
> *continuously beyond measure with incurable grief, you will perish,*
> *in which matters there is no cure of evils.*

"There is no cure" for death. Not only was resurrection impossible, but even resuscitation of the dead to a renewed mortal life,
as in the raising of Lazarus by Jesus, was against the law of Zeus.
Asclepius, son of Apollo and archetypical healer,[47] once raised a
dead man. For his impiety and his breech of "what is proper"
(τὰ ἐοικότα), Zeus incinerated both him and his patient with a
thunderbolt.[48]

The dead did not cease to exist, however, but spent all subsequent
time, according to Homer, in the house of Hades, the shadowy underworld, as insubstantial shades without strength or pleasure. In
the words of Bremmer concerning the archaic period:[49]

---

the heroes with relevant literature is given by E. Vermeule, *Aspects of Death in Early
Greek Art and Poetry* (Berkeley: Univ. of California Press, 1979) 211, n. 1.

47. *Il.* 11.518: Machaon, the physician in the *Iliad*, is "son of the excellent healer
Asclepios"; also 4.194.

48. For the myth, cf. Pindar, *Pyth.* 3.1–60 (τὰ ἐοικότα in line 59).

49. Jan Bremmer, *The Early Greek Concept of the Soul* (Princeton: Princeton
Univ. Press, 1983) 124.

When we compare the soul of the living with the soul of the dead, we are struck by the negative way the souls of the dead are characterized. On the whole they are witless shades who lack precisely those qualities that make up an individual.

So Achilles describes the constitution of his dead friend Patroklos, who appears to him during sleep requesting burial (*Il.* 23:103–104):

*Ah look now! Something [still] exists even in the dwellings of Hades, a soul and an image, but there is no vital substance in it at all.*

And so later the dead Achilles, after being revived by a draught of blood given by Odysseus, describes himself and his companions in Hades, "where the senseless dead abide, unreal images of perished mortals" (*Od.* 11. 475–476).

Immortality in Homer, therefore, was not to be gained by enviable afterlife,[50] but by κλέος ἀνδρῶν, "fame among men," reputation and remembrance among the living especially through poetry and cult.[51] The most important example of this in Homer is that of Achilles' two destinies: he may choose either to return home to Phthia and live a long, prosperous but anonymous life, or fight and die young at Troy but gain as compensation κλέος ἄφθιτον, "unwilting fame" (*Il.* 9.413). Such fame was communicated especially through poetic song, the rehearsal by bards of the ideals of culture and the great deeds of ancestors. This form of immortality was important

50. A few fortunate individuals of this age were allowed to enter the Elysian Field at the far West of the earth. So Menelaos, as son-in-law of Zeus by marriage to Helen, is granted this boon (*Od.* 4.561ff.); cf. Hesiod, *Erga* 167ff., and Vermeule, *Death*, 72. Cf. the discussion of body/soul by Corrigan, "Body and Soul," 360–383.

51. Examples for poetry include *Theognis* 237–252; Tyrtaeus 12.31–32; Simonides 99.1; cf. also the discussion of immortality conferred by the songs of Pindar in Frank J. Nisetich, *Pindar's Victory Songs* (Baltimore: Johns Hopkins Univ. Press, 1980) 42–47. The tomb itself was also an important signifier of the hero's past life and honor. On the relationship of epic, cult, and the "life" of the hero, especially Achilles, cf. Gregory Nagy, *The Best of the Achaians: Concepts of the Hero in Archaic Greek Poetry* (Baltimore: Johns Hopkins Univ. Press, 1979) passim, but, e.g., 341–342.

throughout the Greco-Roman period,[52] and was countered by those espousing the doctrine of the immortality of the soul.

## From Homer to Plato

The concept of the divine evolved between Homer and Plato, from the immanence of the Olympians to a view of a god behind the gods. How early such a concept arose is unclear, but was not without precedent even in epic language. That the gods were petty squabblers and immoral revelers was a polemical caricature used by philosophers and later by Christians.[53] Yet the figure of Zeus was quite capable of bearing the role of supreme god among the gods and god of justice in the archaic age.[54] Hesiod especially viewed Zeus as the god of justice. He tells, for example, of the servants of Zeus, 30,000 immortal watchers, who watch over human judgments and wicked deeds while roaming everywhere on the earth (*Erga* 252ff.), and of his rewards and punishments for those deeds. Even so, the gods who had controlled all the phenomena of nature, who stood behind rain, wind and lightening, began to recede before the notion of probable causation.[55]

The many gods were seen as culturally dependent, manifestations of one essential being; the gods began a transformation into the one god of all the cosmos. Xenophanes,[56] in a famous fragment (15 Diels), declared that:

52. And into the twentieth century; cf. Albert B. Lord, *The Singer of Tales* (New York: Athenaeum, 1978).

53. As early as Xenophanes (frag. 11 Diels): "Homer and Hesiod have attributed to the gods all things which are shameful and a reproach among humans: stealing and committing adultery and deceiving one another." The charge by Christians is especially strident among the apologists: cf. Justin Martyr, *1 Apol.* 21; Tatian, *Oratio ad Graecos* 8, 21; Athenagoras, *Legatio* 20–21; Tertullian, *Apologeticus* 15; Minucius Felix, *Octavius* 24.

54. Cf. Hugh Lloyd-Jones, *The Justice of Zeus* (rev. ed.; Berkeley: Univ. of California Press, 1983) 1–54, esp. 35.

55. Cf. G. E. R. Lloyd, *Early Greek Science: Thales to Aristotle* (New York and London: W. W. Norton, 1970) 9, 54; S. Sambursky, *The Physical World of the Greeks* (Princeton: Princeton Univ. Press, 1959) 51; Ernest L. Abel, *Ancient Views on the Origins of Life* (Rutherford: Farleigh Dickenson Univ. Press, 1973) 50.

56. Cf. Edward Hussey, *The PreSocratics* (New York: Charles Scribner's Sons, 1972) 13ff. Hussey surmises Hebrew or Persian influence for the origin of monotheism in Greece (p. 14). One wonders at the lack of mention of Egypt.

*If oxen <and horses> or lions had hands*
*or could draw with hands and complete the works which men do,*
*horses would draw pictures of gods like horses, and oxen like oxen,*
*and they would make the bodies (of their gods)*
*the sort which they themselves have in form.*[57]

Thus the gods of Homer and the poets are perceived to be mere projections of the limited experiences of humans, as they would be, in this sarcastic *reductio ad absurdum*, even for animals. The corollary is that "there is one god, among gods and humans the greatest, not at all like mortals in body or in mind" (frag. 23 Diels). A younger contemporary, Heracleitus, although critical of Xenophanes in other respects,[58] held a similar view: "That which is wise alone is one; it is unwilling and willing to be called by the name of Zeus" (frag. 32 Diels). The Zeus of Olympus was becoming something larger, more remote, and conceived in less material and anthropomorphic terms. Greek philosophical monotheism conceived of a god encompassing not only all the gods, but all the universe itself.

Among some of the more creative thinkers, the notion of the cosmos itself changed, and the physical distance to the realm of the gods increased dramatically: Zeus "moved" from the top of Olympus to the outer sphere of the stars. Astronomy and philosophy combined to develop a new cosmology, turning from the egg-shaped three story universe of tradition to the concept of the geocentric cosmos. The earth changed its shape, from a flat disc surrounded by and floating on Oceanos,[59] to a sphere fixed in the center

57. This is supported by the observation that (frag. 16 Diels): "Aethiopians say that their gods have snub noses and black hair; Thracians that their gods have grey eyes and red hair."

58. Frag. 40 Diels: "Great learning does not teach one to have intelligence; for it would have taught Hesiod and . . . Xenophanes. . . ."

59. Oceanos surrounds the earth, and is the source of all other waters (*Il.* 21.195ff.). Poseidon, as god of the sea, in Homeric terms is the "earth shaker" (ἐννο-σίγαιος, 13 times in *Iliad*); he "rocks" the earth by his waves, causing earthquakes. Herodotus, writing during this change, is able to say that he does not believe there is such an Ocean, but that it was invented by poets (2.23). Cf. also, Lloyd, *Greek Science*, 9. For the similar three-story cosmos of the Bible, cf. Tikva Frymer-Kensky, "Biblical Cosmology," in Michael Patrick O'Connor and David Noel Freedman, eds., *Backgrounds for the Bible* (Winona Lake, Ind.: Eisenbrauns, 1987) 231–240.

of the universe, surrounded by the heavenly spheres.[60] Heaven, formerly a hard surfaced dome a few thousand feet above the earth, became a vast sphere containing all the lower heavenly spheres and contained only by god; Hades of necessity was reduced in importance from one third of the world egg to occupy only the interior of the earth itself or ascend from under the earth to the sublunar regions. These changes in cosmology and theology were important for subsequent developments in the concept of the soul.

The psyche ($\psi \upsilon \chi \dot{\eta}$) in archaic Greece was conceived of as a material substance, very fine and akin to air and aether, but material nonetheless. No concept of immateriality yet existed in Greece;[61] even the gods had bodies, and could, for example, engage in sexuality with humans or be wounded in battle.[62] The $\psi \upsilon \chi \dot{\eta}$ was not even the single bearer of human essence apart from $\sigma \hat{\omega} \mu \alpha$ ("body"), but was conjoined with other organs ($\theta \upsilon \mu \acute{o} \varsigma$, $\phi \rho \acute{\epsilon} \nu \epsilon \varsigma$, and $\nu \acute{o} o \varsigma$[63]) as the

---

60. By the time of Plato this notion is already in place. His myth of Er (*Rep.* 10.616c ff.) describes the universe as the "spindle of necessity" surrounded by eight nested whorls which revolve around the central axis, representing the heavenly spheres revolving around the earth as axis.

61. Cf. R. Renehan, "On the Origins of the Concepts Incorporeality and Immateriality," in *GRBS* 21 (1980) 105–138: " . . . no Greek word for that concept yet existed" (106). "There is in fact no evidence to suggest that any Greek in the sixth century was in a position to define the soul as an immaterial being" (107). There are no "securely attested examples" (129) of the word $\dot{\alpha} \sigma \acute{\omega} \mu \alpha \tau o \varsigma$ ("bodiless, immaterial") before Plato. Much of what follows on immateriality in Plato is inspired by this excellent article.

62. So Aphrodite, after deceiving the other gods into sex with mortals, is driven by Zeus to lust for Anchises, and bears him a son, Aineas (*Homeric Hymn to Aphrodite*). She is later wounded by Diomedes while trying to save her son at Troy (*Il.* 5.330–362).

63. Et alia. These terms are all but untranslatable, in that they do not correspond well to modern physiology or psychology. Onians has argued persuasively that the $\phi \rho \acute{\epsilon} \nu \epsilon \varsigma$ (singular: $\phi \rho \acute{\eta} \nu$) are properly the lungs, and the word may be translated variously as "heart, mind, wits"; the $\theta \upsilon \mu \acute{o} \varsigma$ is properly the warm and vaporous breath in and from the lungs, and may perhaps be rendered by "passion, emotion, spirit"; $\nu \acute{o} o \varsigma$ is the controlling consciousness in the $\theta \upsilon \mu \acute{o} \varsigma$, and may be translated by "mind, intellect, intelligence, consciousness": Richard Broxton Onians, *The Origins of European Thought* (New York: Arno Press, 1973) 23–83. Cf. also, Bruno Snell, *The Discovery of the Mind in Greek Philosophy and Literature* (trans. by T. G. Rosenmeyer; New York: Dover, 1982) 8–17.

carriers of vitality, emotion and consciousness;[64] it was one element of a composite "soul." It was the "life" of an individual which was lost at death, and it alone survived in Hades as an "image" (εἴδωλον), "the visible but impalpable semblance of the once living."[65] The soul, as "life," could exit the body through any mortal wound, [66] but was often conceived of as "breathed out"[67] through the mouth. So Achilles tells his friends (*Il.* 9.408–409):

> *The soul of a man does not return again, neither by being carried off nor seized, after it has crossed the barrier of his teeth.*

Two suppositions about human nature developed between Homer and Plato which changed dramatically ancient philosophic ideas on life both present and postmortem: the derivation of the soul from the upper world (of air or fire, or the divine); and the opposition of body to soul. The connection of the ψυχή with breath was important for its association with the air, an "air-soul," and the elevation of the soul from the earth and underworld to the status of something akin to the divine, whose proper abode is above. Etymologically the word is likely derived from the idea of breathing (cf. ψύχω "to breathe, blow"). A similar phenomenon existed in Latin vocabulary, where the word *animus* ("soul") is cognate with Greek ἄνεμος ("wind"), and *anima* means first "air, breeze." Orphism, along with the early philosophers Anaximenes and Heracleitus, conceived of

---

64. Note in Latin the comparable *anima, animus*, where the former corresponds to the ψυχή (e.g., Matt 16:25 Vulg.), and the later may be used of emotional states as is θυμός.

65. Onians, *The Origins of European Thought*, 94. Cf. Achilles' description of Patroklos' ghostly return, quoted above.

66. Patroklos draws out with his spearhead the soul of Sarpedon (*Il.* 16.505), and that of Hyperenor exits through a wound in his side (14.518) caused by the spear of Menelaos. LSJ (s.v. ψυχή VII) rationalize the loss of the ψυχή in these passages as a loss of blood, which is clearly not Homeric anthropology; cf. Onians, *The Origins of European Thought*, 94, n. 5.

67. Cf. also *Il.* 5.696f., 22.467; Simonides 52 (Bergk) of Danaë's grief for the "soul breathed forth" (ψυχὰν ἀποπνέοντα) of her child Perseus; the word λειποψυχέω "to swoon"; and the Hebrew concept נִשְׁמַת חַיִּים "the breath of life," Gen 2:7.

the soul as air.[68] Aristotle tells us (*De anima* 410b 28) that the Orphics taught that the soul entered the body from τὸ ὅλον, "the Whole," as one breathed. That the soul after death abides in the air we learn in an inscription concerning the Athenians who were killed in 432 BCE at Potidaea (*IG* I,2 945.6):

αἰθὴρ μὲμ ψυχὰς ὑπεδέξατο, σώ[ματα δὲ χθών].
The aether has received their souls, but their bo[dies the earth].[69]

The soul came to be viewed as something originating in a sphere of being different from, and superior to, that of the body. The concept of the body too underwent change, from a positive vehicle of life, in fact the real self while alive,[70] to a distraction for and even the enemy of the soul. The Orphic idea was that body and soul were foreign to one another, the body being earthly and evil while the soul derived from the divine sphere. This anthropology was supported by a myth which told how humans were made of the dead bodies of the Titans, enemies of Zeus and righteousness who had murdered and eaten the infant divine child Dionysus. For this heinous crime Zeus struck them down with his lightning, and created humanity from their ashes. Humans were thus a mixture of the divine and earthly: they bore the "Titanic nature" in their bodies, but derived their souls from the ingested Dionysus.[71] One of the most famous ancient com-

---

68. Onians, *The Origins of European Thought*, 93; Anaximenes: G. S. Kirk, J. E. Raven, and M. Schofield, *The Presocratic Philosophers* (second ed.; Cambridge: Cambridge Univ. Press, 1983) 158–161, ¶ 160; Heracleitus (for whom the soul is fiery aether): 203–204. Cf. also W. K. C. Guthrie, *Orpheus and Greek Religion* (rev. ed.; New York: W. W. Norton, 1966) 193, n. 21.

69. Cf. Euripides, *Suppliants* 533–534: "The spirit into the aether, but the body into the earth." Also, the tomb inscription, *CIL*, 3.6384: "The ashes have my body; sacred air has taken away my soul."

70. *Il.* 1.3–5 describes the destructive anger of Achilles, which "cast many strong souls into Hades, while it made [the men] themselves prey to dogs and all birds." The opposition is ψυχάς and αὐτούς, "souls" and "themselves;" the souls descend to Hades, while the real persons (= bodies) are eaten, lifeless (= without ψυχή), by animals.

71. "Titanic nature" in Plato, *Laws* 701c. For the myth, cf. Jane Harrison, *Prolegomena to the Study of Greek Religion* (Cleveland and New York: World Publishing, 1959) 492–494, and Guthrie, *Orpheus*, 107ff.

monplaces was the Orphic saying "σῶμα σῆμα," "the body is a tomb."[72] In keeping with such a view of the body, Orphism prescribed an ascetical way of life which included sexual abstinence and vegetarianism.[73] Pythagoras and his disciples, whose connection with Orphism is clear to all but difficult to assess, considered the soul to be immortal, imprisoned in the body, and destined to be reincarnated into various other beings. Orphism stands behind much of later philosophy, and had great influence on Plato.[74]

## Socrates and Plato

It is to Plato's portrayal of Socrates, however, that we owe the major impetus for the spiritual orientation against the body later so emphasized by the ascetic elements in the Church, that "the spirit is the one that gives life; the flesh profits nothing."[75] Socrates felt it his divine mission to persuade his fellow Athenians to concentrate their efforts on the cultivation of the good of the soul over against that of the body. He describes his function in *Apology* 30a-b:

> For these things God orders, as you well know, and I think that no better thing has happened for you in this city than my service to God. For I go around doing nothing other than persuading both the young and old among you not to care for your

72. Found, e.g., in Plato, *Cratylus* 400c; *Gorgias* 493a. That this saying is Pythagorean or Heracleitean and not Orphic is argued by E. R. Dodds, *The Greeks and the Irrational* (Berkeley: Univ. of California Press, 1951) 169, n. 87; and idem, *Plato: Gorgias, A Revised Text with Introduction and Notes* (Oxford: Clarendon Press, 1959) 300. The *Cratylus* passage does, however, seem to me to attribute use of the saying to Orphism.

73. Cf. Euripides, *Hippolytus* 948–954, where Theseus berates his son Hippolytus for his Orphic mode of life which includes these two ascetic behaviors. Also, cf. Harrison, *Prolegomena*, 507f.

74. Cf. G. S. Kirk, J. E. Raven, and M. Schofield, *The Presocratic Philosophers* (second ed.; Cambridge: Cambridge Univ. Press, 1983) 214–238, esp. 215 (for Plato), 220ff. (for Pythagoras); Charles H. Kahn, "Pythagorean Philosophy Before Plato," in A. P. D. Mourelatos, ed., *The Pre-Socratics: A Collection of Critical Essays* (Garden City, N.Y.: Doubleday, 1974) 161–185, esp. 165; and Guthrie, *Orpheus*, 216–221.

75. John 6:63. Cf. Werner Jaeger, *Paideia: The Ideals of Greek Culture* (trans. by Gilbert Highet; Oxford: Oxford Univ. Press, 1943; repr. 1986) 2.38–39.

bodies or property so much as for your soul, how it might be best, . . .

Socrates faced the judicial sentence of death with a peaceful expectation of release from suffering. He instructed his friends to sacrifice on his behalf to Asclepius, the god of healing, on the grounds that his death was a kind of healing from bodily existence (*Phaedo* 118). The superiority of the soul over the body is likewise emphasized in a remarkable passage of the *Laws* (12.959a); we are told that:

> the soul is completely superior to the body, and in life itself the thing which supplies this existence to each one of us is nothing other than the soul; but the body, merely resembling each of us, follows. . . .

Socrates himself did not, apparently, hold any definite doctrine of the afterlife, preferring a mild agnosticism toward the varying theories of postmortem existence.[76] Plato, however, was persuaded that the soul was immortal, immaterial,[77] and the true vehicle for human identity. He tells the myth of Er (*Rep.* 10.614b-621d), in which a soldier killed on the battlefield goes to the world of the dead and then returns to life to tell of his experiences. Er discovers that the natural mode of the soul's existence is reincarnation from body to body, interspersed with thousand-year periods of reward or punishment without the body. The souls of famous individuals are still recognized by Er, but go on to choose other bodies and lives. The soul is not, therefore, something without individuality, but retains its identity, as did the shades of Homer; Plato's souls, however, pass through

---

76. He considers the possibility of death as dreamless sleep, or as an opportunity to discourse with all the famous dead of prior ages; both possibilities seem to him to be positive (*Apology* 40c-41c).

77. *Phaedrus* 246a: "Of necessity the soul is both unborn and immortal"; *Meno* 81b: " . . . the human soul is immortal." Plato does not say *in expressis verbis* that the soul is immaterial, but he does discuss the soul as incorporeal against an argument which ascribes to the soul σῶμά τι "a kind of body" in *Sophist* 247b-d; cf. *Epinomis* 981b. Later tradition also clearly attributed the doctrine of the immateriality of the soul to him. See Renehan, "Incorporeality," 130, n. 65.

an interim period of reward or punishment,[78] and are then reincarnated, becoming "someone else" in the next life. The souls, whether material but insubstantial (Homer et al.), or incorporeal (Plato), possess identity and are recognizable, a point which is important in the interpretation of the appearances of Jesus in John's Gospel.

Plato does address, surprisingly, the issue of "physical immortality," of postmortem physical survival. In his speech on Love in the *Symposium*, Socrates describes the instruction of Diotima to him on Beauty and her (Plato's) views on immortality. Love is defined as a longing for immortality (207a), which in the argument eventually becomes the longing for the immortal world of ideal Beauty and Goodness. But along the way to the ideal world, the discussion passes through the "lower" forms of love, and the desire for physical immortality. Diotima gives a clear presentation of the only possible means of achieving physical postmortem survival (207d, 208a-b):

> . . . the mortal nature seeks as much as possible always to be immortal. But it is possible by this alone: by reproduction, that it always leave behind another new [generation] in place of the old. . . . Every mortal creature is preserved by this means, not at all by remaining the same always, like the divine nature, but by the one departing and growing old leaving behind a new of the sort it was. By this mechanism, O Socrates, she said, what is mortal shares immortality, both the body and all other things. Otherwise it is impossible.

Aristotle shares this view. He tells us in his treatise *On the Soul* that "It is the most natural of acts for living creatures . . . to reproduce another like itself . . . in order that it might share in eternity and the divine in the manner in which it is capable . . . since it is impossible to share in the eternal and divine by continuance [of life]" (*De anima* 2.4. 415a).

---

78. Cf. especially *Gorgias* 523–525 on the benefits of postmortem punishment for souls.

Physical preservation is possible only through progeny; there is no other way. In fact, the only other effective way to immortality in the archaic Greek mind is discussed directly following the *Symposium* passage. But this is the oldest form we have seen, that of κλέος ἀνδρῶν, fame and reputation among one's contemporaries. So Diotima declares in dactylic hexameters that men and women desire nothing so much as glory, "and that deathless fame be established forever" (208c). This, to gain reputation as Achilles had gained "unwilting fame" (κλέος ἄφθιτον; *Il.* 9.413), was seen as an even greater incentive toward self-sacrificial behavior than the welfare of one's progeny in the search for postmortem survival. But it too falls short of the goal which Diotima and Plato are recommending, the eternal world of ideals toward which the soul should strive.[79]

## The Mysteries

Contemporary mystery religions promised a future blessedness, and celebrated "unutterable rites" and "things forbidden to mention,"[80] strictures which have kept some of their rites and ideas hidden to the present day. Representative of the mysteries, and certainly the most popular and long-lived single mystery cult, was that of Demeter at Eleusis. We are told of the initiate at Eleusis in the Homeric *Hymn to Demeter* (480–482):

> Blessed is the one among those on earth who has seen
>   these [mysteries].
> But the one who is not initiated in the rites, and who
>   has no portion [in them],

79. *Symposium* 209e-210a is seen by Jaeger, *Paideia* 2.192, and Renehan, "Incorporeality" 127-128, as one indicator of the division between "the historical Socrates" and Plato's own philosophy expressed through Socrates as the literary spokesman for Plato. Prior to this point Socrates speaks, in this discussion of Love, of the procreation of the spirit, which bears Wisdom and all her sister virtues. After 210a, Socrates as Plato's spokesman speaks of the higher mysteries of Love, which lead to the quest for Beauty as ideal form, eternal and unchanging, from which every earthly beauty takes its substance.

80. Aristophanes, *Clouds* 302: "unutterable rites" (ἀρρήτων ἱερῶν); *Eccl.* 442: "things forbidden to mention" (τἀπόρρητα).

*Never has a fate of similar things after death, down under
the moldy gloom.*

Isocrates, in a famous passage (*Panegyricus* 4.28), praises the double
gift of Demeter, the goddess of grain and of the Eleusinian mysteries. He speaks of her two gifts:

> . . . which are the greatest: the grains, which are the reason
> why we do not live as beasts; and the [Eleusinian] rite, in which
> those who partake have more pleasant hopes both for the end
> of life and all [present] lifetime.

Cicero was an initiate at Eleusis, a Stoic and Platonist, one of many
such highly educated and highly placed men in the first century BCE
and later. In a work inspired by Plato's *Republic*, he imitates this passage while describing the religious laws for his ideal state. He tells us
again of the two gifts, which grant civilization and "a reason not only
for living with happiness, but also for dying with better hope."[81]

What was the "better hope" for the hereafter offered by the mysteries? Many thousands of all social classes were initiated, some into
more than one mystery. Yet early evidence for postmortem survival
in the mysteries is surprisingly ambiguous and inconclusive.[82] One
promise seems to have been that the dead would descend to the underworld as in Homer, but enjoy a better lot, in an improved version
of the old myth. Plutarch writes that some "think that certain initiations and purifications are of help, by means of which, once purified,
they [will] spend their time playing and dancing in Hades in places

---

81. *Laws* 2.36. Cicero himself held a view of the afterlife much influenced by
Plato, characteristic of the Stoicism of his time; see infra.

82. Cf. Walter Burkert, *Ancient Mystery Cults* (Cambridge, Mass.: Harvard Univ.
Press, 1987) 23–24, 75–76. Burkert uses the word "resurrection" here in what can, in
the Greek world, only be a nonphysical sense, to mean "life after death." His burden is not that of this discussion on bodily resurrection, and one can only surmise
that, if it were, his terminology would have been adjusted.

having brightness, pure air and voices" (*Non Posse* 1105b).[83] So Isis promises to Lucius (Apuleius, *Met.* 11.6):[84]

> When you descend to those below, having measured out your lifetime, there also, in the vaulted subterranean world itself, inhabiting the Elysian fields, you will constantly worship me, whom you see, shining in the shadows of Acheron and reigning over the inner Stygian reaches, and propitious to you.

This is clearly a "better hope." But even this improved afterlife did not persuade all. Isocrates, Cicero's model in the passages above, although acknowledging the benefits of the Mysteries, seems himself to have valued most not the hope of immortality promised by them, but that of undying reputation, the "unwilting glory" (κλέος ἄφθιτον) of Homer. For him, reality and tradition demonstrated that the soul was still perishable, material, and dissolved at death along with the body.[85] He writes (*Archidamos* 6.109):

> . . . it is nobler in exchange for a mortal body to receive an immortal reputation, and for a soul, which we will not have in a few years, to purchase such good repute as will remain forever for those who are born from us. . . .

The soul is, in this passage, an impermanent possession, lost at death. It is the "life" which escapes the body at death, much as it had in Homer through a wound. The idea that the soul was immortal had not yet in his time (436–338 BCE) become common philosophical parlance, and never did convince all. Neither were the mysteries for all, nor their promises of blessed afterlife.

---

83. Cf. also Plato, *Rep.* 2.364b–365a, where rites of Orpheus and Musaeus are used to mitigate the afterlife.

84. According to Martin, Apuleius' message was: "Do not be an ass; the religious life under the protection of the great goddess is better": Luther H. Martin, *Hellenistic Religions: An Introduction* (Oxford: Oxford Univ. Press, 1987) 77.

85. Cf. R. Renehan, "Incorporeality," 133.

## Death and Epicureanism

Apart from the influence of Plato, few even among the philosophers subscribed to the doctrines of the immortality, immateriality, and reincarnation of the soul. The idealism of Plato, his theory of immaterial but existent forms, competed at the end of the fourth century with a renewed pre-Socratic naturalism and materialism.[86] Epicurus developed in principle the atomic theory of Democritus. There were for him but two kinds of Being, atoms and void. Void was but the absence of atoms, and therefore literally ἀσώματος, "incorporeal." The soul, like all things other than void, was composed of atoms. Epicurus maintained therefore that "the soul is a finely-particled body,"[87] and in reference to the disciples of Plato, that "those who say that the soul is incorporeal are speaking nonsense."[88] The direct consequence of such a theory was that the person, body and soul, like all other "bodies," was destroyed at death. So Epicurus could deny immortality of the soul and disregard the fear of death:[89]

> The most terrifying of evils, death, is nothing to us, since when we exist, death is not present. But when death is present, then we do not exist. It is nothing, then, either to the living or to the dead, since concerning the former it does not exist, and concerning the latter, they no longer exist.

This was comfort to him and his followers, who could repeat the saying centuries later as a kind of gospel: "Death is nothing to us."[90] So Lucretius (3.37–38) proclaims his master's doctrine, and "drives outdoors headlong that fear of Acheron which disturbs human life at its very foundations."

---

86. Cf. Ludwig Edelstein, *The Meaning of Stoicism* (Cambridge, Mass.: Harvard Univ. Press, 1966) 22.

87. Epicurus' *Letter to Herodotus*, in Diogenes Laertius 10.63.

88. Ibid., 10.67.

89. Ibid., 10.125.

90. Ibid., 10.139. Cf. also Lucretius 3.830: *nihil igitur mors est ad nos neque pertinet hilum*; likewise Cicero, *De Finibus* 2.31.100; Sextus Empiricus, *Pyrrhonism* 3.229.

The Epicurean view of the finality of death was one which also resonated long and widely in the culture at large. Catullus used this theme in his attempt to persuade his coy mistress (5.1, 4–6):

*Let us live, my Lesbia, and let us love.* . . . .

*Suns may set and return:*
*We, when once brief light sets,*
*Must sleep one perpetual night.*

Grave inscriptions often declare the dead to be nonexistent.[91] One commonly found is *NON FUI, FUI, NON SUM, NON CURO:* "I was not, I was, I am not, I don't care."[92] This line became so often used that it was reduced to its first letters only, in both Latin and Greek.[93] Similar in viewpoint is the following Greek epitaph from the Empire:[94]

*ΤΕΤΤΙΑΔΕΛΦΕ / ΕΥΨΥΧΙΟΥΔΙΣ / ΑΘΑΝΑΤΟΣ*
*O Tettius, my brother, farewell! No one is immortal.*

91. "Greek epitaphs are well known to reflect an almost universal pessimism in regard to any life beyond the grave. Only the famous, or those who died gloriously, are assured of immortality, for the only kind of immortality possible is to live on in the memory of posterity": W. K. C. Guthrie, *The Greeks and Their Gods* (Boston: Beacon Press, 1955) 260.

92. Cf. also (from Leonard and Smith, *Lucreti*, 493): *CIL* 5.1939: *NON FUERAM / NON SUM NESCIO NON / AD ME PERTINET* ("I was not. I am not. Not a thing matters to me"); *CIL* 9.4840: *OLIM NON FUIMUS / NATI SUMUS UNDE / QUIETI NUNC SUMUS / UT FUIMUS / CURA RELICTA VALE ET TU* ("Once we were not. We were born, whence [i. e., having left life] we are now at rest as we were, with care left behind. May you fare well also.")

93. Thomas Wilson, *St. Paul and Paganism*, 187, n. 5; and Ramsay MacMullen, *Paganism in the Roman Empire*, 57 and 173, n. 30. Cf. "R.I.P." used on tombstones in English.

94. From the Catacomb of Priscilla; cited from Graydon F. Snyder, *Ante Pacem: Archaeological Evidence of Church Life Before Constantine* (Mercer: Mercer Univ. Press, 1985) 133. Snyder, incredibly, includes this among Christian inscriptions by misunderstanding the first line as "Tettius the [Christian] brother . . . " How this common theme could be made more palatable to Christians is seen on an unpublished grave stele from Egypt in the Boston Museum of Fine Arts, which John Herrmann of the museum dates between the 5th and 7th centuries. It reads, in part: *ΟΥΔΕΙΣΑΘ / ΑΝΑΤΟΣΕΝΤΩ / ΒΙΩ  ΤΟΤΩ* [sic]; "no one is immortal in this life."

## Afterlife in Stoicism

The Stoics drew quite different conclusions from postulates similar to those of the Epicureans. The material cosmos for them was imbued with a divine but also material spirit/Λόγος, spread throughout which gave a structure and goal to the universe. The human being was a microcosm: the material body was suffused with material spirit/soul, as light in air, as the motive and reasoning power.[95] Diogenes Laertius, in his account of earlier philosophers, writes (7.156-7) that Stoics believed that:

> [the soul] is both corporeal and survives death; but it is perishable, while that of the universe is imperishable, of which the [souls] of living beings are parts. . . . Cleanthes [believes] that all [souls] exist until the Conflagration, but Chrysippus that only the souls of the wise [remain].

Stoicism as a whole had no concept of the survival of the body after death, and individual Stoic theorists differed among themselves as to whether even the soul survived post-mortem. Panaetius in the second century BCE seems to have denied any survival at all,[96] while Posidonius, strongly influenced by Plato, accepted the preexistence of the soul, and its subsequent postmortem ascent into the aether.[97]

Cicero, a student of Posidonius, furthered this melding of Stoic notions of the identity of the human and cosmic soul with Platonic notions of the soul's divine origin and immortality. In what is probably the most famous passage in Cicero on the afterlife, the *Somnium*

---

95. Cf. S. Sambursky, *Physics of the Stoics* (Princeton: Princeton Univ. Press, 1987; repr. of 1959 ed.) 16. Zeno drew not only on Heracleitus and Plato, but also Anaxagoras and Diogenes in postulating a Purpose immanent in the material cosmos; cf. Werner Jaeger, *The Theology of the Early Greek Philosophers* (Oxford: Clarendon Press, 1947) 168–169.

96. Cicero, *Tusc. Disp.* 1.32.79: "Panaetius . . . does not approve of this one [Platonic] opinion about the immortality of souls. [He says that] whatever is born dies, and souls are born. . . ." Cf. A. A. Long, *Hellenistic Philosophy: Stoics, Epicureans, Sceptics* (second ed.; Berkeley: Univ. of California Press, 1986) 213, n. 2.

97. Cicero, *Tusc. Disp.* 1.18.42–19.43

*Scipionis* (*De Re Publica* 6.9ff.), the elder Scipio says to his grandson in a dream vision:

> [14] It is surely true, he said, that those who have unbound the chains of the body as if from a prison are alive; but yours, which is called life, is death. . . . [26] Hold this as true, that you are not mortal, but this body is; for it is not you which that form displays, but one's mind is the person, not that form which a finger is able to point at. Know therefore that you are a god. . . .

Thus Stoicism by the time of the early Church was able to meld a materialist view of the cosmos with a notion of immortality and the divinity of the soul. The influence of Plato and Orphism is clear in the division of body from soul, the description of the body as prison, the divinity of the soul, and the cosmology in other parts of the dream.

Cicero uses this "dream" to counter certain time-honored notions. The younger Scipio finds himself in the heavens, viewing the tiny and unimportant earth against the backdrop of the heavenly spheres, listening to the *harmonia* of the music of the spheres. He is counseled to disregard the old notion of immortality by reputation (κλέος ἀνδρῶν), for the reputation "of no one was ever perennial, and it is destroyed by the death of people and extinguished by the forgetfulness of posterity" (*De Re Publica* 6.25). Scipio is able to recognize and speak with both his grandfather and father, demonstrating the survival of the individual personality and outward appearance apart from the body. The grandfather is even capable of "appearing" and instructing his grandson regarding his future, which is far from the Homeric insubstantial "shades" of the underworld.[98]

---

98. Plotinus (*Enn.* 4.7.4) notes that the Stoics "were forced by truth itself" to add to the materialist notion of soul/spirit some (Platonic) idea of intelligence. So the material soul became the whole person, no longer bereft of mental strength as it had been in Homer.

The Stoic doctrine of materiality of the soul had serious consequences for the controversy over the resurrection in the second century Church. The soul was a kind of "body," complete with its mental and spiritual faculties; it was the whole person, but for its expression in fleshly material, which had become devalued and denigrated as a hindrance and disguise of the real person. To Christians trained in such ideas, therefore, "bodily resurrection" was interpreted to mean that the soul was raised, without the flesh.[99]

## Afterlife in the Hellenistic Judaism of Philo

Much of early Hebrew speculation on the state of the body and soul after death had its analogue in Greece, but for the doctrine of bodily resurrection. The same may be said for Greek philosophical ideas on the subject in the Hellenistic Judaism of Philo. In his extensive writings, there is no mention of bodily resurrection;[100] instead one finds the influence of Plato and others, and the doctrine of the immortality of the soul.[101] According to Wolfson, "all the references to resurrection found in the traditional literature of his time were understood by him as being only a figurative way of referring to immortality."[102] Thus Philo interprets Biblical passages on resurrection (Isa 26:19; Dan 12:2) and the hopes of the Maccabean martyrs (2 Macc 7) as references to the immortality of the soul.[103]

One also finds in Philo a strong emphasis on the superiority of soul to body. In an instructive passage, he writes that after death,

99. Cf. Tertullian, *De Res. Carnis* 35.

100. Also no personal Messiah, nor universal judgment day; cf. Samuel Sandmel, *Philo of Alexandria: An Introduction* (New York and Oxford: Oxford Univ. Press, 1979) 109–110.

101. Cf. Erwin R. Goodenough, "Philo on Immortality," in *HTR* 39 (1946) 85–108.

102. Harry Austryn Wolfson, *Philo: Foundations of Religious Philosophy in Judaism, Christianity, and Islam* (second printing, revised; Cambridge, Mass.: Harvard Univ. Press, 1948) 1.404.

103. References in Wolfson, *Philo*, 1.404. For a discussion of the type of salvation offered in Philo's brand of Judaism, cf. E. P. Sanders, "The Covenant as a Soteriological Category and the Nature of Salvation in Palestinian and Hellenistic Judaism," in Robert Hammerton-Kelly and Robin Scroggs, eds., *Jews, Greeks and Christians: Religious Cultures in Late Antiquity* (Leiden: E. J. Brill, 1976) 25–44.

"we will hasten to rebirth, to be with the unbodied," and the soul will depart the body, "leaving it bereft of life."[104] As in Plato's *Timaeus* (69c-d), the body and the irrational soul are created not by God but by his agents (*Opif. Mun.* 75). The rational soul derives from the divine world, and is an alien resident in the body. So he writes:[105]

> For the soul of the wise man, when it comes from above from the ether and enters into a mortal and is sown in the field of the body, is truly a sojourner in a land not its own, for the earthly nature of the body is alien to the pure mind and subjects it to slavery and brings upon it all kinds of suffering. . . .

The body is "by nature wicked and a plotter against the soul"; to one who knows the truth and is initiated into the mysteries of the Lord, the body is "wicked and hostile"; it is "an evil and dead thing, tied to" the soul (*Leg. All.* 3.71–72).

The body hinders and obstructs the soul; the object of wisdom is "to alienate itself from the body and its lusts" (*Leg. All.* 1.103). Therefore Philo teaches the wise to look forward to escape from the body at death, to live with "the incorporeal Logoi of the divine world, whom elsewhere it is accustomed to call 'angels'" (*Q Gen* 3.11). The soul will return to its own world of the immaterial from whence it came. But of the substance of the soul, we are told, "So subtle is it of nature, that it affords no handle for the body to grip" (*Cherubim* 115). The body is the enemy of the soul, and dissolves with death; the soul is subtle in substance[106] and immortal. Resurrection of the body, for clear philosophical reasons, is never mentioned.

---

104. *Cherubim* 115. The "unbodied" are the celestial "angels," the powers of God. Cf. the comments on this passage in Erwin R. Goodenough, *By Light, Light: The Mystic Gospel of Hellenistic Judaism* (Amsterdam: Philo Press, 1969) 375.

105. *Q Gen* 3.10. The translation is that of Ralph Marcus, *Philo: Questions and Answers on Genesis* (Supplement 1, Loeb Classical Library; Cambridge, Mass.: Harvard Univ. Press, 1979) 193.

106. The soul is not, surprisingly, ἀσώματος, "immaterial," but λεπτομερής, "composed of small particles," as was aether or fire in ancient conception. Philo is

## Greco-Roman Popular Religion: Heroes and Hero Cult

Outside of the world of epic poetry and the philosophical schools, popular religion displayed continued adherence to ancient ideas and *cultus*, or ancient skepticism,[107] and showed little influence from literature or philosophy. Innumerable small and local cults of the dead, particularly the special dead, the heroes, existed in Greece,[108] almost entirely absent from Homer because of his Panhellenic and aristocratic focus.[109] Shrines for these denizens of the underworld, on the border between human and divine, were common both within and between towns and villages. They exhibited an effective spiritual presence in the daily experience of the living; they could and did function in cult, as protectors and avengers of wrong for themselves and those who sought their assistance.

The places of burial, and the bones of the dead, were loci of power and sites of cultic activity.[110] The departed was seen to remain and somehow "live" at the grave site. So the dead Agamemnon is invoked at his tomb, called from the grave by his children to avenge his own murder and the wrongs done his house by his wife and her paramour.[111] The secret burial site of Oedipus was thought to function as a talisman to protect Athens against its enemies, especially Thebes.[112] The land in which the bones were buried was the "home" of the hero, and by right received his or her blessing and protection. If the bones were moved, the blessing moved also. The bones of Orestes, Agamemnon's son, were sought out and moved from Tegea by the Spartans to their own land. The bones had functioned as a talisman on the side of Tegea in their combats; once the bones were trans-

---

following the Stoics here and not Plato, reflecting a melding of ideas similar to that in Cicero.

107. Fatalism, not the philosophical school. Cf. the inscriptions quoted in the discussion of Epicureanism above.

108. For the hero and his/her cult as "neighbor," cf. Jeffrey S. Rusten, "ΓΕΙΤΩΝ ΗΡΩΣ: Pindar's Prayer to Heracles (*N.* 7.86–101) and Greek Popular Religion," in *HSCP* 87 (1983) 289–297.

109. Cf., among others, W. den Boer, "Aspects of Religion in Classical Greece," in *HSCP* 77 (1973) 1–21, esp. 2–5.

110. Cf. Guthrie, *The Greeks and Their Gods*, 232–235.

111. Aeschylus, *Libation Bearers* 315–465.

112. Sophocles, *Oedipus at Colonus* 1521–1533.

ferred, the blessing was reversed, and Sparta gained the upper hand.[113] It was this function of the dead, to avenge and protect, to curse and to bless, which energized the cult of heroes in the Greek and Roman world from pre-Homeric times to the end of the Empire, and beyond in the cult of Christian saints.[114]

## Cultus of the Dead

One of the more intriguing aspects of ancient custom, and most revealing concerning the substantial existence of the dead, was the *cultus* at the tomb. The dead required, in the first place, proper burial and lamentation, to prevent the disembodied psyche (ψυχή) from returning from the underworld to punish those who thus wronged it.[115] This is visible as early as Homer: Elpenor threatens to become the gods' curse on Odysseus if he fails to give him proper burial, even though Elpenor had died through his own drunken stupidity (*Od.* 11.51–78). The ghost of Patroklos informs Achilles that without his proper burial rites, he was not allowed to enter Hades (*Il.* 23.71–74):

> *Bury me as soon as possible, that I may pass through the*
> *gates of Hades.*
> *The souls, images of those overcome, keep me at a distance*
> *and do not at all allow me to join them beyond the river,*
> *but thus I wander before the wide gated house of Hades.*

We are told that the living were to wash and lay out the corpse, and especially to mourn and lament, and then burn and bury it with

113. Herodotus 1.67f. Cf. the commentary on this passage in W. W. How and J. Wells, *A Commentary on Herodotus* (Oxford: Clarendon Press, 1936) 90–91.

114. Cf. here, for the Homeric period, J. N. Coldstream, "Hero Cults in the Age of Homer," in *JHS* 96 (1976) 8–17; for Herodotus especially, cf. Margaret Visser, "Worship Your Enemy: Aspects of the Cult of Heroes in Ancient Greece," in *HTR* 75 (1982) 403–28; for, among other things, the functions and rituals, and the many minor cults, cf. A. D. Nock, "The Cult of Heroes," in *HTR* 37 (1944) 141–174. Each of these articles is replete with reference to the standard works on Hero-cult.

115. " . . . proper treatment of the dead produces a healthier and more cooperative shade, . . . it is particularly important not to offend those whom you will join": Emily Vermeule, *Aspects of Death in Early Greek Art and Poetry*, 49.

tomb and grave marker, "for this is the privilege of the perished."[116] The word for "privilege," γέρας, is the gift of honor paid to one who has, by worth or station, come to deserve some present or prerogative; it was Agamemnon's usurpation of Achilles' γέρας which set off the tragedy of the *Iliad*.

Piety prescribed that the surviving members of a family care for their dead at the grave site. Relations brought offerings of meat, fish, bread, cakes, wine, oil, water, flowers, et alia, to the tomb and shared them with the deceased, usually on the anniversary of death. Greek art frequently depicts survivors on their way to the cemetery carrying baskets of gifts for the dead.[117] Herodotus relates a story (5.92 η) of Melissa, the dead wife of the tyrant Periander of Corinth, who refused to give an oracle to her inquiring husband, as she was cold and naked. He then burned numerous garments at her grave site as a means of conveying the offering to her, and obtained his information in return. Tertullian mocks this custom of burning as a means both of disposing of the corpse and making offerings: "Is it a sacrifice or an insult when they burn offerings to the burnt?"[118] The dead were often said to be burned in their finest clothing with all their possessions. That the dead were still "alive" is supported even by certain of the words used euphemistically for the grave clothes, *vitalia*, the "living (grave clothes)", and the bier, *lectus vitalis*, the "living (funeral) bed."[119]

116. *Il.* 16.456–457; = 16.674–675; 23.9; *Od.* 24.190; 24.296. Cf. Jan Bremmer, *Soul*, 89ff. Burial was necessary for the soul to be allowed to cross the river of the underworld; we are told that Charon was forbidden to take any unburied soul accross the Styx (*Aeneid* 6.325–328).

117. Cf. Robert Garland, *The Greek Way of Death* (Ithaca: Cornell Univ. Press, 1985) 108–111; also, J. M. C. Toynbee, *Death and Burial in the Roman World*, 61–64.

118. Tertullian, *De Res. Mort.* 1.3. Tertullian and his church nevertheless made prayers for and offerings to the dead as "birthday honors" on the anniversary of the date of their deaths: *De Corona* 3; cf. also *De Monog.* 10; *De Exhort. Cast.* 11. Justin uses this common practice of invoking the dead as a proof that the soul survives death: *1 Apol.* 18; cf. also 24. Eusebius records an instance where worship of the dead martyrs became so common among Christians that the Romans threw their bodies into the sea to prevent the practice (*HE* 8.6; also 5.1).

119. The dead burned with their clothing and possessions: e. g., *Il.* 6.416–419; *Od.* 11.74; 24.65–67; the shroud as "clothing for the living": Seneca, *Epist.* 99.22, Petronius, *Satyricon* 77; the bier as "bed to live on": Petronius, *Satyricon* 42.

Meals for the dead were occasions for family members to express solidarity not only with the departed, but also with each other. In the words of Cumont, "No religious ceremony was more universally performed in the most diverse regions of the Empire than this cult of the grave. At every hour of every day families met in some tomb to celebrate there an anniversary by eating the funeral meal."[120] Tombs were frequently supplied with dining furniture, and especially an offering table. The table was often fitted with depressions and carvings in the shape of saucers and containers for food and liquids. The covering slab of the grave itself was often this table, overlaying the remains of the deceased just below. Holes or tubes[121] through the stone or earth into the grave conveyed the offered food to the dead family member.[122] Concerning the social dimension of the meal for the dead as it continued in the early Church, Snyder writes:[123]

> The celebration was very social. It strengthened family relationships, either blood or primary, by including extended generations. The service itself included anointing of the stone or

---

This normal means of clothing dead souls obviates entirely the need to invent the specious modern difficulty of "the resurrection of Jesus' robe" as an objection to the resurrection of Jesus, or to use this impossibility as support for a theory of "veridical hallucination" as an explanation of the post-Easter appearances, which, for Badham, is the disembodied mind of Jesus communicating to the disciples by telepathy: Paul Badham, *Christian Beliefs about Life after Death* (London: Macmillan, 1976) 32. "Veridical hallucination" may be defended; that is not the issue here. For the ancients Greeks, however, both the robe and the body passed through death in the same manner, yet neither were resurrected or required telepathy to be seen.

120. Franz Cumont, *After Life in Roman Paganism* (New York: Dover Publications, 1959) 55.

121. Pausanias 10.4.10: "The Phocians bring sacrificial animals and pour the blood into the grave through a hole, but the meat they themselves customarily consume on site." Cf. also Onians, *The Origins of European Thought* (272), on the libation tubes into the shaft graves at Mycenae, and the grave reliefs at Sparta which picture the dead with a cup (285).

122. Cf. David Gill, S. J., "*Trapezomata*: A Neglected Aspect of Greek Sacrifice," in *HTR* 67 (1974) 117–137, esp. 121; Sterling Dow and David H. Gill, S. J., "The Greek Cult Table," in *AJA* 69 (1965) 103–114, esp. the drawing on 106; Graydon F. Snyder, *Ante Pacem*, 90–92. Tertullian describes the lavishness of such meals in *De Res. Mort.* 1.2.

123. Graydon F. Snyder, *Ante Pacem*, 91.

*mensa*, antiphonal singing, dancing, the agape or *refrigerium* meal with all the prayers and acclamations attending that.

The dead participant in the meal apparently enjoyed the experience. Iphigenia poured a soothing libation to the dead ($\nu\epsilon\kappa\rhoο\hat{\iota}\varsigma$ $\theta\epsilon\lambda\kappa$-$\tau\acute{\eta}\rho\iota\alpha$).[124] Graffiti of the conviviality of drink (*VIVAS*, "To your health!"; literally: "may you live [well]!") occur frequently.[125] The singing, eating, drinking, dancing and requests to the dead made this occasion an experience of family "life" with one of its honored members.[126]

Comparison of these customs with the resurrection narratives of the New Testament is quite instructive. Offerings of food for and meals with the dead were common and important to the culture at large. The body of the deceased was cremated or buried, yet offerings were poured into the graves in both cases; no question remained as to the state of the physical body: it was gone. There was not even any supporting mythology that the body might somehow survive. Yet these dead without bodies were able to eat, drink and talk with the living. It seems but a small step to the post-Easter events.[127]

---

124. Euripides, *IT* 166. Cf. on libations, inter alia, Albert Henrichs, "The 'Sobriety' of Oedipus: Sophocles *OC* 100 Misunderstood," in *HSCP* 87 (1983) 87–100, esp 93ff.

125. So Graydon F. Snyder, *Ante Pacem*, 126, 128. One wonders about the potential sarcasm of such a saying in this context.

126. The mixing of pagan and Christian ideas may be seen in a third century grave inscription from the Vatican:

DM / *ΙΧΘΥΣ ΖωΝΤωΝ* / LICINIAE AMIATI BE / NEMERENTI VIXIT
To the Underworld Gods / Jesus Christ Son of God Savior of the Living / For Licinia Amiata the we / ll deserving. She lived . . . [number of years not preserved].

There are the symbols of fish-anchor-fish between the second and third lines. Note the dedication of Licinia both to the underworld gods and to Christ. The inscription is found in Charles A. Kennedy, "Early Christians and the Anchor," in *BA* 38 (1975) 115–124, fig. 25.

127. That the dead could eat, and that ghosts when appearing to the living could eat, is a point missed by some New Testament scholars. So, for example, writes Hendrickx: "A ghost would definitely not eat anything": H. Hendrickx, *The Resurrection Narratives of the Synoptic Gospels* (rev. ed.; London: Geoffrey Chapman, 1984) 92. But as early as Homer, the consumption of a draught of blood was the

## The ΕΙΔΩΛΟΝ

One common characteristic of the dead is that they are easily recognized by both the living and other deceased. The dead keep their recognizable form and appearance apart from their bodies because the surviving soul bears the "image" (εἴδωλον) of the body, and is an essential attribute of the soul. It is the visible form of the physical body, and in ancient conception, gave the living body its characteristics and individuality in appearance, as a mold gives specific form to a bronze casting. Etymologically the word is related to εἶδος / εἴδω, meaning "something seen." It could be used of an image in a mirror or a reflection in water; it was often opposed to the "real" thing, yet it looked like the thing itself.[128] The word εἴδωλον is used interchangeably for the word "soul" (ψυχή) in reference to the departed spirit of Odysseus' companion Elpenor (*Il.* 11.51 and 83), and both words are used in hendiadys to describe the spirit of Patroklos when he appears to Achilles to request burial (ψυχὴ καὶ εἴδωλον: *Il.* 23.104).[129] Elpenor appears, in a middle fifth century depiction, life size and identical to his former self in the underworld; the shade of Patroklos is said to be "like to him in everything, in size and beautiful eyes and voice."[130] So Odysseus and Aeneas are able to recognize the dead in the underworld (*Od.* 11; *Aeneid* 6). Pindar in the following passage describes the soul as the "image (εἴδωλον) of life" which survives the death of the body and is derived from the gods (frag. 131.2–4):

---

means by which the insubstantial dead could gain strength enough to speak with intelligence (*Od.* 11.96). The dead, apparently, were never without the ability to eat.

128. The word could be used for the image or copy of a person in a painting of sculpture. Such "images" were often used for religious purposes; thus the word came to mean "heathen idol" through the LXX, and is so used eleven times in the NT: e. g., 1 Cor 12:2.

129. Cf. *Il.* 24.14: "souls, the images of those who have died." In art, the εἴδωλον of a dead hero is often seen as a *homunculus*, a small replica of the hero floating or "running" in the air above the tomb. Cf. the armed and winged εἴδωλον of Patroklos above his tomb in an Attic black-figured Hydria (sixth century) in E. Vermeule, *Death*, 111.

130. Elpenor on a red-figure *pelike* ca. 440, in George H. Chase, *Greek, Etruscan, and Roman Art: The Classical Collection of the Museum of Fine Arts, Boston* (rev. by Cornelius C. Vermeule III and Mary B. Comstock; Meriden, Conn.: Meriden Gravure Co., 1972), 131, fig. 109; Patroklos: *Il.* 23.66.

*And the body of everyone is followed by all-powerful death,*
*But living still there is left an image [εἴδωλον] of life. For this*
*alone is from the gods.*

By the time of Plato, as we have seen, the word "soul" (ψυχή) had
collected all the Homeric mental and emotional functions (θυμός,
φρήν, and νόος, inter alia) into one concept, and was opposed
specifically to the body (σῶμα).[131] Because of his strong emphasis
on the immaterial soul as the real person, Plato describes the body,
in a clever reversal of terminology, as the εἴδωλον of the soul
(*Laws* 12.959b):

And of those who have met their end, it is well said that the
bodies of the dead are mere images [εἴδωλα], but the actual
essence of each of us is called the deathless soul, which goes off
to other gods to render account. . . .

Here, according to the most influential philosopher of antiquity, the
dead body is a mere phantom, "ghostly," and the surviving soul is
the only truly substantial human element. So the soul as an εἴδωλον
of the person could be seen as the real part of the human being, de-
riving from the realm of the gods, while the body was an unsubstan-
tial image. Thus a postmortem appearance in the era after Plato
could be considered as one of substance, as "real," though bodiless
and immaterial. It could, and probably would have been in fact,
more "real" than the body/soul combination of the antemortem per-

131. Cf. Onians, *The Origins of European Thought*, 115: "Whether Orphic or
Pythagorean belief, by assigning a richer existence (more particularly after death)
to the ψυχή . . . and by a doctrine of retribution naturally tending to the identification of the party punished after death (what survives, the ψυχή) with the party
responsible for good or bad deeds in life (the conscious agent), . . . we cannot tell;
but a very important change can now be traced. The ψυχή gradually ceases to be
merely the life or life-soul which it was in Homer and Hesiod, etc., and begins to be
conceived of and spoken of as concerned in perception, thought, and feeling,
which had formerly passed as the work of θυμός, φρένες, and κῆρ in the chest. In it
as a single entity, 'life' and consciousness, which had formerly been divided, . . .
are now united." Cf. also pp. 168, 208, and 253, n. 11.

son, since the soul when embodied was disguised by beauty or wealth: such is Plato's argument in the *Gorgias*, noted in the following section.

## The STIGMATA

The dead retained not only their appearance (εἴδωλον), but, in appropriate instances, even the marks (στίγμα, *stigma*[132]) of the implements which caused their demise. After being stabbed to death by her son Orestes, for example, Clytaemestra upbraids the Furies for not avenging her, directing them to "look at these wounds in my heart" as a means of galvanizing them to action.[133] Ovid tells us the story of Orpheus' descent to the underworld to retrieve his wife Eurydice, who had died of a snake bite to the ankle. After he had sought the grace of Persephone and Hades, and overcome their resistance with his song and lyre, "they called Eurydice; she was among the recent shades, and came with a slow step because of her wound."[134] She still limped as an *umbra* ("shade, ghost") in the underworld. Likewise, Hector's ghost, bearing all the marks of his fatal encounter with Achilles, is seen by fellow Trojan Aeneas in a dream vision which warns and instructs the unwary soldier. His doleful appearance is described in the following poignant words:[135]

---

132. The word was originally Greek στίγμα, "tattoo, mark," and was taken over into Latin as *stigma* with the same meaning, but used primarily of the tattoo mark which designated slaves. Christian Latin, of course, used it for the marks of the death wounds of Christ, whether on his own body or that of a Christian mystic. Here it is used in this later sense of death wounds, retroverted into the era BCE for any postmortem soul.

133. Aeschylus, *Eumenides* 103.

134. Ovid, *Met.* 10.48–49. Plato had used this idea that the dead retained their death-wounds, but applied it to the wounds suffered by the soul from wickedness in *Gorgias* 524a–525a; for commentary and further examples of this theme, cf. E. R. Dodds, *Gorgias*, 379.

135. *Aeneid* 2.272–273, 277–279. Also in the *Aeneid*, Sychaeus shows his sister in a dream his "breast pierced with iron" (1.355); Eriphyle bears the wounds inflicted by her son for her betrayal of her husband Amphiaraus (6.445–446); Dido bears her self-inflicted wound (6.450), and Deiphobus the horrible mutilations inflicted on him by Helen, Menelaos and Odysseus at the sack of Troy (6.494–497). For further examples, cf. Bremmer, *Soul*, 84, n. 31.

In a dream, behold, before my eyes most sorrowful Hector seemed to be present and be weeping copiously, as of old dragged by [Achilles'] chariot, black with gory dust, and pierced in his swollen feet with thongs . . . wearing a squalid beard and hair clotted with blood, and those many wounds he received around the walls of his fatherland.

Hector here not only bears the wound of Achilles' spear which caused his death (*Il.* 22.326f.) and apparently the scars of many previous wounds, but also the marks suffered by his corpse days after he had died, as a result of being dragged behind Achilles chariot: the marks of the leather cords which bound his body to the car, the swollen feet, and the dirt which soiled him.

We must grant to Virgil his poetic license. But the description, while graphic, is hardly out of character with the general conception of the times: the dead retained their *stigmata* as an essential characteristic of their εἴδωλα. A comparison here with the marks on the body of the resurrected Christ is significant. His post-Easter body, we are told, still bore the imprints of the nails on his hands and feet, and the wound in his side. Yet none of the Greco-Roman examples requires or permits the dead individual to have a physical postmortem body. The only type of bodily immortality possible was that of the genetic reproduction of oneself in one's children. Nevertheless, the disembodied souls of the dead bore the marks of their death wounds, and as had Hector in the *Aeneid*, the resurrected Christ bore the mark of the spear in his side, thrust into his already dead body.

## The Problem of the Impalpability of the Soul

Perhaps the most important aspect of the departed soul in connection with the Gospel narratives was its reputation for impalpability. This motif was common in the Greco-Roman tradition and as old as Homer. For example, when Patroklos appeared to Achilles to request burial, Achilles attempted to embrace his companion in the sorrow of his loss (*Il.* 23.99–101):

> *. . . He reached out his hands to his friend,*
> *but could not embrace him. And his soul, like smoke,*
> *went under the earth with a shrill cry.*

Patroklos was like smoke. Startled awake, Achilles declared that he was but "a soul and an image" with "no vital substance at all" (*Il.* 23:103–104).

Another clear Homeric account of postmortem impalpability of the soul is found during Odysseus' description of his visit to the underworld. The hero, after conversing with the blind prophet Teiresias, is met to his great dismay by his mother whom he had left alive on his home island of Ithaka. She informs him that his wife, son, and father were still alive and mourning his absence, and that she for that very cause, the longing for her son, had passed into the house of Hades. Odysseus continues (*Od.* 11.204–208):[136]

> *So she spoke. But I, contriving in mind, wanted*
> *To embrace the soul of my dead mother.*
> *Three times I rushed forward, and my heart bid me to embrace her.*
> *But three times like a shadow or even a dream she flew from my*
>    *hands.*

Odysseus, struck with grief, asks his mother why each time she escapes his grasp, and whether she is merely an εἴδωλον, an image which Persephone has constructed to torment him.[137] She answers him that it is no trick of Persephone (*Od.* 11.218–222):

> *But this is the normal state of mortals, whenever anyone dies.*
> *For the sinews no longer hold the flesh and bones,*
> *But the strong anger of burning fire*

---

136. On the conflicting views of the underworld and redactional history of *Od.* 11, see the chapter "Odysseus and the Underworld", in Denys Page, *The Homeric Odyssey* (Westport, Conn.: Greenwood Press, 1976) 21–51.

137. *Od.* 11.213–214. This question was not as strange a question as it may seem. Apollo had made a copy of Aeneas to replace the hero in battle while he was re-

> *Overcomes them, whenever the spirit first leaves the white bones,*
> *And the soul flutters like a dream flying away.*

The normal state of the Homeric dead is that the body is dissolved and destroyed by burning on the funeral pyre; the soul remains alive in the underworld, but is as a winged and fluttering dream, impossible to grasp. This ancient motif was used by many later authors and was a common theme in the poetic conception of the dead.

It is this theme which stands behind the post-Easter scenes in the Gospels of Luke and John in which the risen Jesus offers himself to be touched by his disciples (Luke 24:39; John 20:27). In both works it is clear that the intention of these episodes is to counter the idea that the risen Jesus was some type of ghost or phantom, that is, a mere risen soul, as would have been the normal expectation in ancient world culture for any appearance of the dead. Thus Jesus materializes postmortem and commands his frightened disciples to touch him and see that he has flesh and bones, directly contradicting the venerable examples of poetic tradition. The authors hereby attempt to support the late first century Christian claim that the resurrection of Jesus was unique in kind, bodily and substantial.

Yet not even this stratagem was secure against objection. Tradition and poetry did not lack examples of palpability among the shades even in the face of this motif to the contrary. Almost all agreed that the dead could receive offerings and prayers from the living, and reciprocally that they could affect the living for good or ill. These facts, acted out in daily religious cult, implied or necessitated that the "doctrine" of impalpability include some contradiction. The dead were in the main conceived of as were the living: resting and waking, conversing with both the living and other dead, eating and drinking, and carrying on postmortem much as they had in life.

---

moved to be healed of his wound (*Il.* 5.451). Earlier in the *Odyssey* itself, Athena made a double (an εἴδωλον) of Penelope's sister, who then appeared to Penelope in a dream in her bedroom, conversed with her, and departed through the locked door (*Od.* 4.796–841).

Game boards, for example, were a common offering in tombs, along with dice.[138]

The dead were even able to engage in sex, apparently, both among themselves and with the living. The Trojan Cycle included an account of the tragic death of Polyxena, daughter of Priam, whom the shade of Achilles claimed as his reward after the sack of Troy. The Greeks sacrificed her on his tomb that she should be his concubine in Hades.[139] The Romans of later times would on occasion sacrifice a woman for every ten dead soldiers as an underworld "camp girl," to provide comfort for the men in the afterlife.[140] In addition, the (dead) hero Astrabacus had sexual relations with and fathered a son by the (living) mother of Demaratus (Herodotus 6.69). She described the hero as being a φάσμα ("ghost, apparition") in the form of her husband Ariston, for whom she mistook him; they clearly touched each other. This episode is modeled, of course, on the penchant of Greek deities in general for sexual relations with humans, whose offspring would then be in some way remarkable: the child Demaratus in the example above became king of Sparta.

One of the main functions of dead heroes was to bless and protect the living as guardians. Josephus retells a speech of the Roman general Titus, who encourages his troops by noting that those who die on the battlefield become guardian souls who, "as good *daimones* and kindly heroes, appear among their own descendants" (*BJ* 6.47). To further this end, when occasion demanded, the souls of the dead and especially those of the heroes received nearly ubiquitous *cultus*. Thus they were expected to fight against the living enemies who threatened their worshippers. The heroes Phylacus and Autonous, for example, who lay buried in shrines at Delphi, rose in defense of the town during an attack of the Persians. They appeared on the battlefield as larger-than-life soldiers and pursued and slaughtered a great number of the enemy (Herodotus 8.36–39). In addition, the

138. Cf. E. Vermeule, *Aspects of Death in Early Greek Art and Poetry*, 80.

139. Euripides, *Hecuba* 36–41, 566–572; according to Proclus, from the *Iliou Persis*: "Then, after sacking the city, they sacrificed Polyxena on the tomb of Achilles" (Allen, *Homeri Opera*, 5.108).

140. Cf. E. Vermeule, *Aspects of Death in Early Greek Art and Poetry*, 55.

dead could also fight each other: Pausanias' description of the painting by Polygnotus included a scene on the bank of the river Acheron; there the soul of a son is being choked by that of his father, as the son while alive had maltreated him and been neglectful of his filial duties (10.28.4–5).[141] Poetry also provides us with examples of the living threatening the dead with harm. Odysseus, at the beginning of his conversations in the underworld, holds a threatening sword over the blood of his sacrifice to ward off the shades of the dead, allowing but one at a time to drink, that he may converse with them in order (*Od.* 11.48–50, 82, 95–96, 231–232).[142] Thus the dead could, on occasion and when necessary, physically touch for good or ill, and be touched by, the living.

Homer had used to great effect the theme of impalpability in his representation of the dead in the scene noted above, the account of Odysseus in the underworld attempting to embrace his mother. Virgil in the first century BCE made use of this Homeric passage in the *Aeneid*, yet his treatment reflects certain significant developments: the "life" in the underworld had by his time become far more substantial, and the dead had become correspondingly more tangible. In Virgil's story, Aeneas enters the underworld in order to speak with his father, Anchises, and to afford the author the preternatural setting for the prophecy of Rome's greatness which is the central theme of the work (*Aeneid* 6.756–885). Still present is the theme of impalpability: in imitation of the Homeric lines quoted above, Aeneas tries three times in vain to embrace his father, and three times he flits away through his grasp, "like light winds and most similar to a winged dream."[143] Yet in *Aeneid* 6 in general the dead are far more

141. Cf. also the enmity continued beyond the grave between Aias and Odysseus (*Od.* 11.541), the two heroes Adrastus and Miltiades (Herodotus 5.67–68), and Aeneas and Dido (*Aeneid* 6.472).

142. A contradiction of this presumption of the vulnerability of the dead is seen in the fifth victory ode of Bacchylides (fifth century BCE). Here, Heracles, during his descent to the underworld to retrieve the hound Cerberus, is about to shoot an arrow in terror at the sudden appearance of the ghost of Meleager. Meleager tells him to quell his fear (Bacchylides 5.81–84): "lest in vain he shoot / from his hands a swift arrow / at the souls of the the dead."

143. *Aeneid* 6.702. The passage in the *Odyssey* required that the weak and witless souls of the dead receive a draught of blood before they were able to speak with

vital and less ghostly, both in "physical" substance and character. On the shore of Acheron, the river of the underworld, Aeneas first encounters a crowd of souls waiting to be ferried across by Charon. These he describes as "mothers and men, and bodies of great-spirited heroes, with life now passed" (6.306–307). He uses the term "bodies" (*corpora*) to describe the souls; the prevailing philosophic outlook of the time held that the soul was a kind of finely particled material "body." These souls by tradition, though not in the *Aeneid* itself, bring an obol with them as payment to the ferryman,[144] and are carried across the river in the same boat in which Aeneas himself sails. They speak readily with Aeneas, thronging about him, poignantly recounting their mutual experiences. The dead even comfort each other: Dido, Aeneas' spurned lover, enjoys mutual love and consolation with her first husband, Sychaeus, after she rejects the weak apologies of Aeneas (6.467–474). Aeneas then passes the places of torture of the wicked dead, where he hears "sobbing, and the sound of cruel beatings, and the clank of iron and the dragging of chains" (6.557–558). The wicked dead are being whipped and scourged in chains, making atonement for their sins. As Aeneas enters the Groves of the Blessed, he sees some of the dead engaging in sports, wrestling, dancing. Some even have their weapons and chariots of old, whose horses graze in the fields (6.642–655).

A similar remarkable description of the substantial nature of the afterlife among "impalpable" shades is found in the works of Lucian in the century following the writing of the Gospels. In his fantasy tale (which he entitles "The True Account") of a journey to the regions of the western ocean beyond the Pillars of Hercules, Lucian describes his fortuitous arrival at the Isle of the Blessed, the eternal home of those who pass the judgment of the judge of the dead and

---

Odysseus and his men (*Od.* 11.147–149). Yet later in the *Odyssey*, in the second Nekyia, the souls are able to speak to each other without such fortification (*Od.* 24.15–204). In *Aeneid* 6 no such requirement appears.

144. The obol appears in Aristophanes, *Frogs* 140, 270; *Birds* 503, and often in later literature and art. The dead are found from the fourth century on buried with an obol in their mouths, that they should not lack the fare for the journey across the river of the underworld. Cf. E. Vermeule, *Aspects of Death in Early Greek Art and Poetry*, 211–212, n. 7.

ruler of the Isle, Rhadamanthys (or Radamanthus). Lucian, while still sailing offshore, hears the sounds of a drinking party in progress; some revelers are singing while others play the flute and lyre in time to the music. On landing he and his companions are bound with chains of roses and led before the ruler, who is occupied in judging three other cases among the heroic dead. First, Ajax, the hero of the *Iliad* who had gone mad and killed himself, is handed over to Hippocrates the physician to undergo a treatment of medicine from the plant hellebore to recover his wits, and then take his place at the banquet of heroes. Next, the court determines that Helen should be the wife of Menelaus and not Theseus, since Menelaus had undergone such trials to regain her at Troy, and since Theseus already had two other wives. Third, the seat of Alexander the Great is placed above that of Hannibal of Carthage at the feast, since he outranked him. Finally the king turns to Lucian and his companions and decides that they are to be allowed to remain on the Isle for seven months and share the activities and feasting of the heroes before being required to leave for Greece.

Released from his gentle bonds, Lucian discovers a city of gold, walled about with emerald on ivory foundations. Within are temples to all the gods, and a river of myrrh which is quite pleasant for swimming. There are baths warmed by burning cinnamon, filled not with water but dew. For clothing, the blessed dead use spider webs, royal purple in color. In short, the inhabitants live and act exactly as do the living. In fact, Lucian and his companions are alive, and share all activities with them: they eat the same food, drink the same wine, sit at the same tables and banquets, swim and bathe, engage in the same sporting and song. Yet regarding the dead themselves, Lucian tells us (*Verae historiae* 2.12):

> They themselves do not have bodies, but are impalpable and non-fleshly, and appear in shape and form only, and though they are bodiless, they nevertheless act and move and think and give forth voice, and their soul, although as something naked, seems entirely to carry on clothed in the semblance of the body.

If, indeed, one did not touch one of them, one would not be able to verify that what one saw was not a body.

Here one sees clearly the greatly enhanced and substantial "life" of the dead, which even the living Lucian and his companions are able to share; yet the old conceit of the impalpability of the soul survives.

The souls of the dead could certainly interact with the living and with each other, in ways exactly analogous to normal life. Instances abound in which the dead were touched and touched others. In Lucian's account, he and his companions are "arrested" and bound by the dead, and led to the king for their judgment; they sit on the same chairs, eat the same food, and much more. The souls of the dead, though described as impalpable, seem not to notice this minor modification: they live and act exactly as do the living, even alongside the living. So it was quite possible, even after the Gospels were written to maintain the postmortem survival of the soul alone and deny bodily resurrection. It was quite within the traditional view to ignore the intent of the post-resurrection physical demonstration scenes in Luke and John, and to continue to interpret these texts in the old manner: Jesus could have been touched, if he so chose; Astrabacus and many other heroes had been.

## Rejection of the *Kerygma* of Resurrection

Against this background of possibilities for post-mortem existence, the witness of the resurrection of Christ was preached, arousing considerable opposition among pagans and Christians alike. In the words of Weltin:[145]

---

145. E. G. Weltin, *Athens and Jerusalem: An Interpretive Essay on Christianity and Classical Culture* (AAR Studies in Religion 49; Atlanta: Scholars Press, 1987) 44. Also, "Resurrection in the flesh appeared a startling, distasteful idea, at odds with everything that passed for wisdom among the educated": Ramsay MacMullen, *Christianizing the Roman Empire* (New Haven and London: Yale Univ. Press, 1984) 12. It became a common theme among the apologists to attempt to counter those among the educated Romans who thought the doctrine was "unbelievable or impossible" (Justin, *1 Apol.* 8); cf. Tatian, *Oratio ad Graecos* 6, Theophilus, *Ad Autol.* 1.8, Athenagoras, *Legatio* 36.

The Jewish idea of resurrection of the whole person was so novel that it boggled the mind of pagan and gentile Christian alike. Many found it quaint, utterly ridiculous, or downright repulsive. Celsus deemed it so degrading that only fools would have thought it up.

In fact what Celsus says in the second century is what any educated Roman or Greek would have said in the first century: "it is not possible that Jesus rose with his body."[146] The logic of the idea was wrong and, given his inherited doctrines of the soul and body, abhorrent: "This is simply the hope of worms. For what sort of human soul would still desire a body that has rotted?"[147] He discounts the Gospel records of the post-Easter appearances as the reports of an hysterical female and another deluded person (Peter?) who either (2.55):

> dreamed and because of his desire hallucinated in his erroneous opinion, . . . or, what is more likely, wanted to astound others with this fairy story, or to provide through this lie an opportunity for other religious beggars.

In his opinion, the reports of physical resurrection could not be true; they had to be either hysteria, dreams, hallucinations, or lies.

As in earlier generations, there were in Celsus' time Christian groups which did not accept the doctrine of physical resurrection.[148]

146. *Contra Celsum* 6.72. The date of Celsus' writing is given as 177–180 by Henry Chadwick, *Origen: Contra Celsum. Translated with an Introduction and Notes* (Cambridge: Cambridge Univ. Press, 1965) xxviii. Origen wrote his reply in the mid-third century. For the epistemological basis of the argument with Origen, cf. Robert J. Hauck, "'They Saw What They Said They Saw': Sense Knowledge in Early Christian Polemic," in *HTR* 81 (1988) 239–249.

147. *Contra Celsum* 5.14. Modern beneficiaries of medical care may overlook how troublesome life in the body was for the ancients. There was almost no effective treatment even for the rich, and no medical care at all for the poor. Thus the question of Celsus, "Who would desire a body . . . ?", would have been met with much knowing approval in his day.

148. In addition to the references below, cf. the various defenses of the resurrection to Christians in, for example, *1 Clement* 24–26; Ignatius (*Smyr.* 2–3); 2 Clement 9; Barnabas 5; Irenaeus, *Adv. Haer.*, *passim*, against gnostic Christians; and the *Acts of Paul*. Athenagoras, *De Res.* argues for the doctrine against Greek philosophical

In his rebuttal of the idea, Celsus writes: "That this doctrine is not shared even by some of you who are Christians proves that it is utterly repulsive and detestable and at the same time impossible."[149] Polycarp, an older contemporary of Celsus, also encountered such Christians, and leaves the impression in his letter to the Philippians that they were quite numerous. After warning against those who deny the flesh of Christ, the cross, and the resurrection, he admonishes (*Ad Phil.* 7):

> Therefore, leaving the vanities of the majority and their false teachings, let us turn back to the word which was handed down to us from the beginning. . . .

For Polycarp, apparently, they were in the majority.[150] Neither he nor Celsus specify who these Christians were,[151] nor does Origen in his reply name them; he says only that they are "those who, although they are called Christians, deny the scriptural doctrine of resurrection."[152] Origen implies that these Christians simply denied the Scriptures, that both they and Origen knew that the clear teaching of

---

objections within and without the Church [if this treatise is by Athenagoras; Grant attributes it to a third or fourth century anti-Origenist: Robert M. Grant, "Athenagoras or Pseudo-Athenagoras," in *HTR* 47 (1954) 121–129].

149. *Contra Celsum* 5.14. The Christian answer to this accusation of impossibility, that "all things are possible to God," was also known to and disparaged by Celsus, and must have been a commonplace (cf., for example, Justin, *1 Apol.* 18–19). It shows, according to Pichler, the philosophical weakness of the Christian position: Karl Pichler, *Streit um das Christentum: Der Angriff des Kelsos und die Antwort des Origenes* (Regensburger Studien zur Theologie 23; Frankfurt am Main: Peter D. Lang, 1980) 149.

150. Tertullian admits that "a great many" Christians claim that resurrection is escaping out of the world, or going out of the body itself (*De Res. Mort.* 17); that is, the ascent of the disembodied soul.

151. Chadwick takes them, probably rightly, to be Gnostics (*Contra Celsum*, 274, n. 7).

152. *Contra Celsum* 5.22. Origen himself, of course, agreed to a large extent with Celsus and these opponents: none of them would allow the flesh to be raised. Origen instead claims that the raised body is identical with the original body of flesh in appearance (the εἴδωλον), but raised in a new spiritual material (*Contra Celsum* 7.32). Cf. on Origens position, J. N. D. Kelly, *Early Christian Doctrines* (rev. ed.; San Francisco: Harper, 1978) 469–474.

Scripture was bodily resurrection, yet they denied it out of stupidity or perversity. The doctrine was the teaching of Scripture to Origen, but that conclusion was based on his method of interpretation. His competitors also had methods of interpretation, and these supported their opposite conclusions; their doctrines by their lights were also quite as "scriptural."

Justin Martyr, writing before Celsus in the mid-second century, fought a battle against similar opponents. In the fragments of his lost work *De Resurrectione*, he argues against those who deny the doctrine by interpreting words of Jesus to mean that there is no bodily resurrection. Using the saying, "For when they rise from the dead, they neither marry, nor are given in marriage, but are like angels in the heavens" (Mark 12:25) the opponents contend that "the angels . . . neither have flesh, nor eat, nor engage in sex; so therefore a fleshly resurrection shall not occur" (*De Res.* 2.10–12). For these antagonists the soul derives from God, while the body is corruptible and not from God (8.27). Justin remarks (10.6–7):

Don't we see ourselves turning backwards, when we hear 'the soul is immortal, but the body is corruptible and no longer able to live again'? For these things indeed we used to hear before learning the truth from Pythagoras and Plato.

The great enemies of the doctrine of the resurrection faced by Justin were none other than the Christian disciples of Pythagoras, Plato, and so many other philosophers whose doctrines we have seen above. Justin's Christ, on the other hand, proclaimed a "new and strange hope" (10.9), different from what the culture expected. Justin identifies his opponents, these champions of philosophical commonplaces, as Jewish Christians, and calls them (in words reminiscent of Paul in 2 Corinthians 11) "apostles" of "the Prince of Wickedness."[153] He likewise warns Trypho against assuming that all Christians are "authentic" Christians (*Dial. Try.* 80):

153. *De Res.* 10.11. They are "of those who crucified our savior, who bear the name of the savior" (10.13).

> For if you have conversed with certain so-called Christians,
> . . . who also say that there is no resurrection of the dead, but
> that at the time of death their souls are taken up into heaven, do
> not suppose that they are Christians. . . .

These "so-called Christians" espouse exactly what Celsus believed, or Cicero, or any other educated individual of the times. Here are Jewish Christians interpreting Jesus' words and professing as Christian doctrine what Greco-Roman culture had taught for centuries. This is what the author of the *Book of Thomas* taught; here is where the Thomas tradition is at home.

Likewise Tertullian, writing between the time of Celsus and Origen (ca. 208) in his treatise *De Resurrectione Mortuorum*, attempts to counter another interpretive means by which the old philosophy was melded with the new. He assails the view of some who called the soul the "soulish body" (*corpus animale*) which was raised in resurrection, and distinguished it from the flesh which was not raised.[154] The issue concerned differing views of Paul's discussion of the resurrection body in 1 Corinthians 15. Paul claims of the body that "it is sown a soulish body; it is raised a spiritual body."[155] Tertullian's opponents identified the "soulish body" (σῶμα ψυχικόν) as the soul alone, and held that this "body" was raised while the physical body remained in the grave. His counterargument faced the difficulty of an old Stoic proposition which both he and his opponents accepted: that the soul is a corporeal substance.[156] If so, his opponents would argue, then

---

154. *De Res. Mort.* 53: "But some argue that the 'soulish body' [of 1 Corinthians 15:44] is the soul, so that they separate the raised body from the flesh."

155. 1 Cor 15:44: σπείρεται σῶμα ψυχικόν, ἐγείρεται σῶμα πνευματικόν. This verse is often translated as: "It is sown a natural/physical body; it is raised a spiritual body." The translation "natural" (NIV; NASB) or "physical" (NRSV) for the word "soulish" (ψυχικόν) obscures for readers of English the very point ("soulish") so important to the ancient argument.

156. *De Res. Mort.* 53.8: "Albeit the soul is indeed a body" (*anima vero etsi corpus*). Tertullian was caught between Plato and the Stoics: in his denial of Plato's doctrine of immateriality, he argues vehemently that the soul is material in *De anima* 5–9. He goes so far as to "call on the Stoics for assistance" in support of his case for the material soul (5), bringing in arguments that the soul could not be tortured in hell if it were not tangible, and even enlisting the support of Lucretius (*De Re-*

the soul is a "body," and could be termed properly a "soulish body." When it is raised and receives the fullness of the spirit, it becomes the "spiritual body." In Tertullian's sarcastic words, these Christians were advocating *animae resurrectionem*, "the resurrection of the soul" (*De Res. Mort.* 53.12).[157] The same texts were being used by Christians of opposing viewpoints to support contradictory doctrines. Visible here is a hermeneutical method, a way of interpreting texts and traditions, which denied the fleshly resurrection of the body while it accepted the teaching of Paul and his "spiritual body" ($\sigma\hat{\omega}\mu\alpha$ $\pi\nu\epsilon\nu\mu\alpha\tau\iota\kappa\acute{o}\nu$; 1 Cor. 15:44 ); this "resurrection body" was the Greco-Roman corporeal soul.[158]

That the ancients could easily interpret the very resurrection texts themselves in non-physical terms is missed by some modern interpreters. According to Craig, for example, "The notion of resurrection is unintelligible with regard to the spirit or soul alone. The very words imply resurrection of the body."[159] Such a contention is shown to be false by the very controversy itself: to many Christians of the first and later centuries, not only was the idea of physical resurrection odious, but the "very words" used to assert it were understood to teach otherwise.

The counterargument of the Church took the form of a virtual justification of the flesh, which required no small amount of creative thought given the negative view of the flesh in both the culture and the Scriptures. The argument grew especially sharp in the later sec-

---

*rum Natura* 1.305): "Nothing except a body is able to touch or to be touched." Tertullian argues for "Traducianism" in *De anima* 23–41, that the material soul is transmitted physically from parents to children.

157. For a modern Christian meditation on the subject much more in the spirit of the ancient "heretics" than that of Tertullian, cf. John B. Cobb, Jr., "The Resurrection of the Soul," in *HTR* 80 (1987) 213–227.

158. The controversy lasted into the fifth century at least: Gregory of Nyssa refutes Stoic denial of the possibility of resurrection in *On the Making of Man*, 25; Jerome fights against a Christian who teaches the Stoic doctrine of the immortal soul using the Scriptures, in *Epist.* 108.24. Tertullian tells us that in his time "No others, indeed, deny salvation to the corporeal substance than the heretics of a second deity," identifying these as followers of Marcion, Basilides, Valentinus, and Apelles (*De Res. Mort.* 2.2).

159. W. L. Craig, "The Historicity of the Empty Tomb of Jesus," in *NTS* 31 (1985) 39–67 [the quote is from p. 41].

ond century. Irenaeus argues that the fleshly body, once raised by the Spirit's instrumentality, becomes the "spiritual body" (*Adv. Haer.* 5.7.2). So it is for him "the flesh possessed by the Spirit" which inherits the Kingdom of God (5.9.3). Athenagoras clearly feels embarrassment at this Christian claim, and attempts to have it both ways: he declares that "even if we have flesh, it will not seem so; we shall be heavenly spirits" (*Legatio* 31). Tertullian argues that, since all humanity will be resurrected to face judgment, the flesh by itself is not denied resurrection but only the Kingdom of God, if it is without the Spirit (*De Res. Mort.* 50). Accordingly, the phrase "Resurrection of the Flesh" was added to the Old Roman Creed as part of the catechism and baptismal liturgy. Such argumentation laid the foundation for the views of the later Church, in which Paul was understood to mean by the "spiritual body" the same fleshly body of earthly life raised from the grave and controlled by the Spirit. Thus "resurrection of the flesh" could be said of a "spiritual body."[160]

Some of Tertullian's main opponents were the disciples of Marcion, against whom he wrote a rebuttal, *Adversus Marcionem*, in five books. Marcion, in concert with his doctrine of a docetic Christ, also denied the doctrine of physical resurrection. Yet he was one of the most "scriptural" Christians of his day, collecting the Pauline epistles, and editing a version of Luke. His hermeneutical method was to remove those parts of the texts which contradicted his presuppositions, and then to explain as a literalist what remained according to his own theology. Marcion's method was a violent expedient, but his case reveals how easily even the most uncompromising of the traditions and texts which described the physical resurrection of Jesus could be viewed as teaching "spiritual" resurrection. One example will serve as an illustration.

Marcion's Gospel included part of the post-resurrection appearance of Jesus to the assembled disciples (Luke 24:36–43).[161] Verses

160. Cf. H. Clavier, "Brèves remarques sur la notion de σῶμα πνευματικόν," in W. D. Davies and D. Daube, eds., *The Background of the New Testament and Its Eschatology* (Cambridge: Cambridge Univ. Press, 1964) 342–362; and J. N. D. Kelly, *Early Christian Creeds* (third ed.; New York: Longman, 1972) 163–165.

161. Hoffmann's insightful comments on the passage stand behind this discus-

37–38 describe the incredulity of the disciples who think that they are seeing a ghost, and Jesus' rebuke of their doubt. Verse 39 reads in canonical Luke:

*See my hands and feet, that I am myself. Touch me and see that a spirit does not have flesh and bones as you see that I have.*

Here is one of the Gospel's strongest proofs of physical postmortem existence for Jesus; yet Marcion was able to overturn its meaning. Tertullian describes his interpretation as follows:[162]

So he wants the passage to read thus: "a spirit does not have bones, as you see me being," as though he is referring to a spirit "as you see me being," that is, not having bones, like a spirit.

Marcion's understanding of the saying has Jesus tell the disciples to try to touch him and see that they can't, since he, as any spirit, does not have flesh and bones. He uses the received tradition and text, yet is able to advocate "resurrection of the soul."

The assertion of the resurrection was a central feature of much of the early proclamation of Jesus from the beginning. The earliest record of the message which survives, 1 Cor 15:3–5, contains this claim. The question arises: How could early Christians who heard from the be-

---

sion: R. Joseph Hoffmann, *Marcion: On the Restitution of Christianity. An Essay on the Development of Radical Paulinist Theology in the Second Century* (AAR Academy Series 46; Chico: Scholars Press, 1984) 119–123. Cf. also David Salter Williams, "Reconsidering Marcion's Gospel," in *JBL* 108 (1989) 477–496.

162. *Adv. Marc.* 4.43.7:
Vult itaque sic dictum: "spiritus ossa non habet, sicut me videtis habentem," quasi ad spiritum referatur "sicut me videtis habentem," id est non habentem ossa, sicut spiritus.
The Latin *habeo*, like the Greek ἔχω, may also have the sense "to be," "to be constituted in a certain manner," etc. Thus Marcion's interpretation of this passage could stand in either language (and accordingly I have translated the different forms of the word *habeo* as both "have, having" and "being"). The text is that of Aem. Kroymann, *Q. S. Fl. Tertulliani. Adversus Marcionem. Corpus Christianorum: Series Latina. Tertulliani Opera: Pars I* (Turnholti: Typographi Brepolis, 1954).

ginning the preaching of the resurrection have denied it? This very formulation of the question, however, betrays a later Christian bias toward physical resurrection which was (all but) absent at the outset and took generations to develop in the Church. Comparison of the texts and ideas in the survey above with the resurrection narratives of the New Testament reveals that there was a wide field for divergence of opinion between the two extremes of complete denial of postmortem survival (Epicureans, Sadducees) and that of fleshly reconstitution. The mode of resurrection was ill-defined, and disparate communities were able to preach and believe differently, just as they had before the advent of Jesus and his movement.

The idea that the very flesh of the premortem individual should survive the grave was new in the Empire, and to many, abhorrent. The reaction of Celsus showed that the idea of physical reconstitution was odious to the Greco-Roman mind. The Christian examples given above (heretical by later formulation) illustrate some of the hermeneutical methods used in the second century to interpret biblical traditions and texts in accord with accepted Greco-Roman models. Christians in Corinth in the mid-fifties CE, Christians of the Thomas tradition, and many others both within and without the Great Church, for more than four subsequent centuries were able to "deny" such a resurrection. In fact they were not denying it at all; they were interpreting it in categories which their own culture had developed through centuries of philosophical and religious experience. As late as the fifth century, Jerome complains that even in the Eastern creeds, which had matured on the very soil of Greek philosophy, continued to use the terms "resurrection of the body" where the Western versions used "resurrection of the flesh." He complains (*Epist.* 84.5):

> They use the world "body" instead of the world "flesh", in order that the orthodox person, hearing them say "body", may take them to mean "flesh", while a heretic will understand that they mean "spirit".

The Eastern fathers were clearly not heretics, but pragmatists. They understood the need to leave room for compromise, for many of them from the beginning had seen in the resurrection of Jesus a spiritual, not physical, phenomenon.

But these two categories themselves, spiritual and physical, were far from mutually exclusive: the soul itself was a material "body." The message of the Church, under the pressure of controversy over the next several generations, eventually became a message of the resurrection of the physical flesh. But when, as in Philo, the language of resurrection was heard as the time-honored concepts of the postmortem soul and immortality, then all that the tradition reported about Jesus was received in faith without reference to the flesh. Each of the physical activities claimed for the post-Easter Jesus by the writers of the gospels were common religious inheritance for the postmortem soul. Any Semitic or Greco-Roman soul could appear to the living, still bearing the recognizable form of the body. Any soul could pass through closed doors, give preternatural advice, and vanish. Did Jesus appear to and instruct his disciples after his crucifixion? So Patroklos appeared to Achilles, Samuel to Saul, the elder Scipio to his grandson, as did numerous others to their survivors. Did the resurrected Jesus eat broiled fish, and a meal with his disciples? Any soul could, and often did, eat with friends and relatives in the repasts of the cult of the dead, a practice perhaps especially common among Christians.[163] The post-Easter body of Jesus still displayed the imprints of the nails on his hands and feet, and the wound in his side. Yet such would have been the normal expectation for the dead: their souls would, like Hector, have borne their death wounds. That Jesus was "real" after death, in fact more real than while disguised in a body, followed naturally from speculation about the soul as the "real" person, and the body as its mere prison or tomb.

Early Christians could doubt, and there is evidence that they did doubt, any or all of these elements according to their preconceptions

---

163. Eusebius tells us (*HE* 8.6) that the Romans threw the bodies of martyrs into the sea to keep Christians from worshipping the dead.

about death and survival. Among those Jews who inherited the idea of bodily resurrection, the preaching of the doctrine posed little difficulty. Among others, Jew and non-Jew, for whom bodily resurrection was unimagined and outside of cultural expectation, and for whom the body was a negative and temporary element, interpretation of the traditions surrounding the resurrection could still have led to faith without difficulty, but for one element: the poetic conceit that the soul beyond the grave could not be handled. Shades, εἴδωλα, could do all things as we, and more, but were reputed to be impalpable. Here is the motivation for the notices in the post-Easter appearance stories concerning the handling of Jesus. The writers of Luke and John were careful to include physical demonstrations, the offer of touching the body of Jesus, to obviate the interpretation already current among Christians that Jesus had raised as a spirit. Herein lies the motivation for the Doubting Thomas pericope, with its grossly physical demand and response. But even these proofs were insufficient, and interpreted otherwise.

As this study will demonstrate, the *Gospel of Thomas* declares that the body will not be raised by so interpreting the sayings of Jesus. In John, a Johannine version of the same sayings claims the opposite. In fact, several aspects of John and *Thomas* may be seen as points in a "conversation" between the two communities. The *Book of Thomas (the Contender)* argues vehemently against those who hope for the resurrection of the body, drawing heavily on the Greek philosophical tradition. The *Acts of Thomas* is itself in the midst of the battle, between the two sides, suffering "orthodox" revision of its romantic teaching of bodily asceticism in the present and denial of an embodied future. The original denial, however, was not made by these authors and their community, but by the *kerygma* of the flesh, which had first to contradict "immortality of the soul," and was then opposed in counterpoint. This controversy is visible, in ascending levels of stridency, within the Thomas literature. It is also visible between the communities of Thomas and John, and in the disagreement of Jesus and his disciples with Doubting Thomas in the Gospel of John.

# Chapter Two

# Thomas and the Appearance Stories in John

Thomas is an enigmatic figure. For all the literature and tradition surrounding him outside the canon, the only book in the New Testament in which the person of Thomas appears as a character is John's Gospel. Elsewhere in the New Testament the name is found only on the lists of the twelve disciples of Jesus in the Synoptic Gospels and Acts,[1] but Thomas as an individual does not participate in any of the stories or activities of these works. Outside of John we would not know of his existence except for the appearance of his name on the apostle lists. In this he is not unique; but for the lists we would not know of five others of the twelve disciples: neither Philip, Bartholomew, James the son of Alpheus, Thaddeus, nor Simon the Zealot appear as anything more than names. In addition, a mere one verse description of a call to discipleship from his tax booth elevates Matthew above this gallery of the near-anonymous (Matt 9:9).

If one were to ask which disciples are important for the Synoptic Gospels, an answer could be readily given. In general, "the disciples," meaning the Twelve considered as a group, are the main partners of Jesus. Other than the Twelve as a whole, only Peter, James and John are of moment, and, of course negatively, at the end of Jesus' ministry, Judas Iscariot. In Matthew, the disciples stand together for the community.[2] Yet Peter speaks often for the group, and it is clear that Peter is the central figure among the disciples.[3] He is the confessor of

1. Matt 10:3; Mark 3:18; Luke 6:15; Acts 1:13.
2. For Luz, the disciples in Matthew are "transparent"; "behind them stand Matthew's community. *Mathetes* is an ecclesiological term": Ulrich Luz, "The Disciples in the Gospel According to Matthew," in Graham Stanton, ed., *The Interpretation of Matthew* (IRT 3; London: SPCK and Philadelphia: Fortress Press, 1983) 110.
3. " . . . Matthew presents the disciples as a nameless, faceless, collective unity. Against this backdrop of anonymity Matthew gives a portrait of Peter . . . the only disciple who is emphasized": Michael J. Wilkins, *The Concept of Disciple in Mat-*

Christ and the Rock on which the church is to be built (Matt 16:16–18). One could say that Matthew is a Peter Gospel, that it was written to emphasize his role in a community which found his influence and person important as a standard or rallying point.[4] In Mark, the disciples together in the main surround and follow Jesus, participate with him in his ministry and act as his interlocutors. Their main literary function seems to be failure: failure to understand, follow, or believe.[5] Peter, James and John find a place, but the main character is decidedly Jesus himself, without serious emphasis on any other individual. The Gospel of Luke is of course the first volume of a two-volume work, Luke-Acts, which follows the ministry of both the earthly Jesus in the Gospel, and the heavenly Jesus in Acts, as the Spirit in the Church. Among the Twelve, the most influential disciple is Peter, but his role in the narrative of Acts is taken over first by James, the brother of Jesus, and then by the new apostle, Paul. It is Paul who eventually occupies center stage, supported and encouraged, according to the apologetic reconstruction in Acts, by the Jerusalem contingent of Peter and James.

If one examines, however, which disciples are important in John's Gospel, a very different picture emerges. The Twelve still appear, but gone is the troika of Peter, James and John of the Synoptics. James is not mentioned at all. In fact, the name "John" in John's Gospel never

---

thew's Gospel as Reflected in the Use of the Term Μαθητής (Leiden: E. J. Brill, 1988) 223; see 173–216 for Peter. Also, cf. Jack Dean Kingsbury, "The Figure of Peter in Matthew's Gospel as a Theological Problem," in *JBL* 98 (1979) 67–83.

4. Cf. Eduard Schweizer, "Matthew's Church," in Graham Stanton, ed., *The Interpretation of Matthew* (trans. by Robert Morgan; IRT 3; London: SPCK and Philadelphia: Fortress Press, 1983) 135–137; also R. Brown, Karl P. Donfried, John Reumann, eds., *Peter in the New Testament* (Minneapolis: Augsburg and New York: Paulist Press, 1973) 75–107.

5. Cf. T. J. Weeden, "The Heresy that Necessitated Mark's Gospel," in *ZNW* 59 (1968) 145–158; J. B. Tyson, "The Blindness of the Disciples in Mark," in *JBL* 80 (1961) 261–268; Norman Perrin, *The Resurrection According to Matthew, Mark, and Luke* (Philadelphia: Fortress Press, 1977) 31; and Robert C. Tannehill, "The Disciples in Mark: the Function of a Narrative Role," in *JR* 57 (1977) 386–405. For a more positive picture of the disciples representing the new family of God in the Markan community, cf. John R. Donahue, *The Theology and Setting of Discipleship in the Gospel of Mark* (Milwaukee: Marquette Univ. Press, 1983) 35; and David J. Hawkin, "The Incomprehension of the Disciples in the Markan Redaction," in *JBL* 91 (1972) 491–500.

occurs, but was hidden, according to later tradition, by the title "the disciple whom Jesus loved."[6] Peter does occur, as he must in any account of Jesus' ministry. Yet his brother Andrew brings him to Jesus; he is upstaged in the narrative by Nathaniel, by the Woman at the Well, the Man Born Blind, and later by Mary, Martha and Lazarus, none of whom even belong to the Twelve. In the most important section of the Gospel, the Farewell Discourses beginning in chapter 13, Peter is joined by Philip, Thomas and Judas in asking significant questions about Jesus' departure and identity. Thus the circle of conspicuous disciples in John, though overlapping somewhat, is quite unlike that in the Synoptics.

We learn from Gal 2:7 that apostolic spheres of influence were assigned to Peter and Paul, Peter to minister to the Jews and Paul to the Gentiles.[7] We learn also that a particular (erroneous, from Paul's viewpoint) doctrinal position was attributed to "certain people from James," identified with "the party of the circumcision" (2:12). Likewise, a doctrinal position was attributed to Paul. He relates a "slander" told about his teaching in Rom 3:8:[8]

Just as we are slandered and as certain people relate that we say "Let us do wicked things so that good things may result."

---

6. John 13:23; 21:7, 20. Not all agree that the traditional ascription of the title to John, son of Zebedee (Irenaeus, *Adv. Haer.* 3.1), is justified. Sanders, in an interesting article, makes a case for Lazarus: J. N. Sanders, "Who Was the Disciple Whom Jesus Loved?," in F. L. Cross, ed., *Studies in the Fourth Gospel* (London: A. R. Mowbray, 1957) 72–82; also F. V. Filson, "Who Was the Beloved Disciple?," in *JBL* 63 (1949) 83–88. Matthias is chosen by E. L. Titus, "The Identity of the Beloved Disciple," in *JBL* 69 (1950) 323–328. Others consider him an originally historical, but literarily paradigmatic, figure: P. Minear, "The Beloved Disciple in the Gospel of John," in *Nov T* 19 (1977) 105–123; William H. Brownlee, "Whence the Gospel according to John?," in James H. Charlesworth, ed., *John and Qumran* (London: Geoffrey Chapman, 1972) 193 ["not just Lazarus, but every disciple"].

7. Paul reiterates this point of Gentile ministry in Rom 15:16. Acts, curiously enough, has both Paul and Peter ministering to the Gentiles, at least in the early period (9:15; 15:7). We are not told of a formal shift.

8. The "parties" in 1 Corinthians 1–4 are further examples of the same tendency. Another such passage is found in Acts 21:20–21, where the author relates James giving to Paul the viewpoint of Palestinian Jewish Christians against him:

You see, brother, how many myriads there are among the Jews who have believed, and all are zealots for the Law. And they have heard about you, that

This is early evidence for the beginning of a phenomenon quite well attested in the following century, that of doctrines and religious orientations associated with the names of individual apostolic figures. By that time, literature and tradition were produced in the name of apostles or other significant figures in a "school" tradition which reflected not only traditions attached to the apostle, where such information survived, but also subsequent developments within the communities who looked to individual apostles as guarantors of their doctrines and ways of life.[9] Series of writings, produced over time by different generations and often competing groups, were composed in the name of Peter, Paul, John, James, Thomas, and others,[10] which reflect not only a core of early tradition, but also accretions and modifications tending in different religious directions made by later claimants to the teaching of these apostles.[11] The development of the Thomas tradition also follows this pattern, and includes literature, sphere of influence, and specific doctrinal orientation.

The import of these observations is that the significant figures found in the Gospels are not accidentally present, but are emphasized or placed in the background with reason: they were consequential for the communities which produced the records of their faith. These Gospels were each written more than a full generation after the events they describe, when most, if not all, of the actors involved were dead. With due consideration given to sources and traditions inherited by the writers, the choice of what was to be included was consciously made, and reflects the events of the life of Jesus through the prism of the authors' present community concerns. The apostolic figures chosen represent focal points for their respective communities, centers of inspiration for later generations around

---

you teach apostasy from Moses to all the Jews who live among the Gentiles, telling them not to circumcise their children nor walk in the customs.

9. Cf. H. Koester, "La tradition apostolique et les origines du gnosticisme," in *RTP* 119 (1987) 1–16.

10. Cf. the survey of the different "schools" by Terence V. Smith, *Petrine Controversies in Early Christianity* (Tübingen: J. C. B. Mohr, 1985) 9–20.

11. Cf., for example, Marcion and 1 Tim for two different directions in the Pauline tradition.

which the spiritual ideals of each group coalesced. One need but recall the importance of James for Jerusalem and later Jewish Christians, and the efforts expended by the author of Acts to demonstrate
his apostle's (Paul's) unity with him; or the (later) importance of Peter for Rome; or, in the present case, of John and Thomas for the literature which bears their names.

One of the more calculating and artistically deft aspects of John's
Gospel is its creation and manipulation of characters. We meet
uniquely, for example, Nicodemus, the Man Healed at Bethesda, the
Samaritan Woman at the Well, the Man Born Blind, and others.
Each of these characters provides the background and occasion for
the Jesus of John to declare his mission, person, and message. In addition, they furnish the writer with stimuli for the famous Johannine
discourses, and allow him to fulfill his stated purpose to convince
primarily other Jews to "believe that Jesus is the Christ."[12] But not
only are they foils for the character of Jesus; they also represent
facets of John's religious world. They are themselves models and sur-
rogates of people and situations in John's own day.[13] So in the case of
the Man Born Blind we see, according to Martyn, the rejected Johannine Christian (as the once-blind man), the Christian preacher
of John's present time (as Jesus), and the Jewish authorities (as "the
Jews") who ejected them from their synagogues; Nicodemus likewise represents the secret believer of the synagogue.[14] Two much

12. John 20:31. Cf. C. K. Barrett, *The Gospel of John and Judaism* (trans. by D. M.
Smith; Philadelphia: Fortress Press, 1975) 1–19, esp. 17–18.
13. So Borgen interprets John 6: "John 6 reflects the actual situation in the Johannine Church": Peder Borgen, *Bread from Heaven* (Supp. to NT 10; Leiden: E. J.
Brill, 1981) 184; likewise, John F. O'Grady, "Johannine Ecclesiology: A Critical Evaluation," in *BTB* 7 (1977) 36–44, esp. 42. The same has been said of the other
Gospels. For example, "Mark is always moving at two different levels: at the histori-
cal/physical/geographical level of Jesus' presence in Galilee and at the symbolic
level of a series of references to the experience of the early Christians in the Gentile
world;" in H. Hendrickx, *The Resurrection Narratives in the Synoptic Gospels* (rev.
ed.; London: Geoffrey Chapman, 1984) 11; cf. also 13.
14. J. Louis Martyn, *History and Theology in the Fourth Gospel* (rev. ed.;
Nashville: Abingdon, 1979) 18, 28, 35, *et al*; Nicodemus: 116, 121. Also, M. De Jonge,
"Nicodemus and Jesus: Some Observations on Misunderstanding and Understanding," in *BJRL* 53 (1971) 338–358; idem, "Jewish Expectations About the 'Mes-

more significant characters, however, frame the Gospel as a whole; they stand in a somewhat similar relationship to the community of John, and are used by the author in similar ways: John the Baptist and Doubting Thomas.

## John the Baptist as a Literary Character in John

John tells his readers in 20:31 that he composed his book with a specific purpose, that they should "believe that Jesus is the Christ," and thus "gain life in his name." Such a positive intent, however, also had its negative and polemical side. There were those who did not so believe, and they were not only "the Jews": members of other religious communities, Christian and otherwise, also populated John's world. John created characters which addressed the issues presented to his church by these communities also. The most prominent—and the first—example of this polemical use of character in the Gospel is John the Baptist. We are able to see the Gospel writer's treatment of the Baptist as the application of his "positive" goal in a polemical manner. The prominence of the Baptist in John is also an indication of his importance, not only in the time of Jesus, but also the importance of his followers to the Johannine community in the late first century.

John the Baptist, as one may reconstruct from the New Testament and other sources, was a prophetic figure who himself was the inspiration of a religious movement contemporaneous with the early Christians.[15] Josephus tells us (*Antiquities* 18.117–119) that the Baptist attracted large crowds and that Herod feared lest the following he inspired lead to sedition. John gathered disciples around himself, calling on them "to come together in baptism" (βαπτισμῷ συνιέναι: 18.117). Herod's reason for seeing the sect as a political danger, according to Josephus, was that the crowds "seemed to do everything

---

siah' According to the Fourth Gospel," in *NTS* 19 (1973) 262–263; and Jouette M. Bassler, "Mixed Signals: Nicodemus in the Fourth Gospel," in *JBL* 108 (1989) 635–646, who sees Nicodemus as the archetype of "marginality" (645–646).

15. Cf. Charles H. H. Scobie, "John the Baptist," in Matthew Black, ed., *The Scrolls and Christianity* (SPCK Theological Collection 11; London: SPCK, 1969) 58–69.

by his [John's] counsel."[16] To put an end to the unrest, Herod had him killed. Nevertheless, John the Baptist inspired a movement[17] which appears to have predated the ministry of Jesus, and gathered around himself many of the same disciples to whom the preaching of Jesus also appealed. His followers continued to meet together in his name long after his death, and were a competing factor in the life of the Gospel writer and his community.[18]

The movement of John the Baptist had great influence on Jesus and his followers. Jesus was baptized by John (Mark 1:9–11 and parallels), and may have been one of his early disciples.[19] Indeed, Bultmann postulated that the Gospel writer was himself a convert from among the disciples of the Baptist, and took over a hymn used among them for his prologue.[20] D. Moody Smith, following Bultmann's lead, sees the Signs-source which underlies John's Gospel as having been composed as a missionary document to convert the

16. *Antiquities* 18.118. The Baptist is clearly founder of a movement; J.A.T. Robinson proposes that it was called "the way of righteousness" (cf. Matt 21:32), much as the early Christian movement was called the Way (Acts 9:2), in idem, "The Baptism of John and the Qumran Community," in *Twelve New Testament Studies* (SBT 34; London: SCM, 1962) 20.

17. If traditions among the Mandaeans have historical basis, then Herod's action did not put an end to the sect: his followers may still be found today in southern Iraq. Cf. V. Schou-Pedersen, "Überlieferungen über Johannes den Täufer," in Geo Widengren, ed., *Der Mandäismus* (*Wege der Forschung* 167; trans. by Almut und Rüdiger Schmitt; Darmstadt: Wissenschaftliche Buchgesellschaft, 1982) 206–226.

18. They are still opposed to Jesus to the present day, according to the claim of the Mandaeans. Cf. on Mandaeanism, Kurt Rudolph, "Zum gegenwärtigen Stand der mandäischen Religionsgeschichte," in *Gnosis und Neues Testament* (ed. Karl-Wolfgang Tröger; Berlin: Gütersloher Verlagshaus, 1973) 121–148; a resumé of which is found in idem, "Probleme einer Entwicklungsgeschichte der mandäischen Religion," in *Le Origini dello Gnosticismo*, ed. U. Bianchi (Leiden: E. J. Brill, 1967) 583–596; and idem, *Gnosis* (trans. and ed. by Robert McLaughlin Wilson; San Francisco: Harper and Row, 1983) 363f.

19. So argues Dodd from the description of Jesus by John, Ὀπίσω μου ἔρχεται ἀνήρ, "a follower of mine is coming": C. H. Dodd, *Historical Tradition in the Fourth Gospel* (Cambridge: Cambridge Univ. Press, 1963) 272–275.

20. Cf. R. Bultmann, *The Gospel of John: A Commentary* (trans. by G.R. Beasley-Murray et al.; Philadelphia: Westminster Press, 1971) 18. This is clearly possible, especially if, as Brown postulates, the unnamed disciple of 1:40 is the author himself: Raymond E. Brown, "John the Baptist in the Gospel of John," in idem, *New Testament Essays* (New York: Paulist Press, 1965) 134.

Baptist's followers to Jesus.[21] John the author of the Gospel, on this model, was thoroughly conscious of the importance of, and conversant with, the Baptist's movement and used earlier material directed toward the conversion of these sectarians in his own efforts toward the same goal.

It is important to understand the method of John the Gospel writer in his portrayal of the Baptist: he makes him deny his own importance in God's eschatological plan, and puts into his mouth words which witness for Jesus and direct his own disciples to Jesus. But the witness of the Baptist in John conflicts with evidence concerning the historical survival of the movement: if the Baptist had actually been proclaiming the priority of Jesus, why did anyone continue to follow John once Jesus, as the Gospel has it, had been revealed at his baptism, and John began sending his followers to Jesus? One sees readily that this witness in the Gospel is a reinterpretation of the preaching of John in terms of a new-found faith in Jesus. Other early Christians saw in John the figure of Elijah;[22] the Gospel of John does not assign to the Baptist even this honor: he is made to deny that he was the Christ, Elijah, or the Prophet.[23]

John the Baptist himself had preached righteousness and ethical behavior (according to Josephus), and the coming of one after him who would judge such behavior (according to the Synoptics); the Christians naturally took this to mean Jesus.[24] He founded his own

21. Cf. D. Moody Smith, "The Milieu of the Johannine Miracle Source: A Proposal," in Robert Hammerton-Kelly and Robin Scroggs, eds., *Jews, Greeks and Christians: Religious Cultures in Late Antiquity: Essays in Honor of William David Davies* (Leiden: E. J. Brill, 1976) 178. The Signs-source ascribes miracles to Jesus only, in contradistinction to John who did no miracles (John 10:41), demonstrating that Jesus was the miracle working Prophet who was to come.

22. Matt 11:14; 17:9–13; Mark 9:13; Luke 1:17, 76.

23. John 1:21. Cf. J. Louis Martyn, "We Have Found Elijah," in Robert Hammerton-Kelly and Robin Scroggs, eds., *Jews, Greeks and Christians: Religious Cultures in Late Antiquity: Essays in Honor of William David Davies* (Leiden: E. J. Brill, 1976) 181–219, esp. 183–187.

24. The one to whom John was in fact referring is open to question. Koester takes him to mean God, while Robinson, Brown, and others take John to mean Elijah: H. Koester, *Introduction to the New Testament*, vol. 2: *History and Literature of Early Christianity* (Philadelphia: Fortress Press, 1982) 71; J. A. T. Robinson, "Elijah, John and Jesus," in *NTS* 4 (1957–58) 264; Brown, "John the Baptist," 139–140.

group which still competed with that of the Johannine Christian community sixty years after the deaths of the two founding figures (Jesus and the Baptist). From the viewpoint of the Jesus movement, John the Baptist had clearly announced the coming of Jesus, had "prepared his way" by preaching repentance to Israel, and had initiated Jesus' ministry by baptizing him. He had then been (divinely?) removed by martyrdom so that Jesus could take his rightful, superior place. John could therefore, in Synoptic interpretation, fulfill the role of Elijah and announce the coming of the Christ.[25] The disciples of the Baptist, however, saw their founder himself as a messiah-like figure who would be followed by the apocalyptic end, not as a mere "opening act" for Jesus. So they continued to meet in John's name, and came into conflict with the disciples of Jesus over their own separate identity.[26] The author of the Gospel of John (a former Baptist disciple?), after his own conversion, took it upon himself to convert members of the sect to Jesus. He did this by casting the Baptist as a character in his Gospel who denied himself and bore witness to Jesus, contrary to what he likely did in fact. John created a revised "history" of the Baptist as a means of influencing the Baptist's community in his own day.[27] This portrayal of the Baptist at the beginning of the Gospel is a paradigm for the understanding of the figure of Thomas at the end of the Gospel.[28]

25. The positive valuation of the Baptist in Q is contrasted with that of the Gospel of John by James M. Robinson, "Basic Shifts in German Theology," in *Int* 16 (1962) 84–85.

26. The picture in Acts of the disciples in Ephesus who knew only the baptism of John is a case in point. But see Ernst Käsemann, "The Disciples of John the Baptist in Ephesus," in idem, *Essays on New Testament Themes* (trans. by W. J. Montague; Philadelphia: Fortress Press, 1982) 136–148.

27. Cf. Benjamin W. Bacon, *The Gospel of the Hellenists* (Carl H. Kraeling, ed.; New York: Henry Holt and Company, 1933) 411f.

28. A similar retroversion of the writer's present into the "past" of the Gospel account of Jesus may be seen elsewhere in John. The story of the Man Born Blind (ch. 9) points to the exclusion from the synagogues (and worse) for the confession of Jesus as the Christ. While synagogue exclusion was not unknown in individual cases earlier (cf. Acts 17–19), the decree made at Jamnia (*ca.* 85 CE) and contained in the Blessing of the *Minim* ("heretics") was one effective means by which this exclusion was accomplished on a wide scale. As an example and comfort to those excluded ones circa 90, the "Jews" of the Gospel exclude the Man Born Blind for his witness to Jesus by means of their own ban (9:22; 12:42; cf. 16:2). Further examples

## *Thomas as a Literary Character in John*

The figure of Doubting Thomas is also a character created by John, representing a community in the "present" of the author which, like that of John the Baptist, was in competition with his own. The real Thomas, like John, was also an historical figure in the life of the early church. According to Church tradition, he made disciples after the death of Jesus, as had the Baptist before, and as did other disciples of Jesus. Again like the Baptist, and uniquely so among his fellow disciples, he preached a distinctive message which bound his community to himself and his name; his followers also survive into the present, in India, and are still called Thomas Christians.[29]

Thomas appears three times in John, exclusive of chapter 21. In John 11:16, as Jesus is departing to go to Bethany and raise Lazarus, Thomas speaks the desperate words, "Let us also go, that we may die with him." Thomas expects that not only he but Jesus and his fellow disciples will also die in Judea as Lazarus had died, where "the Jews" were just seeking to stone Jesus (11:8). Yet Jesus is not stoned, nor do any of the disciples die; instead one of Jesus' greatest miracles occurs in the raising of Lazarus. Thomas is here singled out by the author of

---

of such compositional technique may be seen, among others, in the Samaritan Woman of ch. 4, and in Peter of ch. 21.

For the date and ban, cf. J. Louis Martyn, *History and Theology*, 50–62; 156–157; and William Horbury, "The Benediction of the *Minim* and Early Jewish-Christian Controversy," in *JTS* 33 (1982) 19–61. A contrary view (that the division between Jew and Christian was a long process and not the result of one decision at Jamnia) is given by Reuven Kimelman, "*Birkat Ha-Minim* and the Lack of Evidence for an Anti-Christian Jewish Prayer in Late Antiquity," in E. P. Sanders, ed., with A. I. Baumgarten and Alan Mendelson, *Jewish and Christian Self-Definition. Vol. 2: Aspects of Judaism in the Greco-Roman Period* (Philadelphia: Fortress Press, 1981) 226–244. For John and the Samaritans, cf. Edwin D. Freed, "Did John Write His Gospel Partly to Win Samaritan Converts?," in *Nov T* 12 (1970) 241–256; and James D. Purvis, "The Fourth Gospel and the Samaritans," in *Nov T* 17 (1975) 161–198. For Peter of ch. 21, cf. Raymond E. Brown, "'Other Sheep Not of This Fold': The Johannine Perspective on Christian Diversity in the Late First Century," in *JBL* 97 (1978) 15.

29. Cf. P. J. Podipara, *The Thomas Christians* (Bombay: St. Paul Publications, 1970). The Thomas Christians of India are not today of the same theological outlook as their earlier Syrian fellows; they were forcibly converted by the Portuguese from Syrian Nestorianism in the sixteenth century, and by the Jesuits and Carmelites to fellowship with Rome in the seventeenth century. Many are still allied with the Jacobite Syrian Orthodox Church.

John as the only one of the twelve disciples named; he is shown to be wrong, and wrong in the specific context of resurrection. In John 14:5, in response to a statement of Jesus, Thomas declares himself to be ignorant of both the (postmortem) destination and "way" of Jesus. In John 20:24–29, Thomas alone of the Eleven fails to see the risen Jesus; he is alone in his doubt, and alone in his demand to touch the wounds of Jesus; he alone is rebuked for unbelief. As a character in John, Thomas is cast as one who is wrong, ignorant and unbelieving.

Yet Thomas was early the spiritual father of a Christian community, much like that of the community of John. The community produced widely used literature in the name of Thomas: the *Gospel of Thomas* survives in at least two recensions,[30] in two languages,[31] and contains very early forms of the sayings of Jesus, stamped with its own independent theological outlook;[32] the *Book of Thomas (the Contender)* carries on and develops traditions found in the *Gospel*, and was likewise translated into Coptic;[33] the *Acts of Thomas* is found in scores of manuscripts in several languages, and was used not only by Christians of various theological persuasions, but also by Mani and his followers.[34] The city of Edessa was by the fourth

30. Perhaps as many as three. The Greek and Coptic texts show such differences, and the Naasenes may have used their own version; cf. H.-Ch. Puech, "The Gospel of Thomas," in Edgar Hennecke, *New Testament Apocrypha* (Wilhelm Schneemelcher, ed.; English trans. by R. McL. Wilson; Philadelphia: Westminster Press, 1963) 1.284. Attridge is cautious, but does recognize the possibility of differing recensions: Harold W. Attridge, "The Gospel According to Thomas. Appendix: The Greek Fragments," in Bentley Layton, ed., *Nag Hammadi Codex II, 2–7* (Leiden: E. J. Brill, 1989) 1.99–101.

31. The *Gospel of Thomas* is preserved at least partially in both Greek and Coptic. Layton makes a cogent argument that the *Gospel of Thomas* must at one time have existed also in Syriac, since it was used by the author of the Syriac *Acts of Thomas* and Mani: Bentley Layton, *The Gnostic Scriptures* (Garden City, N.Y.: Doubleday, 1987), 377.

32. Cf. esp. Koester, "Introduction: The Gospel according to Thomas," in Bentley Layton, ed., *Nag Hammadi Codex II, 2–7*, 38ff.

33. Cf. John D. Turner, *The Book of Thomas the Contender* (SBL Dissertation Series 23; Missoula: Scholars Press, 1975); idem, "The Book of Thomas the Contender Writing to the Perfect: Introduction," in Bentley Layton, ed., *Nag Hammadi Codex II, 2–7* (Leiden: E. J. Brill, 1989) 2.173–178.

34. Cf. A. F. J. Klijn, *The Acts of Thomas* (Leiden: E. J. Brill, 1962); G. Bornkamm, "The Acts of Thomas," in Edgar Hennecke, *New Testament Apocrypha* (Wilhelm

century the "City of St. Thomas," and the repository of his bones.[35] Legends were composed surrounding his missionary activity in the East and India.[36] There was a Thomas Christianity,[37] much as there was a Pauline or Johannine Christianity, centered in the East in the general geographical area[38] in which the community of John arose. The figure of Doubting Thomas in John and the *Gospel of Thomas* allow us to see that these two communities, like that of John the Baptist and John, were in debate in the later part of the first century.

John 19:31–20:31 contains the burial and resurrection appearances of Jesus to his disciples. Like the preceding passion narrative, these stories combine traditional material found also in other Gospels with material unique to John. They bear the stamp of Johannine thought and redaction, and in more than one passage the special concerns of the Johannine community. Nicodemus, a character unique to John, in this section joins Joseph of Arimathea in preparing and burying the body of Jesus. Joseph appears in each of the Synoptics, and his story is traditional. Nicodemus, however, is part of John's special material and concern, for he represents those

---

Schneemelcher, ed.; English trans. by R. McL. Wilson; Philadelphia: Westminster Press, 1963) 2.425–531.

35. Cf. Walter Bauer, *Orthodoxy and Heresy*, 11, n. 24. Also, J. J. Gunther, "The Meaning and Origin of the Name 'Judas Thomas,'" in *Muséon* 93 (1980) 118–119.

36. Most notably, the *Acts of Thomas*. Also Eusebius, *HE* 1.13.4, 11; 2.1.6; 3.1.1; 3.25.6. Cf. J. B. Segal, *Edessa 'The Blessed City'* (Oxford: Clarendon Press, 1970) 63–66.

37. A creative but speculative reconstruction of the community which used the *Gospel of Thomas* is offered by Bruce Lincoln, "Thomas-Gospel and Thomas Community: A New Approach to a Familiar Text," in *NT* 19 (1977) 65–76. Cf. also the doctoral dissertation of Stephen J. Patterson, *The Gospel of Thomas within the Development of Early Christianity* (Claremont Graduate School, 1988) 175–314.

38. *Thomas* was identified as Egyptian by Dom Aelred Baker, "Pseudo-Macarius and the Gospel of Thomas," in *VC* 18 (1964) 225, but Edessa is generally considered to be the place of composition. Cf. Helmut Koester, "*GNOMAI DIAPHOROI*: The Origin and Nature of Diversification in the History of Early Christianity," in James M. Robinson and Helmut Koester, *Trajectories through Early Christianity* (Philadelphia: Fortress Press, 1971) 126–143; L. W. Barnard, "The Origins and Emergence of the Church in Edessa during the First Two Centuries A.D.," in *VC* 22 (1968) 165; A. F. J. Klijn, "Christianity in Edessa and the Gospel of Thomas," in *NT* 14 (1972) 70–77, answering Barbara Ehlers, "Kann das Thomasevangelium aus Edessa stammen?," in *NT* 12 (1970) 284–317; Han J. W. Drijvers, "Facts and Problems in Early Syriac Speaking Christianity," in *Second Century* 2 (1982) 157–175, esp. 158, n. 7.

among the leaders of "the Jews" who secretly believe in Jesus but fear to confess him publicly (John 12:42-43). He does finally, however, show his faith openly in this act of piety, and the character "Nicodemus" completes his function in the Gospel as an example to other Jewish leaders. Likewise, in the most obvious example of redactional concern, the author introduces the Beloved Disciple into the story of the visit to the tomb by Peter (John 20:2-8). The similar story in Luke 24:12[39] relates the run to the tomb by Peter alone.[40] In the Johannine version, the Beloved Disciple races with him, and precedes Peter to the tomb. He is the first to look into the tomb, the first to see the empty linen wrappings, and the (first?) one who believes (20:4-5), although Peter is allowed to enter the tomb ahead of him (20:6-8). The author of John has added the Beloved Disciple to this traditional story of Peter's visit to the tomb in order to give him standing equal, or superior, to that of Peter in the eyes of his own community.[41]

So it is with the story of Doubting Thomas: Thomas as a character, like Nicodemus and the Beloved Disciple, is unique to John; in John alone Thomas has substance and function.[42] This observation is important for understanding not only the tradition history of John 20, but also the meaning of the Doubting Thomas pericope. John

39. This verse (Luke 24:12) is one of the "Western non-interpolations" according to B. F. Westcott and F. J. A. Hort, *The New Testament in the Original Greek. Vol. 2: Introduction [and] Appendix* (Cambridge and London: Macmillan and Company, 1881; second ed. of vol.2, 1896) 175-177. B. Metzger (and the editorial committee of the UBS Greek NT) properly view John and Luke as having "drawn upon a common tradition": Bruce M. Metzger, *A Textual Commentary on the Greek New Testament: A Companion Volume to the United Bible Societies' Greek New Testament (third edition)* (United Bible Societies, 1971) 184.

40. Luke 24:24 ["some of those who were with us went to the tomb . . . "] may be support for a tradition according to which Peter did not go alone to the tomb, or that others went subsequent to his visit alone. If the former is true, then John's redaction inserted the Beloved Disciple as Peter's unmentioned companion. However, "some" may simply mean Peter and then others later.

41. Such a purpose seems also to lie behind the story of Peter and the Beloved disciple in John 21:20-23, mentioned above. Cf. Raymond E. Brown, "'Other Sheep Not of This Fold,'" 15.

42. Thomas is included in the apostle lists of the Synoptics and Acts, as one of the Twelve, but he does not participate as an individual actor in any of the episodes of those works: Matt 10:3; Mark 3:18; Luke 6:15; Acts 1:13.

speaks to the community of the Baptist through the character of the Baptist, to the believing but fearful Jews through the character of Nicodemus, and assures his own community by means of the Beloved Disciple. So he speaks to the rival community of Thomas Christians and to his own community concerning issues of conflict between them through the figure of Doubting Thomas.[43]

## The Appearance Stories and John 20

One important question is whether or not the Doubting Thomas pericope was inherited by the author of John: is it a redaction of a preexistent Thomas story, or a new composition of the author?[44] Examples of both types of characters and editorial activity are present in John. John the Baptist, as we have seen, is clearly a traditional figure who received a Johannine revaluation. Nicodemus, the Woman at the Well, the Man Born Blind, and the Beloved Disciple, among others, are as far as we know Johannine creations without Synoptic counterpart. The question of tradition behind the character Thomas

43. This list in no way exhausts John's use of characters or his target groups; recall the Samaritan Woman at the Well. In addition, Richter, Martyn, and Brown, among others, have attempted with considerable success to isolate successive stages in the development of the Johannine community, visible (among other aspects) in Johannine characters. Cf. J. Louis Martyn, *History and Theology*; and "Glimpses into the History of the Johannine Community," in idem, *The Gospel of John in Christian History* (New York: Paulist Press, 1978) 90–121; Raymond E. Brown, "Other Sheep"; G. Richter, "Präsentische und futurische Eschatologie im 4. Evangelium," in Peter Fiedler and Dieter Zeller, eds., *Gegenwart und kommendes Reich: Schülergabe Anton Vögtle* (Stuttgart: Verlag Katholisches Bibelwerk, 1975) 117–152; A. J. Matill, Jr., "Johannine Communities Behind the Fourth Gospel: Georg Richter's Analysis," in *TS* 38 (1977) 294–315.

44. The pericope is seen as wholly a creation of the author of John by C. H. Dodd, *The Interpretation of the Fourth Gospel* (Cambridge: Cambridge Univ. Press, 1953) 430; and Robert T. Fortna, *The Gospel of Signs* (SNTSMS 11; Cambridge: Cambridge Univ. Press, 1970) 142–143; it is viewed as a manipulation of existing tradition by R. Bultmann, *The Gospel of John*, 693. Hartmann, followed by Dauer, sees it as a creation from materials found in the *Vorlage* of John 20 itself, from which both group appearances were constructed: G. Hartmann, "Die Vorlage der Osterberichte in Joh 20," in *ZNW* 55 (1964) 197–220; and for a full discussion, cf. Anton Dauer, "Zur Herkunft der Tomas-Perikope Joh 20,24–29," in Helmut Merklein and Joachim Lange, eds., *Biblische Randbemerkungen: Schülerfestschrift für Rudolph Schnackenburg zum 60. Geburtstag* (Würzberg: Echter-Verlag, 1974) 56–76.

is important in order to determine whether and to what extent the author has manipulated his inheritance, if such there was. An inherited tradition implies a church concern wider in time and community. If there was none, and the story is a Johannine creation purely, then we should look to the later part of the first century and the community of John specifically for the locus of meaning.

In either case, however, the depth of editorial reworking and the use to which John puts his characters makes "inheritance" seem a moot point. The figure of the Baptist, one person whom it is possible to compare with outside sources, bears little resemblance in John to the picture reconstructed from other evidence. It is difficult to find any Johannine character who is simply "historical," an example of historical description in some modern sense; John's method of composition and the nature of "history" in the ancient world all but preclude such a notion.

John is writing a "true history," an idea which is confused with "accurate description of historical events" by ancient as well as modern readers of ancient texts. "True history" is the writing of the past in terms of the demands of the present, not seldom in heroic or archetypal categories. Often the ancients mixed myth and "the meaning of the story for us" with memory, creating written history controlled by cultural presuppositions. Few means were available to writers of history to assist in producing accurate descriptions; fewer writers *wished* to produce such works. Historiography had a "point," which was exhortation and the promotion of one's own truth, be it religious, political or philosophical. A classic example is the story of Solon and Croesus in the opening book of the *Histories* of Herodotus (the "father of history"). Solon, the Athenian wise man, travels to the court of Croesus, the hubristic ruler of Lydia, and warns him of the dangers of arrogance and prosperity; Croesus declares him a fool, but later loses his kingdom and confesses in a moment of repentant remorse that Solon had been correct. It is a beautiful story, well written, and full of pathos. The Athenians are encouraged by their ancient wise man and present historian; their ideals are shown to be "true," and the foreigner, the "other," submits to their wisdom. The reader is greatly edified, and not in the least bothered by the fact that Solon and Croesus lived decades apart and the two likely never met at all.[45] So freedom in characterization, speech content, and wording, even the creation of events to some extent, was part of the discipline of "history"; John is writing well within the expectations of his culture.

Both from the nature of ancient "history," and an examination of characterization as a literary device in John, one properly expects that the figure of Thomas expresses a Johannine concern. One may ask, in fact one is remiss not to ask, what that concern is and what the "message" of Thomas is, much as we are able to ask the same concerning the Baptist or other characters in John. The most often repeated interpretation is that Thomas the Doubter stands for Doubt. On the contrary, however, John the Baptist does not stand for Baptizing. Put in this glib way, one sees how much more remains to be said of each character. Thomas does doubt, and John does baptize; those are aspects of each character. But neither action is well suited as a description of the meaning of the character in John's Gospel.

### Tradition and Structure of the Appearance Narratives

The Doubting Thomas pericope is placed among the resurrection appearances of Jesus. The appendix of John 21:14 numbers the Sea of Galilee appearance to the disciples[46] as the third, making that to Thomas the second. Yet neither of these two appearances are found in the other Gospels. What, then, was the tradition inherited by John, as far as can be determined from our sources? We can make a rather simple structural analysis of the episodes which constitute the Gospel appearance accounts, beginning with Easter morning, in or-

---

45. This discussion of the writing of history in antiquity is to some extent *contra* the over-credulous essay of A.W. Mosley, "Historical Reporting in the Ancient World," in *NTS* 12 (1965–66) 10–26.

46. John 21:14: "This is now the third time Jesus appeared to the disciples after he rose from the dead." "To the disciples" is an important phrase here, since the first actual appearance of Jesus in John is to Mary Magdalene, making the total in John 20–21 four appearances in all. Only the final three are "to the disciples."

der to see which episodes John may have had at his disposal. This very limited listing of elements in the resurrection narratives is constructed to show the appearances of Jesus in the canonical Gospels, the theme of doubt, and their relationship to the Final Commission.

| MATTHEW | LUKE | JOHN | MARK/ LONGER ENDING |
|---------|------|------|---------------------|
| *Women go to tomb* | *Women go to tomb Disciples doubt women's report* | *Mary goes to tomb* | *Women go to tomb* |
| Jesus appears to women | Jesus appears to two disciples in Emmaus | Jesus appears to Mary | *[Longer Ending] Jesus appears to Mary and the two* |
| Jesus appears to disciples in Galilee *(disciples doubt)* | Jesus appears to disciples in Jerusalem *(doubt at first)* | Jesus appears to ten disciples in Jerusalem | *Jesus appears to the Eleven in Jerusalem (?) (rebukes doubt)* |
| *Final Commission* | *Final Commission* | *Final Commission* | *Final Commission* |
| | | Jesus appears to Doubting Thomas | |
| | | *[Jesus appears to disciples at Sea of Galilee]* | |

Each Gospel knows of the visit to the tomb by Mary Magdalene: she is named first in the differing lists of women in the Synoptics; in John she is the only woman named in this episode.[47] Both Matthew and John record that the first appearance of Jesus was to Mary (at least).[48] Luke replaces this appearance, for his own reasons, with the story of the disciples on the road to Emmaus.[49] Structurally, how-

47. She does say to the disciples, "*we* do not know where they have laid him" (20:2), showing that John knows the tradition that she did not go alone. An objection that this may be an editorial plural (or the royal "we") is less than compelling.

48. If the Longer Ending of Mark 16:9 is not simply copying from John but reflects (some) early Gospel tradition, then we have there the statement *in expressis verbis*, "he first appeared to Mary Magdalene."

49. Luke 24:34 states that these two tell the disciples assembled in Jerusalem, among whom, one assumes, was Peter, that "the Lord has really risen, and has appeared to Simon." There is no place in Luke's narrative for a private appearance to

ever, there is one appearance before the one to the assembled disciples. This observation is strengthened by the combination in the Longer Ending of Mark of the appearance to Mary (taken from John) and the two disciples on the road (to Emmaus, taken from Luke): only these two advents, one assumes, were available to the author to be combined.

The second appearance, by all accounts,[50] is that to the disciples as a group, gathered either in Jerusalem or Galilee. Matthew, following the tradition in Mark, places this event on a mountain in Galilee (John 21 supports the Galilee location, but places it along the shore of the Sea of Galilee). Luke and John 20 locate this event in Jerusalem.[51] In each of the Gospels, this second appearance (the third for the Longer Ending) is followed by the Final Commission, the sending of the disciples into the world to herald the message of Jesus. The Commission is clearly the climax of the written Gospels and the logical end of the gospel story. The author of the Longer Ending felt the need (as have many moderns since) for such an end to Mark's more laconic, but far more dramatic, account.[52] Nevertheless, he either did not find in his sources a further appearance, or saw the literary impropriety of including any other after the disciples had been commissioned. Neither Matthew, Luke, nor the Longer Ending record any appearances subsequent to the single one in the presence of the assembled disciples.[53] Only John of the Gospels has

---

Peter. This verse may well be an interpolation from 1 Corinthians 15:5; the sense is improved by its removal.

50. Including 1 Cor 15:5; it is, of course, the third for the Longer Ending.

51. For John it occurs specifically in a closed room. On the development of the Jerusalem / Galilee conflict of locale, cf. S.G.F. Brandon, *The Fall of Jerusalem and the Christian Church* (second ed.; London: SPCK, 1978) 41–43.

52. Cf. Andrew T. Lincoln, "The Promise and the Failure — Mark 16:7, 8," in *JBL* 108 (1989) 283–300.

53. 1 Cor 15:5–8 lists seven different appearances, only one of which (the second, to the "twelve") is easily reconciled with the Gospel accounts. Acts 1:3 declares that Jesus appeared to the apostles over a period of forty days after his death, "with many proofs." Here may be unstated some indication of demonstrations like that in Luke 24:39–42 (showing his hands and feet, and eating fish).

added one other: to Thomas.[54] This alone is sufficient to raise suspicion that this appearance is a creation of John.

But there were many other appearances included in other traditions. A simple counting of resurrection appearances mentioned in the New Testament yields a much higher number than the two of Matthew and Luke's Gospel, or the three of John.[55] Bruce Metzger gives the number as eleven, unless, in his opinion, the 500 brethren of 1 Cor 15:6 were present on the mountain of Matt 28:16–20,[56] in which case the number is to be reduced to ten.[57] This calculation leaves out the claim in Acts 1:3 of appearances over a period of forty days,[58] which would seem at least theoretically to raise the number considerably. Yet nowhere else is an appearance to Thomas mentioned. One could claim that Luke knew of more appearances than he gives in his Gospel (as evidenced by Acts 1:3), and that perhaps

54. John 21 has one additional appearance in Galilee. John 21 serves a function in this respect similar to that of the Longer Ending Mark, in melding the traditions found also in the other Gospels. Thus the two locations of Galilee and Jerusalem, separate in Matthew/Mark and Luke/John, are reconciled by adding another appearance in Galilee to the one in Jerusalem of John.

55. Or the different three of the Longer Ending of Mark; or the four of John, if John 21 is included.

56. Such is the position of P. Seidensticker, *Die Auferstehung Jesu in der Botschaft der Evangelisten* (StBSt 26; Stuttgart: Katholisches Bibelwerk, 1967) 79; and idem, "Das Antiochenische Glaubensbekenntnis I Kor. 15, 3–7 im Lichte seiner Traditionsgeschichte," in *TGl* 57 (1967) 286–323. For a related but different reading of this passage, cf. Peter J. Kearney, "He Appeared to 500 Brothers (1 Cor 15:6)," in *NT* 22 (1980) 264–284. A more common interpretation of the appearance to 500 is that it refers to Acts 2 and Pentecost: cf., for example, W. Grundmann, "Das Problem des hellenistischen Christentums innerhalb der Jerusalemer Urgemeinde," in *ZNW* 38 (1939) 45–73, esp. 48f.; S. M. Gilmore, "The Christophany to More Than Five Hundred Brethren," in *JBL* 80 (1961) 248–252; and idem, "Easter and Pentecost," in *JBL* (1962) 62–66.

57. Cf. B. M. Metzger, "The Meaning of Christ's Ascension," in J. M. Meyers, O. Reimherr, and H. N. Bream, eds., *Search the Scriptures: Studies in Honor of R. T. Stamm* (Leiden: E. J. Brill, 1969) 123–124, n. 3. This possibility seems to me to be quite remote, especially since the number of disciples is specified as "eleven" in 28:16. Did 500 disciples walk to a mountain in Galilee on the word of the two Marys, whom no one at all believed in Luke 24:11?

58. Cf. A. R. C. Leaney, "Why There Were Forty Days between the Resurrection and the Ascension in Acts 1:3," in F. L. Cross, ed., *SE*, vol. 6 (Berlin: Akademie, 1968) 417–419.

the appearance to Thomas was one of those. The tradition related by
Paul in 1 Cor 15:5–8[59] relates several others.

Why, then, should the Gospels be limited to such a small number
of appearances? Such a small number must surely be based in the intention of John and the other Gospel writers. They were not com-
posing lists as complete as possible of post-Easter appearances; they
were not telling all they knew.[60] The accounts are based on a double
inheritance: the Galilee appearance, and the discovery of the empty
tomb in Jerusalem.[61] Yet it is quite likely that they did know the
kerygma tradition of appearances (1 Cor 15:5ff.). This is proved at
least for Luke, since he adds an unsupported note on the appearance
to Peter ("The Lord really rose and appeared to Simon": Luke
24:34).[62] The congruence of the accounts (such as it is) shows at least
that they were constrained by their tradition, genre, and individual
purposes to include only so much as they did, even contrary to
claims (1 Cor 15:3–8) for a first appearance to Peter, or another to
James and the Jerusalem apostles. Why of all things is Peter not declared to have been the first to see the risen Christ, especially in
Matthew? And why in Luke is this appearance to Peter not where it
belongs, in the "Western non-interpolation" position of 24:12, but
instead insinuated (if not interpolated) unreasonably[63] into an oth-

59. 1 Cor 15:5–8: "he appeared to Cephas, then to the twelve; then he appeared to
more than 500 brethren at once . . . ; then he appeared to James, then to all the
apostles; and last of all . . . he appeared also to me."

60. " . . . Matthew has composed [his account] from earlier lists of appearances": Reginald H. Fuller, *The Formation of the Resurrection Narratives* (Philadelphia: Fortress Press, 1980), 82.

61. Peter Carnley, *The Structure of Resurrection Belief*, 45. Mark shows this in its
barest form. Matthew adds to Mark the appearances both to the women in
Jerusalem and to the disciples in Galilee. Luke and John move the group appearance to Jerusalem.

62. The kerygma may stand behind John 21, with its "Peter-centered" appearance. Luke adjusts the wording of Mark from "He is going before you into Galilee"
(Mark 16:7) to "Remember when he was in Galilee" (Luke 24:6), in order to bring
the Galilee account into Jerusalem. John 21 attempts to harmonize both locations
by adding a Galilee appearance, yet this "third" appearance (John 21:14) makes far
more sense as the first. We would then have a first appearance to Peter in Galilee.

63. "awkwardly inserted": Ernst Haenchen, *John* (Hermeneia; trans. by Robert
W. Funk; Philadelphia: Fortress Press, 1984) 2.214.

erwise independent and unrelated account of the appearance to the Emmaus disciples (Luke 24:34)?

A possible answer lies in the structure of post-resurrection appearance stories as they have come down to us. The kerygma (1 Corinthians 15) spoke in formulaic language of a set of appearances on the basis of its own traditions and purposes, different from those found in the Gospels. The Gospels had their own separate narrative inheritance. A simple comparison of the Gospels and 1 Corinthians 15 shows that the two traditions cannot be reconciled.[64] The kerygma is concerned with authority and apostleship, in addition to proof of resurrection: Peter and James are given special place.[65] Following that lead, Paul adds his own experience, again demonstrating his authority and apostleship. The appearance to Paul was constitutive of his mission; his authority (parallel to that of Peter and James) was founded on that event. The purpose of the kerygmatic stories has determined their content. If one examines, however, the structure and especially the earliest form of the list, a pattern emerges: one appearance to an individual, and a second to the gathered disciples.[66]

---

64. There is "an almost total lack of correspondence"; and "it is not simply difficult to harmonize these traditions, but quite impossible": C. F. Evans, *Resurrection and the New Testament* (London: SCM Press, 1970) 52 and 128. Harmonization is "a fundamentally mistaken enterprise": Peter Carnley, *The Structure of Resurrection Belief*, 18.

65. The two parallel lists of 'Cephas and the Twelve,' and 'James and all the apostles' are "legitimation formulae" which establish the authority of these leaders; so Ulrich Wilckens, *Resurrection. Biblical Testimony to the Resurrection: An Historical Examination and Explanation* (trans. by A. M. Stewart; Atlanta: John Knox Press, 1978) 12 and 16 (the quote is from 16). But see the critique of Wilckens by Gerhard Delling, "The Significance of the Resurrection of Jesus for Faith in Jesus Christ," in C. F. D. Moule, ed., *The Significance of the Message of the Resurrection for Faith in Jesus Christ* (SBT, second series, 8; trans. by R. A. Wilson; Naperville: SCM 1968) 81–82.

66. Murphy-O'Connor and Perkins see the reference to James et alii as Pauline redaction with the purpose of expanding the circle of apostles beyond the Twelve, thus allowing room for Paul's own apostleship. This, however, does not address the form of the tradition; in fact, if verse 7 is not traditional, then one sees the form operative even in Paul's redaction. Cf. Jerome Murphy-O'Connor, "Tradition and Redaction in 1 Cor 15:3–7," in *CBQ* 43 (1981) 582–589; Pheme Perkins, *Resurrection: New Testament Witness and Contemporary Reflection* (Garden City, N.Y.: Doubleday, 1984) 200. The "direction of the growth [of tradition] was from one witness to many": Howard M. Teeple, "The Historical Beginnings of the Resurrection Faith,"

The early kerygma was preached, and one assumes in large part created, by Peter and James. These two "super apostles" (2 Cor 11:5) were authorities among their respective groups of disciples: Peter among the Eleven, and James among those at Jerusalem. These two are the "individuals" who necessarily merit the initial individual appearances. If 1 Cor 15:5–8 is taken at face value, then each leader was personally commissioned; their respective fellow-but-lesser apostles were then later sanctioned as a group. If that individual commission became part of the preaching and legitimation of each, then it could easily have become part of the early kerygma transmitted by Paul's predecessors. This is exactly the case for Paul himself: he includes in his gospel an account of the appearance of Jesus to him which constituted his mission (1 Cor 9:1; 15:8; Gal 1:15–16), and that appearance became part of the "gospel of Paul" in the tradition which Acts relates (Acts 9, 22, 26).[67]

The Gospel writers, however, were writing for communities decades after these apostles had died. They were not under the same constraints to enforce the authority of Peter and James or Paul. Their churches were outside Jerusalem (even outside Palestine), led by second and third generation converts, among whom women held honored positions. At least Matthew and John found useful the tradition of an initial appearance to Mary.[68] Yet these writers also limited themselves to a structure of the same two basic types of appearances: one to an individual; a second to the gathered disciples.[69] The struc-

---

in David Edward Aune, ed., *Studies in New Testament and Early Christian Literature: Essays in Honor of Allen P. Wikgren* (NovTSup 33; Leiden: E. J. Brill, 1972) 111.

67. Cf. Seyoon Kim, *The Origin of Paul's Gospel* (Grand Rapids: Eerdmans, 1981) 28–29.

68. The reason for the placing of the women (or Mary alone) instead of Peter at the tomb, and therefore as recipients of the first appearance may be that "Mark knew that the disciples fled to Galilee at Jesus' arrest": Teeple, "Historical Beginnings," 117, n. 1.

69. So in John; Matthew and Luke multiply the number to two individuals. Not all interpreters, of course, agree. Leaney ("Forty Days," 419) sees the two appearances as those to the two *groups*, to the Twelve and then to all the apostles (1 Cor 15:5 and 7), balanced by the two group appearances in John, to the Ten and then to the Eleven (20:19 and 26); the individuals are added in Luke and John. Yet no account is made of the individuals in 1 Corinthians.

ture (individual / gathered disciples) is stable: Cephas / the Twelve; James/the Apostles; Mary/the gathered disciples, *etc.*[70]

The point of these observations on structure is that the pericope of Doubting Thomas is a redactional addition to an already complete cycle of post-resurrection events. The cycle, according to the reading above, included two appearances and a Commission, and then ended. A most thorough critique and form-critical analysis of the appearance stories is given by John Alsup, whose work concludes that the *Gattung* of appearance stories arises out of the narratives describing the appearances of the "anthropomorphic" Yahweh in Hebrew tradition. Thus all the examples, individual and group, are told according to a relatively consistent "form."[71] His work does not address the reason for the larger structure, the pattern of the New Testament examples. This pattern (of individual / gathered disciples / commission / conclusion) is not part of the Hebrew inheritance, but belongs to the early Church, and arises from its own tradition and memory. Celsus, in fact, complained that (Origen, *Contra Celsum* 2.63):

> If Jesus had wanted to demonstrate that his power was truly divine, he ought to have appeared to those who maltreated him, and to the one who condemned him, and to all everywhere.

Celsus was right: other appearances were possible, to other audiences, which would have had much greater probative value. Hilary

70. This is consistent with the form-critical analysis of M. Albertz, "Zur Formgeschichte der Auferstehungsberichte," in *ZNW* 21 (1922) 259–269; and L. Brun, *Die Auferstehung Christi in der urchristlichen Überlieferung* (Oslo, 1925). Bultmann does not think that a definite "form" was involved; instead, "It belongs to the very nature of things that the Easter appearances or visions should have been told in the first place of individuals and then of all the Apostles. . . . In the same way, it is natural that the evangelists . . . should put at the end a story of an appearance to all the apostles": R. Bultmann, *History of the Synoptic Tradition* (trans. by John Marsh; rev. ed.; New York: Harper and Row, 1976) 288. But this is not a significant difference: we have "the nature of things" determining the "form."

71. John E. Alsup, *The Post-Resurrection Appearance Stories of the Gospel Tradition* (Calwer Theologische Monographien; Stuttgart: Calwer Verlag, 1975). The close correspondence may most easily be seen in his (far more elaborate) chart included at the end of the volume.

even invents such proofs, claiming: "I am sure that after his resurrection he offered himself repeatedly in the body to the sight of multitudes of unbelievers."[72] That Jesus appeared only to his partisans, to those predisposed to "see" him, has long been a discomfort for apologists of the Church.[73] According to Bultmann, however, it was "natural" that the evangelists should begin with individual encounters and end their stories with a group appearance.[74] If so, it seems even more natural that the end of that group appearance should be the Commission, as a finale to the entire Gospel account. Matthew, Luke and the Longer Ending of Mark end at that point.[75] John, uniquely and for reasons which arise in his own community, adds another appearance to Thomas.[76]

### The Theme of Fear and Doubt

One prominent theme in the stories is the fear and doubt of the disciples at the appearance of the resurrected Christ. The whole idea of a postmortem apparition, as wonderful as it was in proving survival after death, was a terrifying prospect. The women fled trembling and speechless at the mere announcement of resurrection in

72. Hilary of Potiers, *De Trinitate* 3.20.

73. The examples of Paul, the Centurion (Mark 15:39), and to the guards in the *Gospel of Peter*, are exceptions, but not without their own difficulties.

74. R. Bultmann, *Synoptic Tradition*, 288. Goguel has postulated two types of appearances on the basis of the psychology of faith: to those who believe already, and to those who do not, but are influenced by an established faith: Maurice Goguel, *La foi à la résurrection de Jésus dans le Christianisme primitif* (Paris: Librairie Ernest Leroux, 1933) 395. This is a useful concept in the different construction offered here: a first appearance to a faithful individual, whose report then influences his or her group. Cf. Teeple, "Historical Beginnings," 117, for Peter's role as catalyst for the Easter faith of the other disciples. The main catalyst according to Gospel evidence, however, must be Mary Magdalene.

75. The fact that the Longer Ending of Mark does not contain the Doubting Thomas episode, while including Mary alone (from John) and the Emmaus disciples (from Luke) is very suggestive for a redaction critique of John. Did the author of the Longer Ending of Mark not find Doubting Thomas in his sources at all?

76. Many more literary reasons for regarding the Thomas pericope as secondary have been advanced by scholars, centering on the obvious unique elements: the literarily dependent nature of the pericope; the absence of Thomas; the concentration on Thomas of all doubt; the Johannine confession of deity as climax; the blessing on John's community of unseeing believers. Cf. the survey of opinions in the following chapter.

Mark's account (Mark 16:8). "Green dread" ($\chi\lambda\omega\rho\grave{o}\nu$ $\delta\acute{e}os$) overtook Odysseus at the arrival of the ghosts whom he had called up from Hades (*Od.* 11.43); the medium of Endor cried out in fear when the ghost of Samuel appeared at her request (1 Sam 28:12). One may imagine the alarm evoked in an ancient by an *uninvited* apparition of Jesus.[77] In Matthew, the women are told to "stop fearing" at the first apparition (Matt 28:10); at the second, some, if not all,[78] of the assembled disciples on the mountain were doubtful.[79] In Luke, the women fall to the ground in fear at the sight of the angels. The disciples, in turn, think that the report of the women about the empty tomb and the angelic messenger is nonsense, and therefore do not believe them (Luke 24:11). The Emmaus disciples are rebuked at the first appearance by the disguised Jesus for being "foolish and slow of heart to believe" (24:25). At the second appearance, all the disciples are chided for their fear and doubt, even though they have reacted as all sane ancients would have at the appearance, as they thought, of a ghost (24:37–38). The Longer Ending of Mark intensifies this scene: the disciples do not believe the women, nor the two disciples; Jesus therefore "reproached them for their unbelief and hardness of heart,

77. Mark 6:49–50 reports the reaction of the disciples at the sight of Jesus merely walking on the water: they thought he was a ghost and cried out in terror.

78. "Some" is the usual, but only one possible, translation of $o\acute{i}$ $\delta\grave{e}$ $\acute{e}\delta\acute{i}\sigma\tau\alpha\sigma\alpha\nu$ ("But some doubted") of Matt 28:17. A similar expression occurs two verses earlier (28:15), where the soldiers take the money from the Jewish priests and do as they are told, saying that the disciples stole Jesus' body: $o\acute{i}$ $\delta\grave{e}$ $\lambda\alpha\beta\acute{o}\nu\tau\epsilon s$ $\tau\grave{a}$ $\dot{\alpha}\rho\gamma\acute{u}$-$\rho\iota\alpha$ $\dot{e}\pi o\acute{i}\eta\sigma\alpha\nu$ $\dot{\omega}s$ $\dot{e}\delta\iota\delta\acute{a}\chi\theta\eta\sigma\alpha\nu$ ("And taking the money, they did as they were instructed"). The expression $o\acute{i}$ $\delta\grave{e}$ here must mean, "but they [= all of the soldiers]." Thus, the natural reading of $o\acute{i}$ $\delta\grave{e}$ in 28:17 is "but they doubted," meaning all of the disciples. Cf. Robert J. Kwik, "Some Doubted," in *ET* 77 (1966) 181; and I. P. Ellis, "'But Some Doubted,'" in *NTS* 14 (1967–68) 574–580.

79. Matt 28:17: "And when they saw him, they worshipped; but they doubted." Doubted what? Did they doubt the identity of Jesus (John 20:14; 21:4)? His corporeal reality (Luke 24:39)? Their own sanity (Acts 26:24)? We are not told. F. W. Beare notes that the record of doubt in Matthew is different from that in the Thomas pericope: in John, when the disciples see, all (including Thomas) believe; in Matthew, they, or some, doubt even after seeing: F. W. Beare, "Sayings of the Risen Jesus in the Synoptic Tradition: An Inquiry into their Origin and Significance," in W. R. Farmer, C. F. D. Moule and R. R. Niebuhr, eds., *Christian History and Interpretation: Studies Presented to John Knox* (Cambridge: Cambridge Univ. Press, 1967) 164. If so, then this is further evidence of the redactional character of the Thomas story.

because they had not believed those who had seen him after he had risen" (16:14).[80]

In the post-Easter account of John, however, no one is afraid; no one doubts. The Beloved Disciple believes even before he sees Jesus, at the mere sight of the empty grave clothes (20:8). At the first appearance, Mary not only does not fear or doubt, she cries out "Rabboni," and grabs Jesus in embrace (20:16-17). Likewise, the disciples neither fear nor doubt: the only ones whom the disciples fear are the Jews and Romans, and so lock themselves in a room (20:19). At the group appearance (20:19-23), they rejoice when they see Jesus; they are so full of faith that they attempt to convince the only one who does doubt, the only one who was not present: Thomas (20:24-25). The doubt found in the Synoptics and associated with the appearance stories has been transferred from the women and the disciples as a group to Thomas as an individual.

## The Theme of Physical Demonstration

Another theme present in at least part of the tradition is a demonstration of the physical reality of the risen Jesus. In Matt 28:18, when the disciples on the mountain doubt, Jesus merely approaches, and then gives them their Final Commission. Nothing specific is said to identify or done to alleviate their doubt; we are not told why they doubt. In Mark 16:14 the doubt is attributed to "hardness of heart" and is summarily rebuked. In Luke, however, an element is visible which had rather wide currency in the early Church: the disciples think that Jesus is a ghost. To counter their incredulity, Jesus has the disciples touch his body, and he eats a piece of fish to show that he is a physical, not merely a spiritual, presence (Luke 24:39-43). The continuation of Luke's story in Acts is introduced by a description of the period between the resurrection and ascension of Jesus, during which he "presented himself as alive after he suffered [death] by many proofs" (Acts 1:3) to his disciples. The "many

---

80. The Longer Ending of Mark apparently understood the theme developed by Mark of the total failure of the disciples. Cf. Norman Perrin, *The Resurrection according to Matthew, Mark, and Luke*, 35.

proofs" are not specified, but they are at least these demonstrations in Luke 24.

In this passage (Luke 24:37ff.), the issue is that Jesus is not a mere spirit, without flesh and bones, but that he is in fact physically resurrected. He says to his disciples (Luke 24:39–41):

> Look at my hands and feet, that I am myself. Touch me and see, for a spirit does not have flesh and bones as you see that I have. 40 And when he said this he showed them his hands and feet. 41 But they were still incredulous. . . .

The disciples assumed what was to their culture normal and logical: Jesus had died; therefore they were seeing a ghost.

Tradition preserved by the Church Fathers adds some interesting elements relevant to this passage. Ignatius confronts certain unnamed docetists who believe that Jesus merely seemed to undergo the passion. He writes (*Smyr.* 2.1–3.2):

> Just as they think, it will also happen to them, that they become bodiless and *daimon*-like. 3.1 For I indeed know and believe that he was in flesh after the resurrection. 3.2 And when he came to those around Peter, he said to them, "Take hold, handle me and see that I am not a bodiless *daimon*. And immediately they touched him and believed. . . . 3.3 And after the resurrection he ate with them and drank as one who is fleshly. . . .

Eusebius, in the early fourth century, cites this passage (*HE* 3.36.11), but adds that he does not know the source of the saying used by Ignatius. Jerome claims that it is from the *Gospel according to the Hebrews*, and quotes this passage in his own Latin translation from Aramaic.[81] Origen cites the sentence *Non sum daimonium in-*

---

81. Or so he claims, but he is not merely translating. The Latin "clarifies" one point: "those around Peter" (τοὺς περὶ Πέτρον) could mean Peter's disciples without Peter, implying an appearance in the absence of Peter. The Latin, therefore, has

*corporeum* ("I am not a bodiless *daimon*") as being from the *Petri Doctrina*.[82] This is clearly a free saying with a long history. The relationship of the Ignatian passage to Luke 24:39–41 is close, but the differences, especially the phrase "bodiless *daimon*," militate against derivation from Luke (contra Vielhauer). It is far more likely that Luke changed this potentially offensive phrase into "spirit" ($\pi\nu\epsilon\hat{\upsilon}\mu\alpha$) than that Ignatius did the reverse. Both Luke and Ignatius have drawn on a common source.[83] That source sought to demonstrate a material resurrection body by means of physical proofs.

In the early kerygma of 1 Cor 15:3–7, no physical demonstration is mentioned. Paul indeed argues with those who deny the resurrection, but by means of "logical," not physical proofs. For Mark, of course, there is not even a resurrection appearance, but only the promise of one (14:28, 16:7); no physical proof is possible or expected in his literary schema. Neither is there any physical proof in Matthew. Matthew is writing in a context in which physical as opposed to spiritual resurrection seems not to have been a concern. The women do take hold of Jesus' feet and worship (Matthew 28:9), yet this is not used as a proof of resurrection of the body, but as a show of reverence. He includes the story of an earthquake at the death of Jesus, the opening of the tombs, the raising of many bodies of the dead "saints," and their appearance in Jerusalem (27:51–53). Physical resurrections, or resuscitations, were for Matthew apparently commonplace at the death of Jesus. Indeed, if one looks to Matthew's story of the controversy over of the empty tomb and the bribing of the guards, even the "chief priests" (28:11–15) conceded that the body had disappeared. At issue was how to explain the absence of the body: theft or miracle? Yet there is indication of a con-

---

*ad Petrum et ad eos qui cum Petro erant* ("to Peter and to those who were with Peter"). Cf. the discussion of Jerome and this passage by P. Vielhauer, "Jewish-Christian Gospels," in Edgar Henneke, *New Testament Apocrypha* (Wilhelm Schneemelcher, ed.; trans. by R. McL. Wilson; Philadelphia: Westminster Press, 1964) 2.127ff.

82. Origen, *De Princ.* 1, Intro. 8.

83. So argues H. Koester, *Synoptische Überlieferung bei den Apostolischen Vätern* (TU 65; Berlin: Akademie-Verlag, 1957) 45–56. See also William R. Schoedel, *Ignatius of Antioch* (Hermeneia; Philadelphia: Fortress Press, 1985) 225–229.

trary tradition, for at the final group appearance on the mountain in Galilee "they doubted" (28:17).

Ignatius in Antioch knew of Christians who denied not only the physical resurrection, but also the reality of the passion; Jesus for them did not have a fleshly body on either side of the grave. The community of John also encountered those who denied the flesh of Christ. 2 John 7 is polemical testimony to those "who do not confess that Jesus Christ is come in flesh."[84] One of the purposes of the Gospel of John is to face this very issue: "the Logos became flesh and dwelt among us" (1:14). Docetism, the denial of the physical reality of the earthly, pre-crucifixion Jesus, was a development in the history of the community arising in high Christological speculations.[85] But evidence for denial of physical resurrection at all, the rejection of the *post*mortem physical reality of Jesus, is much earlier, based in the original proclamation of life from the grave.

There were Christians in Greece who denied physical resurrection prior to Paul's letter to Corinth in the mid-fifties; rejection of the idea was a very early phenomenon in the Church. But this is to state the case in reverse. The doctrine of physical resurrection was itself a denial of "spiritual resurrection," which was the basic belief of the surrounding culture. Docetism had to grow and be applied to Jesus as the tradition and Christological speculations developed. "Resurrection of the soul," however, was in place for centuries before Christ, and had to be denied by those preaching otherwise. John, Luke, Ignatius, and their common source, are evidence that a need existed in the early Christian movement for stories of the demonstration of the physical nature of Jesus' resurrection body. In the Gospel of John, the appearance narratives in chapter 20 are part of the early composition, and include physical demonstration as part of

---

84. Cf. also 1 John 4:1–3.

85. Some interpreters place the anti-docetic strains in John quite late. Richter assigns the passages 1:14 and 6:54 to an anti-docetic redactor, not the evangelist: Georg Richter, "Die Fleischwerdung des Logos im Johannesevangelium," in *NovT* 13 (1971) 81–126 and *NovT* 14 (1972) 257–276. Bousset assigns the Thomas pericope to a later redaction on the basis of its Christological confession: Wilhelm Bousset, *Kyrios Christos* (trans. by John E. Steely; Nashville: Abingdon, 1970) 125, n. 25.

their very substance. They are formed from pre-Johannine tradition, and redacted with proofs of physical resurrection as their main point: to say that Jesus was raised from the dead at all meant for John that he was raised physically. In John, for example, not only is the tomb empty, but we are twice told that the linen wrappings are also empty, and that the face cloth is rolled up in a separate place. This alone is sufficient to instill faith into the Beloved Disciple. Not only does Mary (as do the two Marys in Matt 28:9) apparently grab the resurrected Jesus, but he must tell her to "Stop clinging to me!"[86] During the group appearance(s), Jesus makes not one, but two, demonstrations of the physical nature of his body.

Each of these episodes has its analogue in the Synoptic Gospels. But it is in the redaction of the tradition of the group appearance which

---

86. This phrase (μή μου ἅπτου) has been the source of some difficulty. A normal (but not exclusive) reading of the present imperative would command one to stop doing something in progress (i. e., "Stop touching me!"; cf. μὴ γίνου ἄπιστος "Stop disbelieving!" 20:27); cf., for example, Herbert W. Smyth, *Greek Grammar* (rev. Gordon M. Messing; Cambridge, Mass.: Harvard Univ. Press, 1956) paragraph 1841a, p. 410; A. T. Robertson, *A Grammar of the Greek New Testament in the Light of Historical Research* (Nashville: Broadman, 1934) 853; Nigel Turner, *A Grammar of New Testament Greek* (ed. J. H. Moulton; Edinburgh: T. and T. Clark, 1963) 75.

The subsequent statement of Jesus, however, "for I have not yet ascended to the Father" (John 20:17), has given rise to the idea that Jesus was untouchable for John until this ascension, after which he returned to be touched by Thomas. Therefore, some have taken a less normal view of the Greek: Jesus says, according to Bultmann, "'Do not touch me!' in order to restrain her" (*The Gospel of John*, 687; cf. esp. n. 1). In view of Matt 28:9 (in which the two Marys take hold of Jesus' feet) this is unnecessary, and probably wrong; cf. H. Grass, *Ostergeschehen und Osterberichte* (Göttingen: Vandenhoeck and Ruprecht, 1962) 61ff.; R. Brown ["a false problem"], *The Gospel according to John (XIII–XXI)* (AB 29A; New York: Doubleday, 1970) 1011–1017; and Wayne A. Meeks, "The Man from Heaven," 159.

A clever solution is that of Michael McGehee, "A Less Theological Reading of John 20:17," in *JBL* 105 (1986) 299–302, in which he argues that the offensive γάρ ("for I have not yet ascended . . . ") should mean "since" and start a new sentence ("Stop touching me. Since I haven't yet ascended . . . , go tell my brothers. . . ."). This is possible, but rare Greek usage.

A simple reading (and my own opinion), without an abnormal view of the Greek, would allow the sentences to mean: "Let go of me now, for I need to go to my Father, and you need to go to the other disciples. . . ." This implies that Mary has embraced Jesus and is then told to go to the other disciples, as in Matt 28:9–10. The author of John, one must remember, *wants* Jesus to be tangible.

John shared with Luke and Ignatius that one finds the purpose and application of John's emphasis on the resurrection body. In Luke, "the Eleven and those who were with them" (24:33) are present at the group appearance. All of the disciples are startled and afraid; all think that Jesus is a ghost; all doubt, and all are rebuked. No disciple is named or singled out for special censure. In Ignatius, the same is true: the disciples are together, designated as "those around Peter," but no individual disciple is named in the story as deserving of special treatment. In both cases, only one group appearance occurs.

We are now able to answer the question whether John inherited a tradition or created the character of Thomas. John was working with a tradition which specified a limited number of pre-Commission appearances of Jesus: one to an individual, and one to the assembled disciples. It also reported quite understandable doubt on the part of the disciples, and in part of the tradition, proofs of the physical nature of his body. But during the group appearance, the tradition neither singled out nor spoke of the absence of any disciple. It said nothing of a second group appearance for the benefit of Thomas, or his demands, confession, and dominical rebuke. These are innovations of the author. The pericope of Doubting Thomas is a recasting of the character of an historical disciple much like the recasting of the character of John the Baptist.[87] In fact, Thomas in this Gospel is throughout an instrument of the author, used to face concerns of his community in the late first century.

---

87. Many others, of course, have concluded that the Doubting Thomas pericope is an invention of the author, but for very different reasons, mostly literary and stylistic. Cf. the following chapter.

# Chapter Three

# The Pericope of Doubting Thomas
## John 20:24–29

*Interpretation of the Doubting Thomas Pericope*

The classic interpretation of the Thomas pericope is that of descriptive history: the historical Thomas did and said exactly as described in (approximately) 30 CE, and eight days after the resurrection received his own visitation of the risen Jesus. He proves to himself that Jesus was raised bodily, confesses that Jesus is Lord and God, and stimulates the risen Christ to bless those who do not see as he has, yet still believe. Thus the Church Fathers used Thomas to prove physical resurrection,[1] to argue the deity of Christ,[2] to combat docetism,[3] and to draw spiritual lessons (of believing without seeing) for their congregations.[4] Some modern interpreters, indeed, have also concluded that the main motive behind the framing of this passage is the proof of the resurrection,[5] proof of the deity of Christ,[6] or

---

1. Irenaeus, *Adv. Haer.* 5.7; Tertullian, *De Resurrectione*, 34; Origen, *Contra Celsum* 2.61; *Apost. Const.* 3.19; Hilary of Potiers, *De Trinitate*, 3.20; Ambrose, *Satyrus: De Resurrectione* 2.60; Gregory of Nyssa, *On the Making of Man* 25; Jerome, *Epist.* 108.24 *bis*; *To Pammachius against John of Jerusalem* 28; Theodoret, *Dialogues* 2.

2. Novatian, *De Trinitate* 13, 30; Cyprian, *Treatise* 12: *Contra Iud.* 2.6; Athanasius, *Contra Ar.* 2.16.23; 4.35; *Epist.* 59.10; 61.2; Hilary of Potiers, *De Trinitate* 7.12; Ambrose, *De Spiritu Sancto* 3.15; John Cassian, *De Incarnatione* 3.15; 6.19; Theodoret, *Epist.* 83.

3. Tertullian, *De anima*, 17. Cf. *Epist. Apost.* 11–12.

4. Clement of Alex., *Strom.* 2.4.2; Origen, *Comm. in Jn.* 10.27; Augustine, *Tractatus CXXIV in Joannis Evangelium* 121.5; Gregory of Nyssa, *Oration on Holy Baptism* 40.38; *Second Oration on Easter* 45.24; Leo the Great, *Sermon: On the Lord's Ascension II* 74.1

5. R. Bultmann, *History of the Synoptic Tradition*, 288–289; Gerhard Delling, "The Significance of the Resurrection, 92; Howard M. Teeple, "Historical Beginnings," 113.

6. Robert T. Fortna, *The Gospel of Signs*, 143; Murray J. Harris, *Raised Immortal: Resurrection and Immortality in the New Testament* (Grand Rapids: Eerdmans, 1983) 28f.; Reginald H. Fuller, *The Formation of the Resurrection Narratives*, 145.

recommendation of belief without seeing.[7] Others see the author using the Thomas pericope to address more than one of these issues
at once.[8]

Some have reconstructed the emotional state of Thomas the disciple, reading themselves and their own dispositions into his mind
and character. John Chrysostom, for example, invented a personality for Thomas as a straw man to indict (*Hom. Joh.* 87.1):

> Just as believing carelessly and randomly comes of instability,
> so being curious beyond measure and meddlesome marks a
> most materialistic understanding. On this account Thomas is
> to be blamed.

In more modern times, but with kinder intention, B. F. Westcott
writes regarding Thomas' reply to his fellow disciples that he will not
believe without touching Jesus:[9]

> The reply of St. Thomas reveals how he had dwelt upon the ter-
> rible details of the Passion. The wounds of the Lord are for him
> still gaping, as he had seen them. He must be able to reconcile
> that reality of death with life before he can believe.

These projected interpretations are a high compliment for the author
of John, who was able to frame this character so suggestively well
that many are able to find themselves in Thomas, and see themselves
acting (and thinking) through him.[10] The interpretation offered here

7. The last two in Rudolph Schnackenburg, *St John*, 3.329. Also Otto Michel,
"The Conclusion of Matthew's Gospel," in Graham Stanton, ed., *The Interpretation
of Matthew* (trans. by Robert Morgan; IRT 3; London: SPCK and Philadelphia:
Fortress Press, 1983) 32–33 (on John 20:29).

8. More important than the physicality of Jesus are the "Identitätsmotiv,
Zweifelsmotiv, Glaubensmotiv u. a.": Anton Dauer, *Johannes und Lukas* (Forschung
zur Bibel 50; Würzberg: Echter Verlag, 1984) 293; "reality of the resurrection body,"
"faith and sight" and "Thomas' confession": C. H. Dodd, *The Interpretation of the
Fourth Gospel*, 430.

9. B. F. Westcott, *The Gospel according to St. John* (new impression; London:
John Murray, 1908) 296.

10. Cf. J. H. Bernard, *A Critical and Exegetical Commentary on the Gospel according to John* (ed. A. H. McNeille; ICC; New York: Charles Scribner's Sons, 1929)

is of a quite different stamp: the author of John has drawn the portrait of Thomas as an instrument, much as he had fashioned the character of John the Baptist. Are we to claim that the historical Baptist was a humble and self-deprecating man because John has him say, "He must increase, and I must decrease" (John 3:30), in a sentence clearly framed to further the author's evangelistic purpose? Thomas says very little in the Gospel, and only what John writes for him to say. It is far too little to form such elaborate and definite ideas about his (30 CE) historical personality.

Many have seen that Thomas is an archetype, an example representing aspects of spirituality applicable beyond the time of Jesus. John makes use of Thomas, clearly, to speak to his own community in the later part of the first century.[11] John's community did not have the opportunity to see Jesus personally, but had to believe through the word of a chain of witnesses.[12] Jesus blessed those who did not see but believed; John's community of the faithful receives that very blessing of Jesus.[13] By homiletic extension, the same blessing has been delivered to Christians in other communities and times. So Augustine applies to his own spiritual flock Jesus' blessing of those who do not see:[14]

---

2.681: "We can imagine him saying, 'I told you so'"; E. P. Blair, "Thomas," in *The Interpreter's Dictionary of the Bible* (ed. G. A. Buttrick, et al.; Nashville: Abingdon, 1962) 4.631–632: " . . . both a pessimistic outlook and a spirit of intense loyalty and bravery . . . humble and candid . . . somewhat dull"; C. K. Barrett, *The Gospel according to St. John* (second ed.; Philadelphia: Westminster, 1978) 571–572: "loyal but obtuse"; Leon Morris, *The Gospel according to John* (Grand Rapids: Eerdmans, 1971) 852: "too shocked to believe."

11. Indeed, the very time of the appearance to Thomas, the eighth day after Easter, has been seen to signify the "time of the Church": A. Jaubert, "The Calendar of Qumran and the Passion Narrative in John," in James H. Charlesworth, ed., *John and Qumran* (London: Geoffrey Chapman, 1972) 64–65.

12. The purpose of the pericope, according to S. H. Hooke, *The Resurrection of Christ as History and Experience*, 85. Also, Joachim Gnilka, *Johannesevangelium* (Würzberg: Echter-Verlag, 1983).

13. Cf. Ernst Haenchen, *John*, 2.212. Likewise, "The evangelist is here grappling with a theological problem of how the resurrection can become the basis of faith of subsequent believers": C. F. Evans, *Resurrection and the New Testament*, 126.

14. Augustine, *Ep. Joannis* 1.3.

We are here described; we designated. In us, then, let the blessedness take place, of whom the Lord predicted that it should take place. Let us firmly hold that which we do not see, because those tell us who have seen.

In Augustine's view, Thomas, the Doubter who must see to believe, is a negative archetype of faith: he is the one who allows all others to believe without seeing. He represents, for Obach and Kirk, "the struggle of an individual to come to faith."[15] Some have seen the author directing the reader to the nature "of faith itself, which can and may do without appearance."[16] Thomas in this way is a correction of defective types of faith. According to Hunter, he represents "the type of those who demand tangible proof."[17] He corrects, in McPollin's view, those who are "taken up with establishing the miraculous or marvellous aspect of Jesus' appearances."[18]

Each of the Gospels relates the doubt and fear of the disciples facing the post-Easter events. For Mark it is the fear of the women at the message of the angel and the predicted appearance of Jesus in Galilee; in Matthew, the disciples doubt on the mountain; and in Luke, all are afraid and unbelieving at the sudden arrival of the risen Jesus in their midst. This motif of doubt is limited by John to the figure of Thomas alone: neither Mary nor the other disciples doubt. Many interpreters, therefore, have seen the figure of Thomas as a Johannine archetype of Doubt, and have posited that John has personified this theme of the other Gospels in Thomas.[19] For example, Wilckens writes:

15. Robert E. Obach and Albert Kirk, *A Commentary on the Gospel of John* (New York: Paulist Press, 1981) 254.
16. Herman Hendrickx, *Resurrection Narratives*, 52. Similarly, Maurice Goguel, *La foi à la résurrection*, 294; Schnackenburg, *St John*, 3.335; J. Louis Martyn, *History and Theology in the Fourth Gospel*, 95; Dauer, *Johannes und Lukas*, 258–259; I. de la Potterie, "Parole et Espirit dans S. Jean," in M. De Jonge, ed., *L'Évangile de Jean: Sources, rédaction, théologie* (Louvain: J. Duculot, 1977) 197.
17. A. M. Hunter, *The Gospel according to John* (Cambridge: Cambridge Univ. Press, 1965) 189.
18. James McPolin, *John* (Wilmington: Michael Glazier, 1979) 218.
19. John E. Alsup, *The Post-Resurrection Appearance Stories*, 148; P. Perkins, *Resurrection*, 179; R. Brown, *The Gospel according to John (XIII-XXI)*, 1033; Robert

. . . this motif became stronger and stronger as the tradition
continued. In Matthew mention of the doubts 'of some' only
appears quite marginally. In Luke the proof of identity already
dominates the center of the scene. Finally in John it is expanded
into an independent scene which becomes the climax of the entire story of Christ's appearance.[20]

That the pericope of Doubting Thomas could not have originally
been an independent unit inherited by John is clear, " . . . since it
would be unintelligible except in the light of the connecting passage,
xx. 28–9 [*sic*; *l.* 24–25 ?], which in turn presupposes xx. 19–23."[21] So
Haenchen declares that it is "a later insertion into the source" by a
redactor.[22] On the other hand, the passage does contain traditional
elements (doubt, touching the risen Lord), which have led Bultmann
and others to surmise that the source used by John may have contained the story.[23] But a far more persuasive accounting of those elements is that the author created the pericope out of material in the
tradition which stands behind earlier verses of John 20 (and Luke
24), and reshaped it for his own purposes.[24]

One of the aspects of the Thomas pericope often overlooked, and
from the point of view of this study a most important aspect, is the
central issue raised by the character Thomas: he will not believe in

Mahoney, *Two Disciples at the Tomb: The Background and Message of John* 20.1–10
(Theologie und Wirklichkeit 6; Bern: Lang, 1974) 259; Reginald H. Fuller, *The
Formation of the Resurrection Narratives*, 142; Peter F. Ellis, *The Genius of John: A
Composition-Critical Commentary on the Fourth Gospel* (Collegeville: Liturgical
Press, 1984) 295; Benjamin J. Hubbard, *The Matthean Redaction of a Primitive Apos-
tolic Commissioning: An Exegesis of Matthew* 28:16–20 (SBLDS 19; Missoula: SBL
and Scholars Press, 1974) 114, n. 1; Anton Dauer, "Zur Herkunft der Thomas-
Perikope," 71.

20. U. Wilckens, *Resurrection*, 53.

21. C. H. Dodd, *Historical Tradition*, 145. Cf. also Mahoney, *Two Disciples at the
Tomb*, 37, n. 80; Fuller, *Formation of the Resurrection Narratives*, 143.

22. Ernst Haenchen, *John*, 2.60.

23. Bultmann, *John*, 693. Also P. Gardner-Smith, "It is not at all probable that the
fourth evangelist invented it. . . .", in idem, *The Narratives of the Resurrection: A
Critical Study* (London: Methuen and Co., 1926) 86; and idem, *Saint John and the
Synoptic Gospels* (Cambridge: Cambridge Univ. Press, 1938) 82–84; Reginald H.
Fuller, *The Formation of the Resurrection Narratives*, 144–145.

24. Cf. G. Hartmann, "Die Vorlage der Osterberichte in Joh 20," in *ZNW* 55

the physical nature of the resurrection, and must touch the body of Jesus. One can only agree with other interpreters in regard to the separate uses which the author makes of the pericope. Thomas is clearly the vehicle for doubt; he carries the doubt of all the disciples, and by homiletical extension, every believer's doubt. Thomas' faith is such that he must see to believe, and Jesus blesses those who do not see but believe. By homiletical extension, he also blesses John's community and all other believers who have no opportunity to see. But it is in the first case the physical body of Jesus which is at issue. This has led some interpreters to see the purpose of the Thomas pericope as anti-docetic. Richter has assigned the pericope to an anti-docetic redactor who attempted to prevent misinterpretation of the Gospel by a docetism newly arisen in the community.[25] Thyen, similarly, connects several passages, beginning with "the Word became flesh" (John 1:14), with the Thomas pericope in an anti-docetic motive.[26] Not all, of course, agree. While an anti-docetic motive is clearly present in the post-Easter account of Ignatius (*Smyr.* 3:2f.), according to Fuller, incredibly, "This slant is absent from the Gospel."[27]

The Thomas pericope has as its initial point the physical body of the risen Jesus. The apostle Paul had originally offered his defense against those who denied resurrection of the body by declaring that

---

(1964) 197–220; Anton Dauer, "Zur Herkunft der Thomas-Perikope Joh 20,24–29," 58–71. Guillaume has worked out admirably John's use of traditional elements found, and not found, in Luke; cf. Jean-Marie Guillaume, *Luc interprète des anciennes traditions sur la résurrection de Jésus* (Paris: Librairie Lecoffre, 1979) 188–194.

25. Georg Richter, "Die Fleischwerdung des Logos im Johannesevangelium," in *NovT* 13 (1971) 81–126 and *NovT* 14 (1972) 257–276. Such an interpretation is rejected by Schnackenburg, *St John*, 3.335, and mitigated by Dauer, *Johannes und Lukas*, 293; cf. also 442, n. 339. For Lindars, the Thomas pericope belongs to the first edition of the Gospel: Barnabas Lindars, *The Gospel of John* (New Century Bible; London: Oliphants, 1971) 392.

26. Including John 6:48–58, 19:34–35, 20:20: Hartwig Thyen, "Entwicklungen innerhalb der johannischen Theologie und Kirche im Spiegel von Joh. 21 und der Lieblingsjüngertexte des Evangeliums," in M. De Jonge, ed., *L'Évangile de Jean: Sources, rédaction, théologie* (Louvain: J. Duculot, 1977) 261, 277. Cf. also Ellis, *Genius of John*, 296.

27. Reginald H. Fuller, *The Formation of the Resurrection Narratives*, 145.

the body of Jesus had been transformed into a new substance: the body of Jesus, like all others, was "sown a natural body; it is raised a spiritual body" (1 Cor 15:44). So Jesus would "transform our lowly body into conformity with his glorious body" (Phil 3:21). Although Paul had declared that Christ appeared "in the likeness of sinful flesh" (Rom 8:3), still, according to Bousset,[28]

> With his assumption of the σῶμα πνευματικόν, it is only with difficulty that he stays on the borderline between the late Jewish and early Christian materialistic hope of the resurrection of the flesh and the spiritualism of Hellenistic religion. According to his total basic outlook, he apparently stood closer to the latter.

Not only did the early *kerygma* not emphasize the physical nature of the risen Jesus, Paul at least taught something else. The pre-Pauline Christ hymn (Phil 2:7–8) is even less helpful for later orthodoxy. It does not specify that Jesus had a real human body even before the crucifixion: Jesus took only on the "form," "likeness," and "appearance" (μορφὴν . . . ὁμοιώματι . . . σχήματι) of a man, words which gave at least license, if not mandate, to anyone who wished to deny to Jesus human flesh on either side of the grave.[29]

So one branch of the early Christian movement could follow a non-physical risen Jesus, while others began to contend, not only for the body, but for the flesh, of the risen Christ. This development is visible in the Gospel literature: Mark has no appearances or physical demonstrations of the risen Jesus; Matthew has doubters at the final appearance, but no demonstration; Luke (and Ignatius' source) has one demonstration; and John has two. By the time of the writing of the Thomas pericope, divisions in the Christian movement were clearly visible. The original community and proclamation were far

---

28. Wilhelm Bousset, *Kyrios Christos*, 256. Cf. also 336: "But what took place here [at the incarnation] was, according to Paul, at the same time an unnatural connection, from which death has freed Christ himself, and following him, us also."

29. "Marcion's Docetism was founded on Phil ii.7": Ralph P. Martin, *Carmen Christi: Philippians 2:5–11 in Recent Interpretation and in the Setting of Early Christian Worship* (rev. ed.; Grand Rapids: Eerdmans, 1983) 62, n. 1.

closer to a "spiritual" Jesus than to a Jesus raised in the flesh. The early sources either do not specify, or teach something other than a fleshly post-Easter Jesus. The new development in resurrection doctrine was not the appropriation of Jesus by Greco-Roman traditionalists, Docetists and Gnostics to create a phantom Christ, but the directing of the message by the "orthodox" toward the flesh of Christ in order to counter their claims. The position of the Thomas Christians was the earlier one.

### John 20:24–29: Exegesis of the Pericope of Doubting Thomas

As John had used the character of John the Baptist to speak to the community of the Baptist, so he uses the character of Thomas to speak to the community of Thomas. Many of the elements in the story of the Baptist at the beginning of the Gospel had specific reference to issues in his community; they were consciously used by John as part of the overall "message" of this character. So the Baptist denies his own independent role, and confesses the preeminence of Jesus (John 1:15, 20–30). His ultimate programmatic statement is, "He must increase, but I must decrease" (3:30). John has the Baptist deprecate himself, and declare the superiority of Jesus. A similar treatment of Thomas occurs at the end of the Gospel, with similar consequences: Thomas also retreats from his stated position of unbelief, and confesses the (divine) superiority of Jesus, addressing him as "my Lord and my God" (20:28). The following is a selective exegesis of this pericope and the message communicated to the Thomas community by its portrayal of their spiritual champion.

### John 20:24

But Thomas, one of the Twelve, the one called "Twin," was not with them when Jesus came.

### The Absence of Thomas

There is no indication whatever in the preceding narrative that Thomas or any other disciple should have been absent at the appearance of Jesus to the assembled disciples. This information comes not only as a surprise, but as an anticlimax. What is more unsettling is that it strikes one as an impossibility: Jesus has just commissioned the disciples, "sending" them as he himself was sent (20:21); he has fulfilled his promise of the Paraclete, and granted them the spirit (14:16; 20:22); he has given them the authority to forgive and retain sins. Their training is complete; their equipping and authorization are complete. They have now been constituted as full representatives of Christ in the world. And all of this Thomas has missed by his absence.

If this were in fact the author's intention, to exclude Thomas (as he has) from these endowments, or had there been some historical basis for this pericope, what daunting consequences for Thomas and his followers this would have had! Thomas could not have made the transition from disciple to apostle; his followers would not have been forgiven their sins, received the spirit, or inherited the apostolic succession. But these issues are never raised in the text, nor is any mention made of the missed awards. The reader is not told of a subsequent, private commissioning, inspiration, and authorization of Thomas. These "historical" difficulties are invisible. The author's intention is otherwise: according to John's story, Thomas did not see the risen Jesus, and therefore did not believe in the resurrection. Here again is indication of the secondary character of the pericope relative to the tradition, and of the literary creativity of the author.

### "One of the Twelve"

This last point of the creativity of John gives one pause concerning an otherwise apparently harmless expression used of Thomas in this verse: "one of the Twelve." Any of this group of disciples could conceivably have been so described; the group as a whole is designated as "the Twelve" in John 6:67 and often outside of this Gospel.[30] Yet throughout the canonical Gospels, other than this verse, only one

---

30. The earliest occurrence as a *terminus technicus* is 1 Cor 15:5, and then often in the synoptics (cf. Mark 3:16 and parallels). Cf. Karl Heinrich Rengstorf, "δώδεκα," in Gerhard Kittel, ed., *Theological Dictionary of the New Testament* (trans. and ed. by Geoffrey W. Bromiley; Grand Rapids: Eerdmans, 1964) 2.321–328.

other disciple is ever identified as "one of the Twelve": Judas Iscariot. Even in John, Judas, and Judas alone, has already been given this epithet as the one who would betray Jesus.[31] In Mark, Judas is thus signified three of the four times he is mentioned; all four times he is called "the one who betrayed" or is said to be in the act of betraying Jesus.[32] Judas is mentioned five times in Matthew: each time he is the traitor; twice he, and only he, is "one of the Twelve."[33] In Luke, he is named four times: twice he is the traitor (6:16 and 22:48), and twice he is "one of the Twelve" (22:3 and 47).

Why did John use this expression here? Anyone at all familiar with the tradition knew that Thomas was one of the Twelve. The expression is not used of Peter or the Beloved Disciple earlier in the chapter, nor is Mary "not one of the Twelve." If one assumes that the phrase is consciously employed, then certain factors may be noted. First, John uses the Doubting Thomas pericope to recall significant expressions and themes used earlier in the Gospel in other important instances: the designation of Jesus as God ($\Theta\epsilon\acute{o}\varsigma$; recalling 1:1 and 18); the (permanent) incarnation (recalling 1:14); the spear wound in Jesus' side (recalling 19:34); and the theme of faith and sight (recalling 6:30). The pericope as a whole is crafted in more than one respect as a summation of significant elements in the Gospel. The reader, therefore, may be expected to recollect the only earlier use of the phrase "one of the Twelve," and the only use of the phrase in the entire tradition as we have it. Second, the presentation of Thomas in John is not a complimentary portrayal: he is the "fatalist" in John 11 regarding the resuscitation of Lazarus; he is ignorant of the "place" and "way" of Jesus in John 14; and he is the only one

31. John 6:70–71:
Did I not choose you, the Twelve? And one of you is a devil. 71 And he spoke of Judas, son of Simon Iscariot, for this one was about to betray him, one of the Twelve.
In 12:4 Judas is called "one of his disciples, who was intending to betray him." The expression in John is not identical in form with that of the other Gospels: John uses the partitive genitive with $\dot{\epsilon}\kappa$ (producing $\epsilon\hat{\iota}\varsigma$ $\dot{\epsilon}\kappa$ $\tau\hat{\omega}\nu$ $\delta\omega\delta\epsilon\kappa\alpha$) in both 6:71 and 20:24. The other Gospels have the same construction without $\dot{\epsilon}\kappa$: $\epsilon\hat{\iota}\varsigma$ $\tau\hat{\omega}\nu$ $\delta\omega\delta\epsilon\kappa\alpha$.
32. Mark 14:10, 20, 43. He is also mentioned in the passage concerning the calling of the Twelve: 3:19.
33. Matt 10:4; 26:14, 25, 47; 27:3. "One of the Twelve" in 26:14 and 47.

who denies the resurrection of Jesus here. Thus, this expression may be meant negatively, to link subtly Judas Iscariot and Thomas. Third, there are but ten disciples present at the appearance of Jesus in John. In the parallel of Luke 24:33, the Eleven are gathered; only Judas is absent. For John, both Thomas and Judas Iscariot are absent. Finally, and this most interestingly, the very name of Thomas according to tradition was Judas. Both "Thomas" and "Didymos" are simply nicknames, each meaning "twin" in Aramaic (תאומא) and Greek (Δίδυμος) respectively. The given name of Thomas was "Judas."[34] So he is ⲆⲓⲆⲨⲘⲞⲤ ⲒⲞⲨⲆⲀⲤ ⲐⲰⲘⲀⲤ ("Didymos Judas Thomas") in the opening of the *Gospel of Thomas*, ⲒⲞⲨⲆⲀⲤ ⲐⲰⲘⲀⲤ ("Judas Thomas") in the first line of the *Book of Thomas (the Contender)*, and "Judas Thomas" in the opening section of the *Acts of Thomas*. In John 14:22, where "Judas not Iscariot" according to the Greek tradition asks Jesus a question, the Syriac versions have "Thomas" (Sinaitic) and "Judas Thomas" (Curetonian). Thus "Judas the One Who Betrays" and "Judas the One Who Denies" are both and uniquely designated in John by the same expression, "one of the twelve," the second use here recalling the first.

### "The One Called 'Twin'"

The Gospel of John is the only canonical source for the phrase "the one called 'Twin'." The other mentions of this disciple in the Gospels and Acts[35] use "Thomas" as a proper name, without noting that this Aramaic word means anything in Greek. Such a circumstance is the norm in the New Testament: we are not told that "John" means "the Lord is gracious" in Hebrew, or that "Philip" means "lover of horses" in Greek. In John, however, we learn that "Thomas" is an epithet, and as such is translated. Likewise John 1:42 reads, "You are Simon, son of John; you shall be called Cephas (which translated means 'Pe-

---

34. Cf. Tai Akagi, *The Literary Development of the Coptic Gospel of Thomas* (Ph. D. Diss., Western Reserve University, 1965; Ann Arbor: University Microfilms, 1965) 43–51; Helmut Koester, "*GNOMAI DIAPHORAI*, 127–135; John J. Gunther, "The Meaning and Origin of the Name 'Judas Thomas'," 113–148; Han J. W. Drijvers, "Facts and Problems in Early Syriac Speaking Christianity," 160ff.

35. Matt 10:3; Mark 3:18; Luke 6:15; Acts 1:13.

ter')." This phrase "who is called . . . " (ὁ λεγόμενος . . .) is one of the ways John signifies common names or words which had currency in both Aramaic and Greek. For example, one finds the phrases: "the Messiah, the one who is called 'Christ'," and "'Rabbouni,' which is called 'Teacher'" (John 4:25 and 20:16). Both the Aramaic and Greek versions of these terms were common words, and commonly heard. So Judas (Thomas) was called "Twin," apparently both in Aramaic and Greek, to the point that his original name was all but lost.[36]

If the author used this phrase by conscious choice, then there may be some significance behind the fact that John alone designates Thomas as the Twin. John may be familiar with a signature element of the Thomas tradition: at some point in the history of the Thomas community, Thomas the Twin was said to be the twin brother of Jesus.[37] This is clearly stated at the end of the second century in the *Acts of Thomas* 39, where Thomas is addressed by a talking donkey as "Twin of the Messiah." Likewise earlier, in the mid-second century *Book of Thomas (the Contender)*, Jesus says to Thomas (*BTh* 138.8): "It has been said that you are my twin and my true companion. . . ." The relationship of Jesus and Thomas as twins is here shown to be part of an inherited oral tradition ("It has been said . . . ") used by the author of the *Book of Thomas*.[38] How early this relationship became part of the Thomas tradition is impossible to say, but it appears to have been present already in the first century. Negatively, it may underlie the avoidance of the title "Jude, . . . brother of Jesus," in favor of "Jude, . . . brother of James" (= the brother of Jesus) in the incipit of the Epistle of Jude. Koester pos-

36. Cf. James Hope Moulton, and George Milligan, *The Vocabulary of the Greek Testament Illustrated from the Papyri and Other Non-literary Sources* (Grand Rapids: Eerdmans, 1930; repr. 1972) 159. One may compare a case of another type, the *Epistula Apostolorum* 2, where Peter and Cephas are different disciples, illustrating how the meaning and function of double names for individuals could be lost or confused.

37. Cf. Raymond Kuntzmann, "L'identification dans le *livre de Thomas l'Athlète*," in Bernard Barc, ed., *Colloque International sur les textes de Nag Hammadi: Quebec, 22–25 Aout 1978* (Quebec: Laval, 1981) 283f.

38. Cf. John D. Turner, *The Book of Thomas the Contender*, 114–119.

tulates that this identification of Judas, the brother of the Lord (Matt 13:55), with Thomas "is more likely a primitive tradition than a later confusion. Such a primitive tradition was, to be sure, suppressed by later orthodox developments"[39] The choice of "brother of James" for "brother of Jesus" may already be an instance of this suppression.

On the other hand, one may see this relationship as twins as an esoteric tradition in the *Gospel of Thomas* itself. In logion 13, Jesus takes Thomas aside and speaks three (secret) words to him alone.[40] On his return, his fellow disciples ask him what Jesus had told him. He replies:

> If I tell you one of the words which he said to me, you will take up stones and throw them at me, and fire will come out of the stones and burn you up.

The disciples will attempt to stone Thomas if he repeats what he has heard. In John, stoning is the punishment of choice for those who claim equality with deity (John 10:30–33). If one looks to the *Book of Thomas*, the three words which are secrets in the *Gospel of Thomas* appear to have been part of oral tradition, and are declared openly: ⲡⲁⲥⲟⲉⲓⲱ, ⲡⲁⲱⲃⲣ ⲙⲙⲉ,[41] and ⲡⲁⲥⲟⲛ ("my twin, my true compan-

39. Cf. Helmut Koester, "GNOMAI DIAPHOROI," 134.

40. The full text of *GTh* 13 in English translation is as follows:
Jesus said to his disciples: Make a comparison to me and tell me whom I am like. Simon Peter said to him: You are like a righteous angel. Matthew said to him: you are like a wise philosopher. Thomas said to him: Master, my mouth will not at all be capable of saying whom you are like. Jesus said: I am not your master, because you have drunk and have become drunk from the bubbling spring which I measured out. And he took him and withdrew, and spoke three words to him. And when Thomas came to his companions, they asked him: What did Jesus say to you? Thomas said to them: If I tell you one of the words which he said to me, you will take up stones and throw them at me, and fire will come out of the stones and burn you up.

41. Cf. the discussion of this term by Hans-Martin Schenke, "The Book of Thomas (NHC II.7): A Revision of a Pseudepigraphical Letter of Jacob the Contender," in A. H. B. Logan and A. J. M. Wedderburn, eds., *The New Testament and Gnosis: Essays in Honor of R. McL. Wilson* (Edinburgh: T. and T. Clark, 1983) 213–216. Schenke argues against the position of Peter Nagel, "Thomas der Mitstreiter (zu NHC II, 7: p. 138,8)," in *Mélanges offerts à M. Werner Vycichl, Société d'Égyptologie Genève, Bulletin* 4 (1980) 65–71.

ion, and my brother": 138.8 and 10).⁴² What was esoteric and potentially "blasphemous" in the *Gospel of Thomas* is accessible inheritance for the community of the *Book of Thomas*.⁴³

The Gospel of John, unlike the synoptic Gospels, declares that Thomas is called "the Twin." It may be that John is merely translating the name into Greek for his non-Semitic audience. Yet why does he do even that? John wants his Greek readers to know that people are calling Thomas "Twin," not simply that his name was Thomas.⁴⁴

42. This passage was first connected with *GTh* 13 by J. Doresse, *L'Évangile selon Thomas, ou les paroles secrètes de Jésus* (Paris: Librairie Plon, 1959) 141–142. Confidence is impossible in such a case. According to Davies, "It is easy to make clever guesses about the identity of the three mysterious words, or logia, but it will be best to refrain from such guesswork": Stevan L. Davies. *The Gospel of Thomas and Christian Wisdom* (New York: Seabury Press, 1982) 92. Likewise, Émile Gillabert, Pierre Bourgeois, and Yves Haas, *Évangile selon Thomas* (Paris: Dervy-Livres, 1985) 171; and R. McL. Wilson, *Studies in the Gospel of Thomas* (London: A. R. Mowbray, 1960) 112.

Bolder hearts have offered other opinions: Arthur thinks that the three words represent "inspired sayings" of Christian prophets for their community: Richard L. Arthur, *The Gospel of Thomas and the Coptic New Testament*, 23. Grant-Freedman, Nations, Walls, and Ménard point to the three portentous words of the Naassenes, "Caulacau, Saulasau, Zeesar," from Isa 28:10: cf. Robert M. Grant, and David Noel Freedman, *The Secret Sayings of Jesus* (Garden City, N.Y.: Doubleday, 1960) 127; Archie Lee Nations, *A Critical Study of the Coptic Gospel according to Thomas* (Ph. D. Diss., Vanderbilt University, 1960; Ann Arbor: University Microfilms, 1960) 117f.; A. F. Walls, "The References to Apostles in the Gospel of Thomas," in *NTS* 7 (1960–61) 266–270; and Jacques-É. Ménard, *L'Évangile selon Thomas* (NHS 5; Leiden: E. J. Brill, 1975) 99. Puech considers the possibility of "Father, Son, and Holy Spirit": H.-Ch. Puech, "Une collection de paroles de Jésus récemment retrouvée: L'Évangile selon Thomas," in *Comptes rendus de l'Académie des Inscriptions et Belles Lettres* (Paris, 1957) 156. Gärtner thinks that the three words are the unutterable name of Jesus, on the model of the Tetragrammaton: Bertil Gärtner, *The Theology of the Gospel according to Thomas*, 121–125; also Jacques-É.Ménard, *L'Évangile selon Thomas*, 32–33. Giverson cites the three words spoken to Thomas in John 14:6, "I am the way, the truth, and the life": S.Giverson, *Thomas Evangeliet* (Copenhagen: Gads, 1959) 48.

43. This information, if it was not simply lost, was still esoteric in the *Acts of Thomas*. In *ATh* 47, Thomas says, "Jesus . . . [you who] did set me apart from all my companions and speak to me three words, wherewith I am inflamed, and tell them to others I cannot" (the translation is that of G. Bornkamm, "The Acts of Thomas," in Henneke-Schneemelcher, *New Testament Apocrypha*, 2.469). This is a clear allusion to *GTh* 13.

44. Schnackenburg notes that "The translation of the Aramaic name אוּתְמָא [*sic.*; *l.* תָּאוֹמָא] is remarkable, since Thomas and Didymos were also separate names in the Greek-speaking world": R. Schnackenburg, *St John*, 515, n. 37.

No mention is made of whose twin he was, or what that may have signified. Theological speculation on the special and virgin birth of Jesus make the idea that Thomas could have been thought the twin of Jesus shocking or abhorrent to modern ears. But that was not so for all early Christians: the Thomas community at sometime in the second century clearly held that view. There was, however, an early stage in the Thomas tradition during which this twin relationship was esoteric information, as evidenced by its covert nature in the Gospel of the Twin, the *Gospel of Thomas*.[45] At this early stage, the communities of Thomas and John produced their two Gospels. It is enticing to speculate that John knew that the Thomas community, at least, was calling Thomas the "twin," but because of their esotericism, did not yet know why.[46]

*John 20:25*

> The other disciples, therefore, kept telling him, "We have seen the Lord." But he said to them, "Unless I see in his hands the mark of the nails and I put my finger into the mark of the nails and put my hand into his side, I will definitely not believe."

The response of Thomas, that he must touch the hands and side of Jesus, demonstrates that the statement of the disciples to him, "We have seen the Lord," meant something much more substantial than a visionary experience. No difficulty whatever would have been occasioned by the disciples' statement if it had meant: "We have seen the shade of the Lord." The sentence had traditional basis: Paul used it of his own "vision in light" of the post-Easter Jesus in 1 Corinthians 9:1:

---

45. The secrecy concerning the "three words" of *GTh* 13, as it seems to me, has to do with this very relationship. The incipit of the Coptic version of *Thomas* specifically includes the form of the name with both Greek and Aramaic words for "twin": "Didymos Judas Thomas." The word Δίδυμος appears to have been missing in the recension of the Greek fragment, P. Oxy. 654. Cf. J. A. Fitzmyer, "The Oxyrhynchus Logoi of Jesus and the Coptic Gospel According to Thomas," in *TS* 20 (1959) 515; and M. Marcovich, "Textual Criticism on the Gospel of Thomas," in *JTS* 20 (1969) 53.

46. Another, less charitable, possibility exists, suggested to me by Paul Morrisette: the author uses the phrase with sarcasm, knowing full well its implications; Thomas is the "so-called Twin of Jesus."

"Have I not seen Jesus our Lord?" Nearly all ancients believed in postmortem survival of the soul, which was seen on occasion by survivors.[47] Thomas' response, however, shows that John meant the disciples to say, "We have seen the Lord in the same physical body he had before his death." This was an impossibility for both the Greco-Roman world and the Thomas community. Yet the affirmation of the physical incarnation and resurrection of Jesus is one of the burdens of this Gospel.

In concert with the generally negative portrayal of this disciple, John fashions with sarcasm the crass demand of Thomas: he requires a distasteful, even repulsive, method of proof of the physical nature of the risen Jesus. The other disciples were convinced by a mere visual demonstration by Jesus of his hands and side (John 20:20). In Luke 24:39, when the disciples also do not believe that Jesus has a physical body, he says, "See my hands and feet, . . . Touch me and see. . . ." The following verse (24:40), however, says simply that he showed them his hands and feet. They are not said actually to have touched him, and no such odious behavior as probing his wounds is even intimated. In each case, the mere visual demonstration is sufficient. Surely a shake of Jesus' hand or touch of his arm would have sufficed for even the most hardened Philistine to ascertain that the appearance was more than visionary. But John has Thomas demand what no cultured or sane person, ancient or modern, would consider acceptable behavior.

Theological arguments, however, seldom bring out the most charitable traits of the participants involved. During the following century, the level of argumentation descended to remarkable depths in the controversy over the resurrection body of Jesus. The Great Church moved farther and farther toward insistence on the actual identity of the pre- and post-resurrection bodies of all humanity, whether saved or damned. Opponents of such doctrines brought up the obvious difficulties inherent in such ideas. Athenagoras, for example, in the treatise *De Resurrectione*, argues against "men

47. Chapter one examined this belief. Among the exceptions were Epicureans and Sadducees, and the sophisticated Athenians of Plato's day (cf. Plato, *Phaedo* 80e).

who simply do not believe it, others who dispute it, and others who, although they are among those who accept our basic assumptions, are as doubtful as those who dispute it."[48] These, "who mock God . . . as much as the most unprincipled" (9.1), he likens to weeds in a garden and to bodily infections (1.4), and accuses them of giving comfort to the immoral (2.2). They in their turn, to judge from the counterargument, questioned the willingness and ability of God to reconstitute bodies which had been dissolved, eaten by animals and fish, or become part of other human bodies because of the eating of creatures which had eaten humans, or by cannibalism (4.1–4). Athenagoras, in response, invents the specious argument that human bodies reject and do not assimilate human flesh as food, "refuting" his opponents thereby (7.4). Ignatius, not long after the writing of John's Gospel, threatened those who denied Jesus' postmortem body with becoming bodiless and *daimon*-like, as they thought Jesus was (*Smyr.* 2); he claimed that they were blaspheming Jesus, and had been denied by him (5.1–2). The author of 1 John designates similar opponents as being "from the world" and "of the anti-Christ" (1 John 4:2–5). Many more examples of such edifying argumentation could be cited. When one views the Doubting Thomas pericope in this context, John's framing of the crass nature of Thomas' demand becomes understandable: it is one more aspect of a heated and purposely offensive argument over physical resurrection, a controversy which began early in the first Christian century, and lasted for more than four hundred years. The possibility exists that John is merely recasting some sarcasm which he had first heard cast at his own position. Perhaps opponents of physical resurrection had said derisively, "Did the disciples stick their fingers in his wounds?", much as they would later say, "Will God also resurrect your genitalia?"[49]

---

48. Athenagoras, *De Res.*, 2.2. The translation is that of William R. Schoedel, ed. and trans., *Athenagoras: Legatio and De Resurrectione* (Oxford: Clarendon Press, 1972) 91.

49. Yes, according to Tertullian, *De Res. Carnis* 60.

Another unique feature of this verse and the Johannine passion story is the wound in the side of Jesus.[50] This is one further instance of an element found earlier in the Gospel (John 19:34) being recalled and elaborated in the Thomas pericope. The wound in the side is a feature of the earthly Jesus which survives the grave, and indicates for John that the risen one is indeed the very same in body as the one who died. One notes here that the wound in the side of Jesus is one gained by his corpse after death and still retained after his resurrection; recall the wounds suffered by the corpse of Hector retained by his shade (*Aeneid* 2.272–273). John seeks to demonstrate by this motif the continuity of the physical body of Jesus through the transition of death, from passion to appearances.[51] Luke by similar means attempts to prove that Jesus had the very same physical body on both sides of the grave, with the same physical markings gained by human experience. This is a development beyond the conception of Paul, with his teaching on the spiritual body of Jesus (1 Corinthians 15:44). Paul's idea was far too easily interpreted in nonphysical categories, and was readily adopted by those who denied physical resurrection: a "spiritual body" was exactly what they affirmed.[52] Paul's idea, in fact, was itself built on Greco-Roman speculations concerning post-mortem existence which antedated the first century. In the case of John, the retention of wounds alone would also not have proven physical resurrection. Souls of the dead, according to Greco-Roman tradition, normally bore their pre-mortem characteristics, and especially their death wounds.[53] That Jesus as a ghost would appear with wounded side, hands and feet, was what would have been expected in his culture. So John adds the demand of Thomas to

50. Crossan derives this motif from the source of the *Gospel of Peter*, designated by him as the "Cross Gospel": John Dominic Crossan, *The Cross That Spoke: The Origins of the Passion Narrative* (San Francisco: Harper and Row, 1988) 126, 159, 174, and 197. Cf., however, the very interesting review of the textual tradition which describes Jesus as being stabbed in the side by the soldier *before* death, which then became the background of the story in both *GPt* and John, by Stephen Pennells, "The Spear Thrust (Mt. 27.49b, *v.l.* / Jn 19.34)", in *JSNT* 19 (1983) 99–115.

51. Cf. Haenchen, *John* 2, 201.

52. Cf. James M. Robinson, "From Jesus to Valentinus (or to the Apostles Creed)", in *JBL* 101 (1982) 16–17.

53. Cf. the discussion of Greco-Roman views of the soul in chapter one.

*touch* Jesus, the one thing reputed to be impossible in the Greco-Roman tradition concerning the souls of the dead.

We may now look back with profit at the first reference to Thomas in this Gospel, the first time that Thomas doubts resurrection, and note again that John is recalling in the Thomas pericope something found earlier in the gospel. In John 11 we read of the raising of Lazarus. After learning of his friend's illness, Jesus declares his purpose to return to Judea (11:1–7). Against the objection of the disciples that "the Jews were just seeking to stone" him (11:8), he declares, "Are there not twelve hours in the day? If anyone walks in the day he does not stumble" (11:9). This comment may be recast into something on the order of, "Doesn't darkness come at late evening? It's only four o'clock, so there's no problem." The disciples think he might be killed, but Jesus knows that he is in no immediate peril. In the program of John, there is still time; his hour to die had not yet come.[54] He then informs his disciples enigmatically that Lazarus is asleep and that he will awaken him (11:11), referring to his resurrection. The disciples miss the point, so Jesus "tells them plainly, 'Lazarus is dead. . . . Let us go to him'" (11:14–15).

Here Thomas comments to his fellows, "Let us go too, that we may die with him" (11:16). The "him" with whom Thomas resigns himself to die is not Jesus, as is almost universally claimed, but Lazarus: Lazarus is the only one dead at the time, and is the referent of the pronoun "him" in both verses 15 and 16. Lazarus is the only one with whom anyone could die, for Jesus has just declared that he himself is out of danger. The point of the passage, in any case, is to introduce the raising of Lazarus; the purpose of introducing Thomas is that it is the raising of the dead which Thomas will doubt in his most famous moment at the end of the Gospel. So Thomas suggests that not only is Lazarus not going to be raised, but that he and his fellow disciples are going to die along with him. As Lindars

---

54. The author is quite careful to present the closing of the "day" of Jesus, the gathering power of darkness, and the departure of the Light, but it is not at Bethany where this event is to take place. In 12:23, after the triumphal entry into Jerusalem, Jesus says, "The hour has come for the Son of Man to be glorified"; there and then begins the coming of night.

correctly observes: "Thomas's remark must be interpreted in the light of his doubt about the resurrection in 20:24-9. . . ."[55] The Christology of the passage, in addition, viewed as it must be from the perspective of the Johannine church at the end of the century, is not that Thomas and the disciples must die with Jesus, but that they will be raised as was Lazarus; Lazarus receives life after death as an archetype of the Johannine Christian. So Jesus declares, "I am the Resurrection and the Life; the one who believes in me shall live even if he dies" (11:25). The point is that Jesus holds for the church the promise of life in resurrection.[56] Here is the introduction of the disciple Thomas, who doubts the possibility of bodily resurrection, the very theme to be recalled at the end of the gospel in the pericope of Doubting Thomas.

### John 20:26-27

> And after eight days again his disciples were inside, and Thomas was with them. Jesus comes while the doors were shut, and stood in the middle and said, "Peace be upon you." 20:27 Then he says to Thomas, "Bring your finger here and see my hands, and bring your hand and put it into my side; and stop being faithless, but faithful."

The risen Jesus addresses Thomas alone, as though he had heard invisibly the conversation with his fellow disciples a week before. This is a special demonstration for an especially difficult disciple. In the comparable passage in Luke (24:36-43), the disciples also do not believe, and are granted a similar (though much more refined) demonstration of Jesus' physical nature. Yet when they still do not believe ("for joy," we are told in v. 41), Jesus gives them another

---

55. Barnabas Lindars, *The Gospels of John* (New Century Bible; London: Oliphants, 1971) 392. Cf. also Jacob Kremer, *Lazarus: Die Geschichte einer Auferstehung* (Stuttgart: Katholisches Bibelwerk, 1985) 62-63; Alain Marchadour, *Lazare: Histoire d'un récit, Récits d'une histoire* (Paris: Les éditions du Cerf, 1988) 113.

56. Cf. the insightful comments of Martin, who sees the Lazarus narrative as addressing the issue of the delay of the parousia and the death of Christians, much as did Paul in 1 Thess 4: James P. Martin, "History and Eschatology in the Lazarus Narrative: John 11.1-44," in *Scottish Journal of Theology* 17 (1964) 332-343.

demonstration, and eats broiled fish before them (vv. 42–43). In John, however, the atmosphere of joy, and the further effort of Jesus to do an even more remarkable thing (eating fish) to seal their faith, are completely absent. All that remains for Thomas is admonition. Even when he professes faith ("My Lord and my God!"), he is further shamed.

Thomas is described as ἄπιστος, "without faith," in a unique sentence. The Gospel of John uses the verb πιστεύειν ("to believe") more than ninety times, yet Thomas is the only one who is described as ἄπιστος, or told to be πιστός ("believing").[57] In the first instance, these adjectives appear to have a very simple and narrow application: Thomas does not believe that Jesus has risen physically from the dead. In the context of the following four verses, however, the meaning of "belief" has a much wider application: it is the "belief in Jesus"; it refers to the basic method of spiritual approach to God for the Gospel of John as a whole. Thomas is not told to believe in anything, but merely to be "one who believes."

The *Gospel of Thomas* provides an interesting insight into this point: the Coptic words for "believe" (ⲚⲀϨⲦⲈ and ⲦⲀⲚϨⲞⲩⲦ) never occur in the Coptic *Gospel of Thomas* at all; the Greek word πιστεύειν occurs but once, and that is in the mouth of Jesus' opponents.[58] The *Gospel of Thomas* never recommends faith to anyone as a spiritual mode. Disciples in the Thomas community are instead told to "know themselves" (3; 67; 111), to "find themselves" (111), and to "bring forth that which is within them" (70), the "light in a man of light" (24). They are to "seek" until they find "a place in Repose" for themselves (2; 60).[59] This constitutes the disciple as a "single one" (48), who will "stand" (16; 23), and enter the Kingdom (22; 49). The mechanism is the word of Jesus (19), which he "measures out" as a

57. Cf. C. K. Barrett, *St. John*, 572.

58. In transliteration in *GTh* 91; it does not occur in the Greek fragments. *GTh* 91: "They said to him, 'Tell us who you are that we may believe [πιστεύε] in you.'"

59. On "seeking and finding" in the *Gospel of Thomas* and John, among other works, cf. H. Koester, "Les discours d'adieu de l'évangile de Jean: Leur trajectoire au premier et deuxième siècle," in Jean-Daniel Kaestli et al., eds., *La Communauté johannique et son histoire: La trajectoire de l'évangile de Jean aux deux premiers siècles* (Genève: Labor et Fides, 1990) 269–280.

spring of water (13; 108). Whoever hears his words as a disciple and finds their proper interpretation "will not taste death" (1; 19). This same mechanism still holds for the *Book of Thomas* in the next century, in which Thomas is told to "know himself" (138.6ff.), and only once told to "believe the truth" (142.11). The way of hope and faith *in someone else* as a basis for the religious life, the method used by Johannine and other Christians, is in fact condemned (143.38ff.). It is not until the time of the *Acts of Thomas* that faith as a mechanism becomes part of the Thomas tradition, under the influence of the written Gospels and developing orthodoxy (for example, *ATh* 59; 65). Yet the disciple still declares the teaching to be "to seek myself and to recognize who I was and who and how I now am, that I may become what I once was" (*ATh* 15). So in John, Thomas the Unbeliever, who stands for a religious way of life that does not utilize faith as a spiritual mode, is told to "stop being without faith, but one with faith."

One may now better understand another earlier reference in John to the apostle Thomas (the second, after 11:16). John 14 opens significantly with the commands, "Do not let you heart be troubled. Believe in God; believe also in me." Jesus then addresses the disciples concerning his departure to the Father and the place he will prepare for them, making mention of his "coming again" to receive them (14:3).[60] He next adds the enigmatic and apparently unrelated statement (14:4): "And where I go you know the road."[61] This ungram-

---

60. The entire passage under discussion (14:1–7) is as follows:
14:1 Do not let your heart to be troubled. Believe in God, and believe in me. 2 In my Father's house are many residences. If not, I would have told you, because I am going to prepare a place for you. 3 And if I go and make a place for you, I will come again and receive you to myself, in order that where I am you may also be. 4 And where I go you know the way. 5 Thomas says to him, "Lord, we do not know where you are going. How can we know the way?" 6 Jesus says to him, "I am the way and the truth and the life. No one comes to the Father but through me. 7 If you had known me, you would have known the Father also."

61. An important textual variant provides a smoother reading for 14:4: "And you know where I am going, and you know the road" (καὶ ὅπου [ἐγὼ] ὑπάγω οἴδατε καὶ τὴν ὁδὸν οἴδατε.). The text printed in UBS Third Edition and Nestle 26 is both the shorter reading and certainly the *lectio difficilior*, and cannot be explained on the basis of scribal correction. According to the editorial committee, Thomas' re-

matical phrase, "Where I go" (ὅπου [ἐγὼ] ὑπάγω) recalls the earlier identical phrase in 13:36, "Where I go, you cannot follow me now, but you shall follow later."[62] In that case it is the goal of the journey, its destination in the Father, which is the point. The destination is clearly explained in 14:2–3: Jesus is going to his Father's house to prepare a place for the disciples. In 14:5, however, the subject has changed: it is *the way* which is in view. The word order and syntax emphasize clearly the "road", the path or means to the destination, and not the destination itself. Thomas the Ignorant, who had heard Jesus make several (now famous) "I am" statements and speak of his return to the Father on more than one occasion, seems to understand Jesus' comment in pedestrian terms of a literal journey: "Lord, we do not know where you are going. How do we know the road?" (14:5).[63]

There is a mild sarcasm in the language of the text directed at Thomas which depends on the multivalence of the Greek word ὁδός; it may mean both a literal "road, path" and a figurative "way, means, method." Thomas of course is made to understand the word in the literal but incorrect sense. Jesus' reply, however, shows that the statement had nothing to do with a physical journey, but with a method of approaching the divine, in fact the only method allowed in Johannine theology: "I am the Road, the Truth and the Life. No one comes to the Father but through me" (14:6). Thomas, and by extension the Thomas Christians, are told that there is but one way to God: the Johannine Jesus. By implication, the spiritual "way" of the Thomas community, the enlightenment and Gnosis which made Thomas Christians of equal standing with Jesus and granted direct, unmedi-

---

ply, which distinguishes between "where" and "the way" led to the improvement in the text: Bruce M. Metzger, *A Textual Commentary on the Greek New Testament*, 243.

62. Cf. 13:33 and 8:21–22.

63. Dodd takes the reply of Thomas to mean that Thomas does know the "way", but not the destination, as though Thomas were saying, "We know that you are the Way, but we don't know where you are going." So Dodd writes: "What Jesus is saying is,'You know the way: you do not need to know where it leads.'" (C. H. Dodd, *Interpretation*, 412, n. 1). Jesus' reply in 14:6–7, however, makes no sense in such an interpretation. His reply concerns the way and the means, not the destination (vs. 6), and states that Thomas does not know Jesus himself who is the way, not that he does not know the place to which Jesus is going (v. 7).

ated access to God, was futile; it did not result in knowledge of God. The basic reason for its failure was its inadequate (in the Johannine view) understanding of Jesus. So Jesus says, "If you had known me, you would have know my Father also" (14:7). Thomas (and his community: note the plural) did not know the Father because he did not know properly who Jesus was. Thomas and his community could not know God directly by the enlightenment of Jesus' sayings as the *Gospel of Thomas* teaches, but only by the Johannine method of faith in Jesus himself as intermediary. In the continuation of the discussion (14:8–12), the opening commands are reemphasized; it is faith that is the only "road": Thomas and Philip are told to *believe* four more times.

### John 20:28

Thomas answered and said to him, "My Lord and my God!"

Thomas is finally brought to faith, and exclaims that Jesus is his Lord and God. This is the climax of the Christology of the Gospel of John, and recalls the opening verse, "the Word was God." It is also the self-declared title of the Roman emperor in the last decades of the first century,[64] and John here applies it to the one whom he believes deserves the title, as a challenge to the "illegitimate" divinization in ruler cult.[65] Yet this too finds application to the Thomas tradition.

In the *Gospel of Thomas*, the followers of Jesus are termed "disciples" (*GTh* 6; 12; 13; 19, *etc.*). But the process of Thomas spirituality

---

64. For the title θεός in ruler cult, cf. S. R. F. Price, "Gods and Emperors: The Greek Language of the Roman Imperial Cult," in *JHS* 104 (1984) 79–95. Of Domitian, cf. Martin Percival Charlesworth, "Some Observations on Ruler-Cult Especially in Rome," in *HTR* 38 (1935) 5–44, esp. 32ff. For the connection with persecution, cf. Fergus Millar, "The Imperial Cult and the Persecutions," in Willem den Boer, ed., *Le Culte des Soverains dans l'Empire Romain* (Geneva: Fondation Hardt, 1973) 145–175.

65. Suetonius, *Domitianus* 13.2, records of Domitian that "when he would dictate a formal letter, it would begin thus: our Lord and God ordered this to be made" (*cum . . . formalem dictaret epistulam, sic coepit: dominus et deus noster hoc fieri*). Cf. W. Foerster, "κύριος," in Kittel, *TDNT*, 3.1054–1058.

produces an equalization of Jesus and his followers.[66] For example, Jesus is the Light (77), and the disciples are "men of light" (24); Jesus is "son of man" (86), and the disciples become "sons of man" (106); Jesus is the one "who lives" (Intro; 59), and the disciples become "living spirits" (114). In *GTh* 13, Thomas addresses Jesus as "master" (ⲥⲁϩ = "teacher"); Jesus answers, "I am *not* your master, because you have drunk and become intoxicated from the bubbling spring which I measured out." Jesus denies that he is superior to Thomas, since he has fulfilled his discipleship. This is further clarified in *GTh* 108:

> Jesus said, "The one who drinks from my mouth will become as I am, and I myself will become as he is."

Jesus is as the (wine) steward of the water of his own sayings, which constitutes the disciple as the equal of the master.[67] In this context, the confession of the Johannine Thomas to Jesus, that he is both Lord and God, takes on another dimension: if those of the Thomas tradition thought of themselves as the equals of Jesus, they would learn to submit to Jesus as Master, as John hoped, by the example of their spiritual father.

*John 20:29*

> Jesus says to him, "Have you believed because you have seen me? Blessed are those who have not seen and believe."

John ends the pericope with a blessing for those of his own and later times. It is addressed directly to Thomas, as though he were the only one to have seen and believed, and it devalues his faith-based-

---

66. Cf. Jacques-É. Ménard, *L'Évangile selon Thomas*, 206–207; also Stevan L. Davies. *The Gospel of Thomas and Christian Wisdom*, 133–136.

67. The thought is not foreign to the Sayings tradition, though the use made of it in the Thomas tradition is unique; there is ontological equality in *Thomas*. Cf. Luke 6:40: "A pupil is not above his teacher; but everyone, after he has been fully trained, will be like his teacher"; also, with a different application, Matt 10:24–25. Much closer in conception is John 4:14: "Whoever drinks of the water I shall give him shall never thirst; but the water that I shall give him shall become in him a well of water springing up to eternal life"; cf. also 7:37–38.

on-sight. But this is not the point of the Thomas story proper,[68] nor its conclusion; it is the conclusion of the Gospel as a whole. John uses Thomas here to speak to all later Christians. All of the disciples had to see to believe, in all of the canonical Gospels. In this respect, Thomas was not alone. They were all asked to believe the unbelievable, and seeing with their own eyes was a minimum requirement. But later generations had no such opportunity: the time of appearances was past, and they had to rely upon the testimony spoken by others. The conclusion of the Thomas pericope is not for the Thomas community alone, but for all who would read or hear this Gospel, and be asked to rely upon only the witness of John.[69]

That such witness was not wholly adequate, however, may be seen from the further testimony offered. In John 19:35, a redactor adds corroboration: the testimony of the "witness" is declared to be true; "he knows that he is telling the truth, that you may believe."[70] Again,

---

68. Of the several "points" of the Doubting Thomas pericope, the demonstration of the fleshly resurrection of Jesus is the central theme in the debate with the Thomas community. Curiously enough, a friendly objection has been voiced (in conversation) that the physical nature of the resurrection body of Jesus cannot be the issue, since Thomas is not said to have actually touched Jesus. On the contrary, however, one must recall that in the identical situaltion in Luke, when the risen Jesus commands the disciples, "Touch me . . . " (Luke 24:39), they are also not said to have touched Jesus. Yet in both gospels, the point is clearly that if they had, Jesus would have been found to be fleshly. Neither author wished to allow for a docetic or phantom Jesus. One may hope that a description in the gospels of such an action as probing the wounds of Jesus was left out purposely, that it would have offended the ancients as much as anyone; I for one am grateful it is missing.

69. The language of the "seeing and believing" of Thomas is prefigured in the Beloved Disciple, who "saw and believed" (John 20:8) when he entered the tomb of Jesus; yet like the subsequent generations, he did not see *Jesus* and believe, but only the grave clothes. So subsequent disciples who also do not see Jesus are to follow his example of positive and willing faith, not the "forced" faith of Thomas. Cf. Brendan Byrne, "The Faith of the Beloved Disciple and the Community in John 20," in *JSNT* 23 (1985) 83–97, esp. 90.

70. Schnackenburg rightly connects 19:35 and 21:24, and attributes them to the editors of the Gospel (*St. John*, 3.290–292; cf. also Bultmann, *John*, 677–679). Dodd attributes the verse to the author in *Historical Tradition*, 134, n. 1. (cf. also Brown, *John XIII-XXI*, 936 and 1127), but later cannot decide whether this is from the hand of the author or a redactor (*Interpretation of the Fourth Gospel*, 429). Blass-Debrunner note that the verse is missing from two Latin manuscripts, and appear to claim that it should be disregarded on text-critical grounds: F. Blass and A. Debrunner, *A Greek Grammar of the New Testament and Other Early Christian Litera-*

in 21:24, additional supporters assert that the Beloved Disciple was the witness and had written of the gospel events, and "we know that his witness is true." The simple conclusion of the Doubting Thomas pericope was apparently not sufficient in itself to secure faith; doubts still plagued the Johannine community concerning the truth of their testimony and Gospel. The veracity of the Beloved Disciple himself needed support. It is tempting to see here what in fact is visible by other means, that the dispute continued unabated, despite the efforts of the author of John. No notice of the pericope is found in the *Book of Thomas (the Contender)*, written in the next century. One can only assume either that this follower of Thomas did not know the Gospel of John, or that it was purposely ignored. In either case its teaching would have been considered false doctrine. The *Acts of Thomas* does incorporate the "lesson" of the pericope, with significant modification, into its picture of Thomas; nevertheless the basic tenets and modes of Thomas Christianity remain intact. Just as the disciples of John the Baptist continued to follow their spiritual father despite the efforts of the author of the Gospel of John, the community of Thomas was not soon convinced by the pericope of Doubting Thomas.

---

ture (trans. by Robert W. Funk; Chicago: Univ. of Chicago Press, 1961) 152, para. 291.6. Barrett refutes their skepticism, but concedes that "it might be that the gospel was at first issued (perhaps in gnostic circles) without 19:35 and that the verse was subsequently added to secure authority . . . among the orthodox": C. K. Barrett, *St. John*, 558.

# Chapter Four

# The Body and Resurrection
# in the Thomas Tradition
## *The Gospel of Thomas*

One reason why early Christians had such difficulty in convincing their fellows, both Christian and otherwise, of the physical resurrection of Jesus was the lack of a philosophical, logical, or scientific basis for such a claim. All these ways of interpreting the world militated against the idea. Philosophy and religion had in the main declared the soul and body two separate entities, with the soul qualitatively superior to, but imprisoned within, the body. They asserted the immortality of the soul,[1] and its origin and destiny in the divine. The ethereal nature of the soul proved that its home was in the ethereal regions of the gods.[2] They emphasized, in contrast, the mortality and mutability of the body. The earthly body was bonded to the material world: it weighed down the soul, and prevented its ascension to the upper world.[3] In addition, the body with its appetites and passions had a negative spiritual effect on the soul: it blinded, beguiled, and corrupted its natural purity. Logic and observation, for their part, demonstrated that dead bodies did nothing other than decay and disappear over time, if they were not first consumed by the funeral pyre or eaten by animals and birds. Ancients were quite conscientious in their care of the dead, and often gathered the excarnated bones of relatives into family tombs; experience taught them of corpses and the finality of death for the body. Even the dead themselves joined the controversy, appearing in vision and visitation often in epic and cult. These visible dead were by convention impal-

---

1. Cf. for example, Cicero, *Tusc. Disp.* 1.16.38–39.
2. Cf. Cicero, *Tusc. Disp.* 1.17.40–41.
3. Cf. Plato, *Phaedo* 81c-d.

pable shades, some of whom even explained how it was that they had no physical substance, and could therefore not be touched.[4]

It is this cultural inheritance which informs the view of the body in the Thomas tradition. There developed at some time in the first century a docetic view of Jesus, visible in negative through the contrary polemic in Ignatius of Antioch.[5] But the Thomas tradition does not have a docetic Jesus, any more than did Plato have a docetic Socrates. The soul for Plato has its origin in the divine and takes on a body as a "dwelling" or even "prison." It is not unable to undergo suffering, nor does it deny embodiment. The supra-mundane history of the soul and body in Plato is quite similar in outline to the story of both the Living Jesus and the disciple in the *Gospel of Thomas*. Like Socrates, Jesus is not fundamentally different from his disciples, that he alone should "seem" (δοκεῖν) to be physically embodied while his disciples are in fact so. As Jesus is the preexistent savior who comes to earth, takes on a body of flesh (*GTh* 28), then leaves it behind to return to the Father, so the disciple "existed before being born" (*GTh* 19) and will return to the beginning (*GTh* 18), to the Kingdom from which they came (*GTh* 49), after leaving the body behind to its "owners" (*GTh* 21). Just as is the history of Jesus, so is the history of the individual disciple; the two are equalized by self-knowledge meted out by Jesus (*GTh* 13 and 113). He is as a wine steward, measuring out the living water of his secret sayings which constitutes the disciple as his equal: "He who will drink from my mouth will become as I am" (108); his disciples become "sons of man" as he is "son of man" (*GTh* 106).

## Reality of the Earthly Body

That Jesus had a real body, and was not a docetic "semblance" of a human being is clear from several passages in the *Gospel of Thomas*.

---

4. Cf. *Od.* 11.204–222 for the classic passage: Odysseus' mother explains to him why he cannot embrace her post-mortem form.

5. Ignatius, *Trall.* 9–10; *Smyr.* 2–3. Docetism was the view that Jesus merely "seemed" to be human, but was really a divine or spiritual being on both sides of the grave. The term derives from the Greek word δοκεῖν ("to seem to be"). Ignatius argues against those who affirm that Jesus' "suffering was only a seeming" (τὸ

He is the "son of man" (*GTh* 86), a human being with a human lin-
eage and body.[6] His family is spoken of more than once: a disciple
tells him, "your mother and brothers are standing outside" (*GTh*
99); he speaks of his own mother (*GTh* 101), whom he says is termed
a harlot (*GTh* 105); yet a woman from the crowd blesses "the womb
that bore you, and the breasts that nourished you" (*GTh* 79). All of
this has varied non-literal, spiritual meaning and application in the
*Gospel of Thomas* as a whole which directs the reader away from the
flesh and worldly relationships. Nevertheless, it is based on the reality of the humanity of Jesus, in as much as he is the paradigm for his
disciples who must also direct their lives away from their quite real
flesh and human relations to the realm of the spirit. The physical nature of Jesus is apparent also in *GTh* 28:

> Jesus said: I took my stand in the midst of the world, and I ap-
> peared to them in flesh. . . .

Here the preexistence and earthly descent of Jesus is implicit; his
"standing" in the flesh is stated directly. The disciples also "came into
the world" and will "go out again" (also in *GTh* 28). If the collocation of the sayings in *Thomas* is at times a clue to the interpretation
placed on them by the community, then this reading of *GTh* 28 is
strengthened by the following saying (*GTh* 29): "I marvel at how this
great wealth [= the spirit] has made its home in this poverty [= the
body]." The disciples who do not come to self-knowledge are not
only "in poverty" but "are poverty" (*GTh* 3). Their souls are impov-
erished by dependence on the flesh; so Jesus pronounces "woe on
the soul which depends on the flesh" (*GTh* 112; cf. 87).

---

δοκεῖν: *Tral.* 10), who themselves instead of Jesus, he claims, will "be without bodies" (ἀσώματοι: *Smyr.* 2).

6. So Koester, "Introduction: The Gospel according to Thomas" in Bentley Layton, ed., *Nag Hammadi Codex II, 2–7*, 1.43.

## Leaving the Body at Death

The body is not only left behind at death; it belongs to the "owners" and is to be given over to them. In *GTh* 21, Jesus speaks of his disciples as follows:

> They are like little children who inhabit a field which is not their own. Whenever the owners of the field arrive, they will say, "Release our field to us." They strip naked before them in order to release it to them, and they give their field to them.

This is to be interpreted as an allegory: "the disciples (the children) in the world (the field), take off their bodies (their clothing) when the rulers of the world (the masters of the field, the archons?) demand what is theirs, the physical world and material bodies."[7] There is a double action of the disciples stripping themselves in order to release the field, and the giving of the field back to its owners. The "stripping naked" is death, which releases the disciple from the field of the material world, and allows it to be returned to its spiritual rulers. A very similar conception is related in *GTh* 37: the disciples are to remove their clothes, "put them under their feet like little children, and tread on them." Then they shall "come to the son of the Living One"[8] and not fear. This last sentence seems to have both a present and future application: the present application was likely that of the ritual of baptism, during which the candidate was baptized undressed, in a baptismal garment;[9] the future is clearly the removal of the body at death, and the ascent of the soul to the heavenly realms. Baptism had as its basis the enactment in ritual of the "real"

---

7. Dennis Ronald MacDonald, *There is No Male and Female: The Fate of a Dominical Saying in Paul and Gnosticism* (HDR 20; Philadelphia: Fortress Press, 1987) 44. For Ménard, likewise, it is "la délivrance de l'âme emprisonnée dans le corps": Jacques-É. Ménard, *L'Évangile selon Thomas*, 112–113. Cf. also Bertil Gärtner, *The Theology of the Gospel according to Thomas*, 185.

8. An examination of the photographs of the manuscript at this damaged point (39.38) supports a reading at the end of the line 38 of . . . ⲛⲟⲩ ("you will come"), not . . . ⲁⲩ ("you will behold") as is printed by Guillaumont, et al., and Layton.

9. Cf. *Acts of Thomas* 157. Cf. also Jonathan Z. Smith, "The Garments of Shame," in *HR* 5 (1966) 217–238; and D. R. MacDonald, *There is No Male and Female*, 56–63.

drama of death and renewal of life, first of Jesus, and then of the disciple.

## Eschatology and Future Resurrection

The *Gospel of Thomas* refutes directly the conception of an eschatological resurrection of the dead at the end of the age. The community of Thomas certainly knew of those who expected the kingdom of God at the eschaton and a new heaven and earth. In conscious contradiction of such expectation, one finds (*GTh* 51):

> His disciples said to him: When will the Repose of the dead occur? And when will the new cosmos come? He said to them: This thing which you expect has come, but you do not recognize it.

The initial question in an eschatological context to an apocalyptically conceived Jesus would surely have been: When will the *resurrection* of the dead occur? The *Gospel of Thomas* changes even this, since for the Thomas community there is no physical resurrection at all. Its desired state of the individual, both in the present and in the future, is one of Repose (ἀνάπαυσις) of the soul. The disciples are commanded in the present "to seek a place for yourselves in Repose, lest you become a corpse and be eaten" (*GTh* 60). The very "sign of the Father" in the disciple is the present possession of Repose (*GTh* 50), and the reward of discipleship to Jesus (*GTh* 90). A future Repose of the dead is not an eschatological reality: Jesus tells the disciples that their *future* expectation is misdirected; the Repose of the dead is a present reality. When asked when the kingdom would come, Jesus replies, "It will not come by you waiting for it. . . . The kingdom of the Father is spread on the earth and men do not see it" (*GTh* 113).

There is an end to the material cosmos; the heavens and the earth will "be rolled up" (*GTh* 111), but it is the one already "living on the One who Lives" who has no need to fear. Compare *GTh* 11:

Jesus said: this heaven will pass away, and that which is above it
will pass away; and those who are dead are not alive, and those
who are alive will not die.

This saying again addresses the subject of the future resurrection,
and here more clearly in the context of the end of the material world.
The heavens will pass away, and, from the point of view of apocalyptic expectation, the time of the resurrection and judgment will
come. But "the dead" will not live; they are not alive now, and therefore will not be raised then. Those who are now "alive" will never
die; they have no need for resurrection and judgment.[10]

There is a great deal of similarity in this worldview with that of the
Gospel of John, especially the fifth chapter. In John 5, those who believe in Jesus also do not come into judgment, but have "passed out
of death into life," an eternal life which they have as a present possession (John 5:24). Yet as often, these two similar Gospels differ on
fundamental points. John 5:25 declares that "an hour is coming, and
now is, when the dead shall hear the voice of the Son of God and
live." As in the *Gospel of Thomas*, the future eschatological moment
is the present, contrary to apocalyptic expectation. But this is further qualified in John: "all who are in the tombs shall hear . . . and
come forth; those who did good to a resurrection of life; those who
did evil to a resurrection of judgment" (5:28–29). These verses (John
5:28–29) have been seen as added to the tradition on which the
evangelist drew, in an effort "to reconcile the dangerous statements
in vv. 24f. with traditional eschatology."[11] It is clear that "realized
eschatology" has no need for physical resurrection; the future orientation of verses 5:28–29, with its eschatological final judgment, contradicts the present sense of verses 24f. Yet the idea of future physical
resurrection in juxtaposition to present possession of "life" is found
also in the Lazarus story (John 11:23–27). In addition, John is not
averse to using physical resurrection as a corrective to those who are
of contrary opinion, as the Doubting Thomas pericope shows. So

10. Cf. James M. Robinson, "From Jesus to Valentinus," 17–37.
11. R. Bultmann, *The Gospel of John*, 261; also, E. Haenchen, *John* 1, 253.

John creates a tension between present and future,[12] between "spiritual" and "physical" resurrection, in a Christian environment in which representatives of both extremes were to be found. The tension is the conscious choice of an author who would walk between future and realized eschatology, between "orthodoxy" and "heresy."

## The Temple Saying and Resurrection

John chapter 2 includes a pericope built around a saying of Jesus which it shares not only with the *Gospel of Thomas*, but with each of the Synoptic Gospel writers. John 2:19–22 reads:

> Destroy this temple, and in three days I will raise it. The Jews therefore said, 'This temple was built in 46 years, and you will raise it in three days?' But this he said concerning the temple of his body. When therefore he was raised from the dead, his disciples remembered that he said this, and they believed the Scripture and the word which Jesus said.

At the core of this pericope is a damaging saying against the temple which stands in the Synoptic Gospels as a central and fatal political charge against Jesus as revolutionary.[13] The obvious negative implications for the post-Neronian Church of the allegation of anti-temple hostility are mitigated by each of the Gospel writers. In the Synoptics it is preserved only as an accusation alleged by Jesus' enemies: in Mark it is spoken by false witnesses; in Matthew it is again associated with false witnesses, the wording is changed to refer merely to the realm of possibility ("I am *able* to destroy"), and the meaning is directed to the resurrection by emphasis on the phrase "three days"; in Luke it is removed from Jesus entirely and transferred to an accusation against Stephen in Acts.[14] In John, and as we

---

12. Cf. R. Brown, *The Gospel according to John I-XII*, cxix.

13. Cf. S. G. F. Brandon, *The Trial of Jesus of Nazareth* (New York: Dorset Press, 1968) 22–23; also, Ellis E. Jensen, "The First Century Controversy over Jesus as a Revolutionary Figure," in *JBL* 60 (1941) 262.

14. Cf. C. H. Dodd, *The Parables of the Kingdom* (rev. ed.; New York: Charles Scribner's Sons, 1961) 43: " . . . the belief that Jesus had said something of this kind

shall see in the *Gospel of Thomas*, it is applied to the "temple" of Jesus' body.

The saying is followed in Mark by the "blasphemy" of Jesus' claim to be the Son of God. For Mark, the primary basis for the case against Jesus among the chief priests is this blasphemy uttered by Jesus (Mark 14:64; 15:10 adds "envy"). But this assertion of messianic status is connected intimately with the saying concerning the temple.[15] The blasphemy developed out of "false testimony," brought against Jesus just prior, which led to the high priest's questions eliciting that claim. That prior testimony was (14:58):

> We heard him saying, "I will destroy the temple made with hands, and over three days I will build another made without hands."

Thus the first incriminating charge was that of temple destruction. Accordingly, passersby are said to have abused Jesus on the cross with the taunt: "Woe, you who destroys the temple and builds it in three days, save yourself . . . " (15:29–30). Pilate likewise was not concerned with the charge of blasphemy, but in the claim that Jesus was king of the Jews (15:2); so read the inscription over his cross (15:26).[16] His interest was political.

No reference to "made without hands" (Mark 14:58) remains in the taunt of 15:29, nor are the words found in the saying in its other occurrences. Thus interpreters have viewed Mark as indicating an

---

was an embarrassment to the early Church. Mark is concerned to invalidate the evidence at the trial. . . ." Also, for Matthew, F. W. Beare, *The Gospel According to Matthew* (San Francisco: Harper and Row, 1981) 520–521.

15. Interpreters often see the anti-temple saying (14:58) as a Markan interpolation into the passion narrative; for example, cf. N. Perrin, "The Christology of Mark: A Study in Methodology," in William Telford, ed., *The Interpretation of Mark* (IRT 7; London: SPCK/Philadelphia: Fortress Press, 1985) 97–98; Richard A. Horsley, *Jesus and the Spiral of Violence: Popular Jewish Resistance in Roman Palestine* (San Francisco: Harper and Row, 1987) 293; John R. Donahue, *Are You the Christ? The Trial Narrative in the Gospel of Mark* (SBLDS 10; Missoula: Scholars Press, 1973) 136.

16. "The wording of the *titulus* as it is reported in the Gospels is in all likelihood authentic": E. Bammel, "The *titulus*," in idem and C. F. D. Moule, eds., *Jesus and the Politics of His Day* (Cambridge: Cambridge Univ. Press, 1984) 363.

ecclesiastical meaning: he included the words "made with hands" and "made without hands" to allow a metaphorical interpretation of the new temple as the Markan community.[17] Yet the literal interpretation of the saying was the primary issue in the Markan description of the trial, and part of the political charge under which Jesus was condemned. There was a lively expectation of a literal and eschatological "temple made without hands" among certain Jews in the time of Jesus. The destruction of the temple and its (divine) replacement was an apocalyptic hope not uncommon in pre-Christian Judaism. A new temple is outlined in the final chapters of Ezekiel and the Temple Scroll. The temple is destroyed in the prophecy of Dan 9:26; it is destroyed and rebuilt at the eschaton in Tobit 14:4–7. The Lord replaces the temple with one of his own making in 1 Enoch 90 and Jubilees 1:27. The Qumran midrash on 2 Samuel 7 outlines a temple divinely built which would replace the Second Temple.[18] The Qumran Essenes withdrew from the defiled temple and awaited the eschaton and its new one. The phrase "made without hands" is used of the heavenly tabernacle of God (Heb 9:11), and the "house" of the resurrection body, "not made with hands, eternal in the heavens" (2 Cor 5:1). Both of these passages point to the belief that it is a temple made by God which is signified by the phrase "made without hands." As Flusser interprets the midrash on 2 Samuel 7 on the eschatological temple:[19]

> The present temple is evidently desecrated and polluted . . . , therefore in the future there will be revealed 'the House which He shall make in the End of Days, as it is written in the Book of

17. Lohse sees the "temple made without hands" as a reference to the "new people of God," that is, to the Markan community itself: E. Lohse, *History of the Suffering and Death of Jesus Christ* (trans. by Martin O. Dietrich; Philadelphia: Fortress Press, 1967) 83; also, John R. Donahue, *Are You the Christ?*, 109; and idem, "Temple, Trial, and Royal Christology," in Werner H. Kelber, ed., *The Passion in Mark: Studies on Mark* 14–16 (Philadelphia: Fortress Press, 1976) 69. Horsley draws interesting parallels of this "community as temple" with the Qumran sect: Richard Horsley, *Jesus and the Spiral of Violence*, 294–295.

18. Cf. D. Flusser, "Two Notes on the Midrash on 2 Sam. vii," in *IEJ* 9 (1959) 99–109.

19. D. Flusser, "Two Notes on the Midrash on 2 Sam. vii," 102.

Moses: the sanctuary of the Lord thy hands have established, the Lord shall reign forever and ever' (Exod. xv, 17–18). The verse from Exodus is quoted to explain the text of 2 Sam. vii, 11: 'for a house shall the Lord make for thee': the house of the future shall be made by God's own hands, not by human hands.

So the saying in Mark 14:58 was understood to refer to the eschatological temple which God would build to replace the present one at the end of the age.[20]

The saying is placed in the mouths of "false witnesses" (14:57). The fact that "false witnesses" quote Jesus here has led some commentators to conclude that Mark wanted the reader to understand the saying itself as false.[21] Crossan, for example, has concluded that for Mark, "what Jesus truly said is 13:2" ("No stone will be left upon another"), and that the two occurrences in 14:58 and 15:29 are in fact false statements.[22] Aune, on the other hand, thinks that Mark 13:2 is a "truncated version" of the real prophecy of 14:58.[23] Cullmann

20. Cf. K. Schubert, "Biblical criticism criticized: with reference to the Markan report of Jesus' examination before the Sanhedrin," in E. Bammel and C. F. D. Moule, eds., *Jesus and the Politics of his Day* (Cambridge: Cambridge Univ. Press, 1984) 396–397.
The evidence, however, for the apocalyptic hope of a rebuilt temple in pre-Christian Judaism does not convince all interpreters; cf. Donahue, *Are You the Christ?*, 111–112; R. Horsley, *Jesus and the Spiral of Violence*, 293. Neither seem to have noted the "temple made without hands" from Qumran.
21. So argues Theodore J. Weeden, Sr., "The Cross as Power in Weakness (Mark 15:20b-41)," in Werner H. Kelber, ed., *The Passion in Mark: Studies on Mark* 14–16 (Philadelphia: Fortress Press, 1976) 121–129. For Brandon, "certain Christians" were anti-temple, and were responsible for the saying, which was "painful and embarrassing for the original community of believers, who had remained strictly loyal to their national faith . . . ": S. G. F. Brandon, *The Fall of Jerusalem and the Christian Church*, 40. He argues against Schoeps, for whom the original Christians (Ebionites) were strictly anti-temple; cf. H. J. Schoeps, *Theologie und Geschichte des Judenchristentums* (Tübingen: J. C. B. Mohr, 1949) 239. For Taylor, "It is not clear why Mark represents the testimony as false. . . .": Vincent Taylor, *The Gospel according to St. Mark* (London: MacMillan, 1952) 566.
22. John Dominic Crossan, *In Fragments: The Aphorisms of Jesus* (San Francisco: Harper and Row, 1983) 309; "Jesus did not say 'I will destroy the Temple, etc.'" (309).
23. David E. Aune, *Prophecy in Early Christianity and the Ancient Mediterranean World* (Grand Rapids: Eerdmans, 1983) 185–186. Cf. also F. Flückiger, "Die Redaktion der Zukunftsrede in Markus 13," in *TZ* 26 (1970) 404–405; and Rudolf Pesch,

chooses part of each in reconstructing the original: "this temple will be destroyed, and I will build another."[24] Beasley-Murray prefers "to regard our saying [Mark 13:2] and Mark 14.58 as independent."[25]

The use of the saying in 14:58 is intimately connected to its context, and its valuation must be judged against the use of the saying in the confrontation with chief priests and council taken as a whole. "False witnesses" related this Jesus saying, and that inconsistently.[26] But the saying, however quoted, necessarily implied that Jesus was a divine emissary: it meant to the high priest that Jesus was claiming to be the Messiah. He therefore asked, "Are you the Christ?" (14:61). The two elements are interdependent; the second is an interpretation and the very point of the first. The situation is similar in John 2: the cleansing of the temple prompts "the Jews" to ask for a sign of authentication (John 2:18). This is why Luke, in his story of the trial, is able to dispose of the threat to the temple and retain the point, the "blasphemy" of Luke 22:66–71. Any prescient soul could have spoken Mark 13:2 concerning the destruction of the temple, especially after 70 CE; only the Messiah could destroy the temple and rebuild it in three eschatological days. The question of the high priest is the logical inference from the saying. How does the Markan Jesus answer? He accepts the deduction, and replies: "I am [the Christ]; and you shall see the Son of Man . . . coming with the clouds of heaven" (Mark 14:62). In other words, the Markan Jesus *was* this divine emissary, *would* destroy the temple and rebuild it. What the witnesses

---

*Naherwartungen: Tradition und Redaktion in Mk 13* (Düsseldorf: Patmos-verlag, 1968) 91.

24. Oscar Cullmann, *Jesus and the Revolutionaries* (trans. by Gareth Putnam; New York: Harper and Row, 1970) 19.

25. G. R. Beasley-Murray, *A Commentary on Mark Thirteen* (London: Macmillan, 1957) 23. Sanders argues the case for a traditional dominical origin: E. P. Sanders, *Jesus and Judaism* (Philadelphia: Fortress Press, 1985) 71–76. Donahue (*Are You the Christ?*, 109 and 136) maintains that Mark himself composed the saying out of two pre-Markan sayings (one of destroying, and one of the Church as God's temple). For Crossan, 14:58 likely "represents a teaching of the false prophets opposed in 13:6, 21–2, rather than a Markan creation from previously independent traditions . . . ": John Dominic Crossan, *In Fragments*, 310.

26. Mark 14:59 "not even thus was their testimony consistent."

quote is, in the opinion of Mark, genuine in substance.[27] The interpretation, however, that Jesus was a political and religious pretender who had come to overthrow the Romans, that he was an actual present threat to the temple and worthy of death, was according to all the Gospel writers false. Such is the function of the phrase "made without hands," which transfers the destruction and rebuilding out of the political and into the spiritual and divine realms.

Matthew's version accepts as fact that the charge of the witnesses was true. The critical passage (Matt 26:59–61) reads:

> But the high priests and the whole Sanhedrin kept seeking false testimony against Jesus so that they might kill him, and did not find any, though many false witnesses came forward. But finally, after two came forward, they said, "This man said, 'I am able to destroy the temple of God and build it in three days.'"

According to Matthew's account, after much deceitful seeking, the authorities finally found two corroborating witnesses. For the court, this meant that the two witnesses were stating a true accusation.[28] Matthew does not impugn this testimony, and connects to it, even more closely than did Mark, the question of the high priest as to whether Jesus was the Christ. Here the question of the high priest is again the logical inference from the testimony, that Jesus had Messianic pretensions.[29]

---

27. Cf. Donahue, *Are You the Christ?*, 77, 134–136; R. Horsley, *Jesus and the Spiral of Violence*, 293. Weeden objects (among other reasons) on the grounds that when the temple was destroyed in 70, which the Markan community had witnessed, Jesus was absent; "If, then, he is absent in the epoch in which the Temple is destroyed, he cannot be its destroyer," and the saying must be false (Theodore J. Weeden, Sr., "The Cross as Power in Weakness," 126). This is, however, exactly Luke's argument in the mouth of Stephen in Acts 6:14: Jesus will destroy the temple, though he has already ascended to heaven and is present as the spirit in the church.

28. Cf. Eduard Schweizer, *The Good News According to Matthew* (trans. by David E. Green; Atlanta: John Knox Press, 1975) 498; and Daniel Patte, *The Gospel according to Matthew: A Structural Commentary on Matthew's Faith* (Philadelphia: Fortress Press, 1987) 372.

29. Cf. E. Meyer, *Ursprung und Anfänge des Christentums* (Stuttgart, 1921) 1.192.

Matthew, while following Mark's plan, leaves out the Markan reference to "made without hands."[30] He nevertheless mitigates the political implications of the saying in two ways: by changing Jesus' statement to say, "I am able to destroy . . . ," thus relegating it to the realm of possibility instead of threat; and by placing special emphasis on the reference to "three days." The story of setting a guard at the tomb (Matt 27:62–66) is the third reference to "three days" in the passion story (26:61; 27:40, 63). Here even the chief priests and Pharisees in Jerusalem in some way know that Jesus was to rise after three days, information which Jesus in Matthew had spoken to his disciples only, either in northern Galilee (Matt 16:21; 17:23), or privately on the road to Jerusalem (20:19). This third reference to "three days" points the reader to the (soon-to-be) empty tomb, and the correct Church interpretation of the saying: "rebuilding the temple in three days" is "resurrection in three days."

Alone of the canonical Gospels, Matthew has included the story of the guards at the tomb, found also in the *Gospel of Peter*. In this non-canonical work, the Jewish authorities entreat Pilate (*GPt* 8.29–31):

> Give us soldiers that we may watch his sepulcher for three days, lest his disciples come and steal him away, and the people suppose that he is risen from the dead, and do us harm.

There is a connection between the three days and resurrection, but what that connection is remains unexplained by the text. Not enough of the text is preserved to know whether Jesus had previously predicted his rising, or that this prediction motivated the length of time for the standing of the guard. Matthew's version, however, specifies the reason by having the authorities state: " . . . that deceiver said 'After three days, I am to rise again'" (Matt 27:63).

---

30. Matthew preserves here a more original form of the saying according to Nils Alstrup Dahl, "The Passion Narrative in Matthew," in Graham Stanton, ed., *The Interpretation of Matthew* (IRT 3; London: SPCK and Philadelphia: Fortress Press, 1983) 47. Aune chooses Mark 14:58 as the more original, since it includes the words "made without hands," and thus must refer to the "temple" of the "eschatological community of the New Israel": David E. Aune, *Prophecy in Early Christianity*, 174.

Emphasis on this phrase is visible in Matthew even in his redaction of an earlier prediction by Jesus of resurrection on the third day. In Mark, after Jesus' declaration that he would be killed and then after three days rise again, "the disciples did not understand the statement, and were afraid to question him" (Mark 9:32). In the parallel in Luke, not only did they not understand, but the statement "was hidden from them in order that they not perceive it" (Luke 9:45); only after the resurrection is the reference explained, first by the angels at the tomb, and then by the risen Jesus himself (Luke 24:7 and 46). Matthew, however, has the disciples not only understand the reference, but become "very sad" at the news of his impending death (Matt 17:23). Thus the reference is not hidden from anyone, or misinterpreted. The chief priests and Pharisees could understand also, secure the tomb, and help prove the resurrection.

Luke, in an effort to portray Jesus and the early Christians as obedient and non-revolutionary Roman subjects, has removed from the gospel entirely[31] this reference to the destruction of the temple, and placed all the calumny of revolutionary activity into the mouths of the Jewish elders.[32] All the representatives of Rome, contradicting the accusations of the Jewish authorities, find him completely innocent: Pilate declares him guiltless three times (Luke 23:4, 14, 22); Herod returns him without charge (23:15); after Jesus' death, the Roman centurion praises God and declares, "Certainly this man was innocent" (23:47).[33] On his way to the cross, Jesus does predict the destruction of Jerusalem, but the prediction in no way implicates him or his followers in revolution: it says nothing about Jesus as agent of the destruction.[34] Luke does, however, know the saying as a

31. And placed it in Acts 6:14; cf. R. Pesch, *Die Vision des Stephanus: Apg. 7,55–56 im Rahmen der Apostelgeschichte* (StBS 12; Stuttgart: Katholisches Bibelwerk, 1966) 44–45.

32. Cf. Gerhard Schneider, "The political charge against Jesus (Luke 23:2)," in E. Bammel and C. F. D. Moule, eds., *Jesus and the Politics of his Day* (Cambridge: Cambridge Univ. Press, 1984) 403–414; Stanley Hauerwas, "The Politics of Charity," in *Int* 31 (1977) 259.

33. For δίκαιος as "righteous" rather than the more usual "innocent," cf. Robert J. Karris, "Luke 23:47 and the Lukan View of Jesus' Death," in *JBL* 105 (1986) 65–74.

34. Luke 23:28–29: "Daughters of Jerusalem, stop weeping for me, but weep for yourselves and your children. For behold, the days are coming when . . . "

political accusation against Jesus and the early Christians. In Acts 6:14, an accusation is brought against Stephen, again by "false witnesses," who declare him guilty:

> For we have heard him say that this Jesus, the Nazarene, will destroy this place and alter the customs which Moses handed down to us.

Luke has not only transferred the saying itself to Acts, but also its context of a trial, complete with false witnesses, before the Sanhedrin. Yet Stephen is the one who is accused, not Jesus. The indictment against Stephen is made after the death, resurrection and ascension of Jesus. The destruction alleged can only refer to some type of act from heaven. Luke's use of the saying is, therefore, no longer a "political" statement at all.

This early saying attributed to Jesus was interpreted in two opposing ways. The Synoptic Gospels relate that Jesus was accused of, and in part condemned for, revolutionary activity on the basis of a literal interpretation of the saying. The accusation threatened the disciples also; we are told that they fled in terror at the arrest of Jesus. The *Gospel of Peter* 7.26 quotes the escaping disciples as saying: "we were sought after by them as evildoers and as persons who wanted to set fire to the temple."[35] Stephen, according to Acts, was indicted on a charge of anti-temple polemic. The beginning of hostilities against the Church in Rome was for the same type of political incendarism: Nero accused the Christians of having set fire to Rome.[36] The fact that the Gospels defend Jesus and the Church against such an accu-

---

35. Quoted from Chr. Mauer, "The Gospel of Peter," in Edgar Hennecke, *New Testament Apocrypha* (Wilhelm Schneemelcher, ed.; Eng. trans. by R. McL. Wilson; Philadelphia: Westminster Press, 1963) 1.185. Cf. Mauer's introduction, ibid., 179–183; and Ron Cameron, ed., *The Other Gospels: Non-Canonical Gospel Texts* (Philadelphia: Westminster, 1982) 76–78.

36. Tacitus, *Annals* 15.38–44. Tacitus explains that "those [Christians] who confessed were arrested" (15.44). He does not exhonorate them, even though he is quite interested in placing the blame on Nero himself. The accused Christians could, perhaps, have confessed under torture to a crime they did not commit. The other possibility nevertheless remains.

sation shows that the issue was still alive near the end of the century and later. It clearly continued into the second century: Justin defends the Church against charges of political aspirations, based on the Roman misunderstanding that the Christian hope of a Kingdom of God was to be an actual political entity (*1 Apol.* 11). But some in the Church soon after Easter interpreted the saying as a prediction of the resurrection.

*Elements in the Temple Saying*

The saying itself is found seven times in our literature in four different contexts.[37] Taken together in all its versions, it is composed of at least four separate elements: the temple destruction; its rebuilding; the specified time of three days; and the application to the resurrection. It is clear that originally these elements were not all connected: the destruction of the temple was the original point, not the resurrection, and is predicted elsewhere;[38] two versions of the saying seem to lack (or contradict) rebuilding;[39] the prediction of "three days" is found in several other passages unconnected to this saying or the temple,[40] and a version of this saying is twice found without the reference to three days; in these same two passages, destruction of the temple is alleged for Jesus without reference to resurrection.[41]

The early saying, to those apocalyptically oriented and literal minded, may have meant, "I, as God's representative (Messiah or

37. Mark 14:58; 15:29; Matt 26:61; 27:40; Acts 6:14; John 2:19; *GTh* 71.
38. Mark 13:2 and parallels; Luke 19:44.
39. Acts 6:14; *GTh* 71. Donahue argues that the destruction and rebuilding portions of the saying (Mark 14:58) were originally two separate sayings: *Are You the Christ?*, 105–107. Gaston thinks that *GTh* 71 "goes back to a tradition which knew the temple saying only in the sense of destruction": Lloyd Gaston, *No Stone on Another: Studies in the Significance of the Fall of Jerusalem in the Synoptic Gospels* (NovTSup 23; Leiden: E. J. Brill, 1970) 152.
Neither of these two texts (Acts 6:14 and *GTh* 71), however, stands without a rebuilding implied. In Acts 6:14, where Jesus is to destroy "this place," he must still "alter the customs which Moses handed down," which certainly implies a new *cultus*, and reflects the new temple of the other versions. Only *GTh* 71 has no "rebuilding" at all, and that for polemical theological reasons; it was composed to contradict the promise of rebuilding interpreted as bodily resurrection.
40. Mark 8:31; 9:31; 10:34; Matt 16:21; 17:23; Luke 9:22; cf. 24:6, 46; John 2:19.
41. Acts 6:14; *GTh* 71.

Son of Man), will destroy this sinful temple at the immanent *eschaton*, and replace it with another, divinely-constructed one (as God has long promised through the prophets)." The new temple would be the future temple of the reign of God, awaited by apocalyptic Jewish groups especially.[42] John's collocation of the saying with the temple cleansing would then make excellent sense and be clearly motivated: Jesus would be redeeming the temple from its "sinful abusers" in both present and future.[43] The Gospels do not lack other references by Jesus to the destruction of the temple (Mark 13:2; Matt 24:2; Luke 21:6), nor accusations of revolution (John 11:48; 19:12), evidencing a memory that Jesus was *regarded* among some as an agitator with designs on the temple. *Gospel of Peter* 7.26 ("we were sought after . . . as persons who wanted to set fire to the temple"), in addition, does seem to build on a tradition of the charge of anti-temple revolution. Thus Jesus would have appeared to such as these (and to the Romans) to be an apocalyptically oriented, anti-temple activist.[44]

42. Cf. Harvey K. McArthur, "'On the Third Day,'" 81–86. Reitzenstein connected this destruction with the hope in pre-Christian Baptist (< Mandaean) circles of a Messiah-Man who would destroy the temple; the myth was then transferred to Jesus. He is followed by R. Bultmann, *History of the Synoptic Tradition*, 120–121, and 401. Cf. W. Bousset, *Kyrios Christos*, 74–76, who presents a discussion of this position, without taking sides.

43. John's application of the saying to the resurrection would still be redactional.

44. S. G. F. Brandon has championed the view that Jesus and the early Christians sympathized with the ideals of the Zealots, in *The Fall of Jerusalem and the Christian Church* (London: SPCK, 1951) and especially *Jesus and the Zealots* (Manchester: Manchester Univ. Press, 1967). Opposing views are held by many others: cf. the discussion of the Jesus movement as a "radical theocratic movement" which would end all other rule, "even the rule of the Romans and priests," by the kingdom of God: Gerd Theissen, *Sociology of Early Palestinian Christianity* (trans. by John Bowden; Philadelphia: Fortress Press, 1978) 59. Hengel argues against political revolutionary aims for Jesus, and that he was instead looking exclusively for a divine kingdom: Martin Hengel, *Christ and Power* (trans. by Everett R. Kalin; Philadelphia: Fortress Press, 1977) 15–21; so also Adolf Harnack, *Militia Christi: The Christian Religion and the Military in the First Three Centuries* (trans. by David McInnes Gracie; Philadelphia: Fortress Press, 1981). Yoder sees Jesus as a nonviolent, pacifist revolutionary; his trial is a demonstration of "the political relevance of non-violent tactics"; "God's will for God's man in this world is that he should renounce legitimate defence": John Howard Yoder, *The Politics of Jesus* (Grand Rapids: Eerdmans, 1972) 59 and 100; cf. also the several essays in E. Bammel and C. F. D. Moule, eds., *Jesus and the Politics of his Day* (Cambridge: Cambridge Univ. Press, 1984).

But soon, in fact contemporaneously, the saying was interpreted otherwise, as a metaphor for the resurrection. Important for this development was the inclusion of the reference to three days. Jesus, according to the canonical Gospels, predicted his resurrection after three days several times before his arrest and trial. Yet the early kerygma in 1 Cor 15:4 ("and he was buried, and he was raised on the third day according to the Scriptures") declares the resurrection on the third day as an event in itself, unconnected to any saying. The phrase "three days" is based in that passage on interpretation of the Scriptures, not on a prophecy of Jesus, or even on a reference to historical remembrance, as if the meaning were "on the third day, as we recall it happened." The Church interpreted the events, meaning, and timing of the resurrection on the basis of the Scriptures and read this interpretation into the reports of the passion and Easter events. We are told several times (as in 1 Cor 15:4) that this understanding came only after the events, through the Scriptures. In John 2:22, after the saying about the temple destruction, we read:

> When therefore he was raised from the dead, his disciples remembered that he had said this, and believed the Scripture and the word which Jesus had spoken.

Concerning the triumphal entry, John 12:16 concedes:

> His disciple did not understand these things at first, but when Jesus was glorified, then they remembered that these things were written about him and they did these things to him.

The Paraclete, sent according to John after Jesus' resurrection, taught the disciples "all things" and brought all Jesus had said to their remembrance (John 14:26). So the disciples found both the life and death of Jesus illuminated by the new Spirit and a new understanding of the Scriptures.

The disciples are said not to have understood at the time the predictions of Jesus' death and rising after three days (Mark 9:32). Luke twice states that this prediction was divinely concealed from them, that they might not understand (9:45; 18:34). Only after the resurrection, in the Emmaus story, does the risen Jesus explain to the two disciples "the things concerning himself in all the Scriptures" (Luke 24:25-27). In the following appearance to all the disciples, "He opened their minds to understand the Scriptures" (Luke 24:45). Thus the prediction of the three days is seen to have been of special importance to the Church in allowing the saying of the temple destruction to be interpreted metaphorically of the resurrection of Jesus' body, and in grounding that metaphor in the Scriptures. Of the seven occurrences of the saying, two only do not include a reference to three days: Acts 6:14 and *GTh* 71. In Acts 6, however, such a reference would make no sense, since Jesus had already been raised. It is Stephen who is accused of declaring that Jesus would destroy the temple, and that destruction could only have been from heaven, apocalyptically. In the second instance, the author of the *Thomas* passage removed the reference because of a special theological position: Jesus is declaring that the "house" would *not* be rebuilt, and that requires no time limit.[45]

Matthew's account is an interesting compromise, a medial stage in the interpretation of the saying between a literal and a metaphorical understanding: Matthew includes both the prediction of the destruction of the temple and rending of the veil from Mark,[46] and

---

45. An argument that the expression "three days" was a post-Easter addition of the Church to the saying may still be falsified. If there was in the first century, as Flusser claims, a lively expectation that the resurrection and restoration would occur three days after the eschaton, as there was in later Rabbinic interpretation, the phrase may be original to the saying: D. Flusser, "Two Notes on the Midrash on 2 Sam. vii," in *IEJ* 9 (1959) 99–109. The story of Jonah and Hosea 6:2 were early used of the resurrection, but how early is unknown. This possible inclusion of the three day eschatological reference would have made the Church's metaphorical use of the saying even easier.

46. Matt 24:2 and 27:51 from Mark 13:2 and 15:38. On the veil, cf. Harry L. Chronis, "The Torn Veil: Cultus and Christology in Mark 15:37-39," in *JBL* 101 (1982) 97–114; M. De Jonge, "Matthew 27:51 in Early Christian Exegesis," in George W. E. Nickelsburg with George W. MacRae, S. J., eds., *Christians among Jews and Gentiles: Essays in Honor of Krister Stendahl on His Sixty-Fifth Birthday* (Philadelphia: Fortress Press, 1986) 67–79; and Dennis D. Sylva, "The Temple Curtain and Jesus' Death in the Gospel of Luke," in *JBL* 105 (1986) 239–250.

emphasizes the "three days" to make pointed reference to the resurrection of the body of Jesus. This last element especially assisted the church in defending itself against political suspicion. A bare statement of temple destruction and the title "King of the Jews" could be used as accusations of political revolution. The added specification of the three days, with its fulfillment in resurrection and support in the Scriptures, made such an accusation far less cogent. It furthered the claim that the Jewish and Roman authorities in their spiritual blindness had misinterpreted both Jesus' prediction and title, and wrongfully proceeded to crucify him. In Mark and Acts the saying was used (though not exclusively) of the actual temple; Matthew balanced the interpretation of the saying between literal and metaphorical, between temple and resurrection; the Gospels of John and *Thomas* move entirely into metaphor.

### *"Destroy this Temple" in John 2:19*

The use of the saying by John (2:19) is remarkably different from that in the Synoptics. Instead of placing it at the end of Jesus' ministry, on the night before he is killed, John locates it at the beginning of his story, just after his first sign at Cana of Galilee. It is not a basis for accusation which Jesus' opponents attribute to him, but a statement boldly made by Jesus himself. In Mark, it had led to his crucifixion for political reasons. In John, the "danger" of allowing Jesus to speak such a revolutionary word is obviated by giving it a wholly different meaning and function. It is set in a context not of political turmoil, when the temple is in possible danger and troops, courts and executioners are in attendance. Instead it follows a passage (2:14–17) in which Jesus cleanses the temple; not only is he not destroying it, he is preserving and returning the temple to its proper function. Even the Jewish authorities recognize the divine stamp of his acts, and ask for a "sign" of authentication of his heavenly authority and mission. In this context, the saying makes no literal or political sense: Jesus acts to preserve the temple function, and when asked for a sign, tells his questioners to destroy it so he may raise it in three days. If one may judge from their sarcastic retort (2:20: "This temple was built in 46 years, and you will raise it in three days?"), John is implying that the Jews take him for a fool. They do not, therefore, accuse him of revolution, nor is the accusation of temple destruction brought up again at his trial.

The author of John makes another subtle change which again serves to remove any suspicion from Jesus as revolutionary. In each of the other uses of the saying, Jesus himself is the one who says that he will destroy the temple. He is the destroyer; he is the culprit (Mark 14:58: "I will destroy this temple. . . ."). In John, however, when asked for a sign, Jesus tells *the Jews* to destroy the temple themselves, and he will rebuild it (John 2:19: "Destroy this temple and in three days I will raise it up"). They would be the destroyers and he the rebuilder, much as they had been the defilers and he the one who had cleansed and restored the temple just prior. Thus again there is no stigma in assigning this saying to Jesus.

John, unique among the Gospels, tells us explicitly that Jesus uttered this saying concerning his body and the resurrection: "he was speaking of the temple of his body" (2:21). No such thing is stated *expressis verbis* in the Synoptics. For them, the primary original reference was to literal temple destruction, and that was the issue to be combated or mitigated by editorial activity. But John turns the statement into a metaphor, which is impossible in its context to take literally (or by "the Jews" even seriously). It refers to his body, which the authorities do in fact destroy by crucifixion. It becomes, therefore, no threat to the community. Mark directed the saying toward the Christian community as the "temple made without hands." John gives it the meaning it had come to signify for the Johannine Church: the resurrection of Jesus' body. This is in accord with his own special emphasis on the actual physical incarnation and resurrection of Jesus. Thus John's redaction removes Jesus as destroyer, presents Jesus as speaker directly, and applies it specifically to the resurrection of his physical body.

## GTh 71: "I will Destroy this House"

The *Gospel of Thomas* also preserves a version of this saying of the destruction of the temple which displays several interesting and sig-

nificant features when compared to the various canonical instances.
*GTh* 71 reads:

ⲡⲉⲍⲉ ⲓ̅ⲥ̅ ⲍⲉ ϯⲛⲁϣⲟⲣ[ϣⲡ ⲙ̅ⲡⲉⲉ]ⲓ ⲏⲉⲓ
ⲁⲩⲱ ⲙ̅ⲛ̅ ⲗⲁⲁⲩ ⲛⲁϣⲕⲟⲧϥ .[........]

Jesus said: I will destr[oy this] house,
and no one will be able to build it [. . . .]"[47]

First to be noted is that it is spoken directly by Jesus, as in John. Second, as in all other versions excluding John, Jesus is the destroyer.
Third, the word for "temple" here is "house." Fourth, and most striking, the complementary second line is radically altered: all the other
versions are directly contradicted, and the reference to three days is
removed.[48] Matt 26:61 alleged that Jesus said he was able to destroy
and rebuild; here Jesus declares that no one will be able to rebuild.

That Jesus himself speaks the saying associates this version with
John. John is the only other Gospel to allow Jesus to utter the saying
directly. If it is true (as argued above) that the saying was viewed as
having dangerous political implications, then this directness connects it with a non-literal meaning. The other Gospel writers seek to
avoid placing the saying in Jesus' mouth because of its negative con-
notations. A *Sitz im Leben* in which no such avoidance is attempted
implies that no such implications are associated with the saying: it is
metaphor only.

Jesus is the destroyer in *Thomas*. Again, this is the heart of the
revolutionary charge, and the central hazardous point. John, in allowing Jesus to utter the saying, changed the role of destroyer from
Jesus to "the Jews": Jesus tells the Jewish authorities to destroy the

---

47. The Coptic text is quoted from Bentley Layton, ed., *Nag Hammadi Codex II,*
*2–7* (Leiden: E. J. Brill, 1989) 1.80. The Guillaumont edition adds to the end of the
second line a further restoration, and notes a partially preserved letter at the end of
the saying: ⲁⲩⲱ ⲙ̅ⲛ̅ ⲗⲁⲁⲩ ⲛⲁϣⲕⲟⲧϥ .[ⲁⲛ ⲛⲕⲉⲥⲟ]ⲡ: "and no one will be able
to build it [again]": A. Guillaumont, *et al.*, *The Gospel according to Thomas: Coptic*
*Text Established and Translated* (New York: Harper and Row, 1959) 41.

48. There is not enough space in the final lacuna for any expression of time containing ϣⲟⲙⲛ̅ⲧ ⲛ̅ϩⲟⲟⲩ ("three days").

temple. *Thomas* allows Jesus to claim directly that he will destroy. This again points to a non-literal meaning for the saying.

The word for "temple" in five of the versions other than the *Gospel of Thomas* is *ναός*,[49] an expression which seems early to have become integral to the saying. Mark, for example, normally uses the word *ἱερόν* ("temple, holy place") for the temple, which occurs nine times. He also uses "house" (*οἶκος*) for the tabernacle in 2:26, and for the temple within his quotation of Isa 56:7 (as in the LXX) at Mark 11:17. Only in this saying, however, is the word *ναός* used.[50] Thus Mark inherited the saying with the word *ναός*, and retained this word in his use of it against his normal habit.

The major reason for the inclusion of the saying in the *Gospel of Thomas* is clearly the final line: "no one will be able to [re-]build it." This is the point and the issue of import. It is here that the Thomas community corrects the tradition, and debates with other Christians. In the other versions it is Jesus who will rebuild the temple; in *Thomas* no one at all will rebuild: not Jesus, not God, not the community.

Eliminated in concert with the change of the final line is the reference to three days. This specified time is in the New Testament a cipher for the resurrection of Jesus, and in rabbinic interpretation for the general eschatological resurrection.[51] The Coptic did have some expression following the last preserved words, "no one will be able to build it." The conjectured restoration "again"[52] would be, if sound, the response to the time limit. Thus the rebuilding would not take place "again," either after the crucifixion or at the eschaton.

The saying in *GTh* 71 has changed the word *ναός* ("temple") to what one assumes was *οἶκος* ("house") or *οἰκία* ("residence") in the Greek *Vorlage* of the Coptic translation. No Greek fragments have been found of saying 71 in *Thomas*. The Coptic ΗΕΙ ("house") is

---

49. Acts 6:14 does not use the word "temple" at all, but "this place" (*τὸν τόπον τοῦτον*).

50. And in its reflex in the rending of the temple veil (15:38); cf. Donahue, *Are You the Christ?*, 104–105; also Weeden, "The Cross as Power in Weakness," 123.

51. Cf. Harvey K. McArthur, "'On the Third Day,'" 82ff.

52. [ΑΝ ΝΚΕϹΟ]ΪΙ: A. Guillaumont, *et al.*, *The Gospel according to Thomas*, 41.

used to translate several terms, most commonly οἶκος and the related term οἰκία (for example, John 2:16 and Job 4:19 LXX respectively). Which of several possible terms stood in the Greek *Vorlage* behind *GTh* 71 is difficult to determine with confidence.[53] None of the ten examples of ΗΕΙ ("house") in *Thomas*[54] is supported by a Greek fragment. If one compares the four passages in the canonical Gospels which have parallels to the *Thomas* "house-sayings," the evidence is curiously divided.[55] Where Mark is the source, both Matthew and Mark have οἰκία (*GTh* 48: Mark 3:25/Matt 12:25; *GTh* 35: Mark 3:27/Matt 12:29); Luke changes this to οἶκος (Luke 11:17) and αὐλή (11:21). Where Matthew and Luke are using Q, Matthew has οἰκία (*GTh* 21b: Matt 24:43), and οἰκιακοί, a derivative of οἰκία (*GTh* 16: Matt 10:36); Luke has οἶκος in both instances (Luke 12:39 and 52). In support of a theory that Luke is consciously changing the vocabulary of his source is the fact that in the temple destruction saying itself (Acts 6:14) he has, instead of ναός ("temple"), τὸν τόπον τοῦτον, "this place." Thus, if one were forced to choose which of these two words stood in the Greek *Vorlage* of *GTh* 71, οἰκία would seem the more likely option.

Not all interpreters have considered this substitution of "house" for "temple" in *GTh* 71 a "change" at all. For some it is apparently a mere variation in expression which leaves the saying with essentially the same import against Herod's temple as it had in the Gospel trial

53. ΗΕΙ, according to W. Crum, *A Coptic Dictionary* (Oxford: Clarendon Press, 1939; repr. 1972) 66, translates οἶκος ("house" in many senses), οἰκία ("residence"), οἰκόπεδον ("building site"), αὐλή ("hall"), σκηνή ("tent"), μυχός ("innermost part of a house"), ὄροφος ("roof"). ⲡ̅ⲓⲉ is used for both ναός and ἱερόν in the Coptic Bible. ⲙⲁ ("place") is used to translate τόπος ("place") and means "temple" in Deut 12:2, just as in Acts 6:14.

54. Sayings 16, 21 bis, 35 bis, 48, 64, 71, 97 and 98.

55. *GTh* 48: Jesus said: If two make peace with one another in this one house, they will say to the mountain, "Move away," and it will move.

*GTh* 35: Jesus said: It is not possible for one to enter the house of a strong man and take it by force unless he binds his hands; then he will ransack his house.

*GTh* 21b: If the owner of a house knows that a thief is coming, he will keep awake before he comes, and will not allow him to dig through into his house of his kingdom to take his goods.

*GTh* 16: I have come to cast divisions on the earth. . . . There will be five in a house; three will be against two and two against three. . . .

narratives.[56] Arthur, for example, attributes the mention of Samaria in *GTh* 60, along with "hostility to the Davidic dynasty reflected in log. 40 and the opposition to the temple which seems to be present in log. 71" to a Samaritan provenance for the *Gospel of Thomas* as a whole.[57] Interpreted within *Thomas* itself, however, saying 40 is better seen as opposition to a competing religious way of life; no mention is made of the Davidic dynasty (*GTh* 40):

> Jesus said: A vine was planted outside of the Father, and since it is not established, it will be uprooted and destroyed.

The *Gospel of Thomas* rails against, among other things, fasting, prayer, almsgiving, and special diet (*GTh* 6, 14 and 104); against keeping the Sabbath (27); and against the Pharisees and Scribes (39). The way of life in question clearly includes Jewish practice, found both outside and within the Christian community. The image of the vineyard and its destruction is ancient within prophetic tradition, symbolizing Israel and the exile (Isa 5:1ff.; Ezk 19:10ff.; Ps 80:8ff.). Both the Gospels of John and *Thomas* use the image in similar ways. In John 15:1, Jesus declares: "I am the *true* vine," thus excluding the false vine which in context is the religion of "the Jews." The *Gospel of Thomas* says much the same thing, but in negative terms: this false vine will be uprooted.

In addition, if *GTh* 71 were referring to Herod's temple, then it would be saying something never mentioned within *Thomas* theology as a whole: the central shrine of Judaism would be destroyed by Jesus and never rebuilt. This implies an apocalyptic context, with Jesus as eschatological Son of Man (or the like). But the *Gospel of Thomas* is of a very different stamp; its worldview does not include Jewish apocalyptic expectation, but the (realized) presence of the kingdom in the disciple and the world. It even sarcastically devalues the prevailing view of the kingdom taught by the (Jewish and Christian) religious leaders: "If those who lead you say to you, 'Behold, the

---

56. So David E. Aune, *Prophecy in Early Christianity*, 173.
57. Richard L. Arthur, *The Gospel of Thomas and the Coptic New Testament*, 21.

kingdom is in heaven,' then the birds of heaven will get there before you" (*GTh* 3). When the disciples ask when the (eschatological) kingdom will arrive, Jesus replies: "It will not come by you waiting for it; they will not say, 'See, here!,' or 'See, there!' On the contrary, the kingdom of the Father is spread out on the earth and people don't see it" (*GTh* 113). Thus a literal interpretation of *GTh* 71 as an anti-temple saying would have little place in the context of the *Gospel of Thomas* as a whole.

In addition, *Thomas* never mentions the temple elsewhere in any saying, and the word "temple" (ⲣⲡⲉ) never occurs. The word for "house" (ⲏⲉⲓ) is found ten times,[58] but it never refers to the temple. In saying 21b, the "house" is specifically identified with the individual disciple. After stating that the knowing householder will not allow a thief to dig through his house, it reads:

> But you also, watch against the world; bind up your loins with great power, lest the robbers find a way to come to you. . . .

"To you": the reference is to individuals, pictured as souls indwelling their bodies as a householder dwells in a house (cf. 103).[59] Saying 98 is also best interpreted in this light:

> Jesus said: The kingdom of the Father is like a man who wants to kill a great man. He drew his sword in his house, and thrust it into the wall in order to know whether his hand would be strong enough. Then he killed the great man.

Here the sword is the (ascetic) will and power of the individual soul, which is tested against the "house" of the body. Once it has shown

58. Sayings 16, 21 bis, 35 bis, 48, 64, 71, 97 and 98. In sayings 16 and 64 the word is used of a literal house. In saying 35 it is the "house" of the strong man whose hands are to be bound, which is the world. In saying 97, it is the end of a journey, at which time an inspection takes place; it appears to be the end of the journey of life, reached at death.

59. Cf. Hans Jonas, *The Gnostic Religion: The Message of the Alien God and the Beginnings of Christianity* (second ed., rev.; Boston: Beacon Press, 1963) 55–56.

that it can overcome the body, then the soul is able to overcome the "strong man." Likewise, saying 48 reads:

> Jesus said: If the two make peace with one another in this single house, they will say to the mountain, "Move away," and it will move.

Here again the "house" is the body, in which the soul and heavenly counterpart are to be united, constituting the disciple as a "single one," the goal of *Thomas* spirituality. Interpreted within the *Gospel of Thomas* then, the word "house" is never the temple, but either a literal private house, the world, or the body; and half the examples refer to the body.

If the word "house" refers to the body in Saying 71, then the change in the *Gospel of Thomas* from "temple" to "house" is clearly motivated. *Thomas* is not in the least concerned with an eschatological destruction or rebuilding of the temple. Early in the Church the saying was applied to the resurrection of Jesus. It was at this stage that the Thomas community inherited and adjusted the saying according to its own presuppositions. The words for "house" (οἶκος, οἰκία, and others) had a common double metaphorical application: the temple of the Lord, and the human body as "house" of the soul.[60] The word "temple" (ναός), however, denoted more strictly the dwelling place of deity. When applied to the body, it had a more divine application, and in Paul referred to the body as the "temple of the Holy Spirit," not the soul.[61] While the two words "temple" and "house" could be seen in one sense as synonymous, as both words could apply to the temple, the change of vocabulary in *Thomas* allowed interpreters of the saying more easily to transfer its referent to the body.

---

60. For example, as "temple of the Lord": often in the LXX as a translation of בֵּית יְהֹוָה: 1 Sam 1:7 οἶκος κυρίου; cf. Matt 12:4, John 2:16. As "human body" the related word οἰκία (which is more strictly "residence" than οἶκος, which had a broader application) is more common: Job 4:19 LXX; 2 Cor 5:1. Cf. the discussion of O. Michel, "οἶκος, οἰκία," in Kittel, *TDNT*, 5.119–134.

61. 1 Cor 3:16 and 17; 6:19. Cf. the discussion of O. Michel, "ναός," in Kittel, *TDNT*, 4.880–890.

*Gospel of Thomas 71 as Denial of Bodily Resurrection*

The apostle Paul and his opponents in 1 Corinthians 15 show that some early Christian thinking on the resurrection did not include the reconstitution of the flesh. The apologetic which is seen in the appearance narratives of the Gospels of Luke and John developed after a controversy had evolved among Christians as to the actual substance of the body of the risen Christ. Both the controversy and the emphasis on flesh sharpened into the second century and later. The "trajectory" was clearly from nonphysical to fleshly resurrection, and its development began among Christians in an ill-defined inheritance among Jews before the rise of Christianity and extended into the fifth century at least.

The *Gospel of Thomas* is another early witness to a Christianity which did not accept physical resurrection. The import of *GTh* 71 is that the body of Jesus will not be raised.[62] Gärtner has written a very perceptive treatment of this saying which recognizes its connection to John 2:19. His work is burdened, however, by the supposition that *Thomas* is late and thoroughly (second-century) Gnostic, and therefore heir to the docetism common in that period. He states, for example, that "the Gnostic Jesus despised the body, since it was in any case an apparent body, which shall be destroyed, and has no value while it exists."[63] But this interpretation contains its own contradictions: there is no need to despise an "apparent" body, or to declare that an "apparent" body will never be raised. This is also to miss the point of the controversy in the Church. Here the difference between the second century Gnostic systems and the Thomas tradition becomes clear. Jesus in the New Testament and the *Gospel of Thomas* had a real body. The controversy was whether his *real* body was or was not raised. In *GTh* 28, Jesus declares, "I appeared to them in flesh." This is no docetic "seeming." The very next logion (*GTh* 29b) has Jesus say, "I marvel at how this great wealth has made its home in

---

62. Cf. Lloyd Gaston, *No Stone on Another*, 152: "In the understanding of the Gnostic editor, the word 'house' in all probability refers to the body as the house or prison of the soul. The saying then [*GTh* 71] is a polemic against the concept of bodily resurrection."

63. Cf. Bertil Gärtner, *The Theology of the Gospel According to Thomas*, 173.

this poverty." The body is *real* poverty, not "apparent" poverty. It is a mere dwelling of the soul which will not survive death. There is no need whatever to invoke second century Gnostic systems to account for this ubiquitous ancient world commonplace.

The controversy over the spiritual or physical resurrection of Jesus was already heated by the middle of the first century. Mark applies the saying behind *GTh* 71 to the temple and the Markan community, and Luke literally to the temple in Acts. The application of the saying to both the temple and the resurrection is found in Matthew. There was still some divergence of opinion about its (proper) import at the time of the writing of the canonical Gospels. John, however, understands it to apply to the body of Jesus, and makes it say that his body will be raised. This was formerly a free saying, without a context, as in the *Gospel of Thomas*: ναός, the word for "temple" in the saying, is not part of Johannine vocabulary: it occurs only here (2:19) in the Gospel, and not at all in the epistles; neither is ναός Markan vocabulary. Even in the trial narratives it is a free saying: the false witnesses state that Jesus had (somewhere and sometime) spoken it. But John has picked it up and appended it as the sign required by the story of the temple cleansing.[64]

John and *Thomas* alone use the saying directly as a reference to the body of Jesus. The *Gospel of Thomas* is not quoting John, as the differences in verbal expression and primary features in *Thomas* demonstrate. The use of the saying in reference to physical resurrection and its counter stem from an early period of Church history, earlier by a generation in fact than the Gospel of John. The Thomas community used a version of the saying which applied to the body of Jesus, but changed it to deny his physical resurrection. Thus the "history" of the saying in John and *Thomas* began with some early metaphorical application of the saying to the body of Jesus. The Thomas community then adjusted the saying to fit its own view-

---

64. Why the temple cleansing is where it is in John is another problem. Mark and John cannot be reconciled. Brown recognizes that theology or ignorance has motivated the contrasting placement of the event: R. Brown, "The Problem of Historicity in John," in idem, *New Testament Essays* (New York: Paulist Press, 1965) 153f.

point by changing "temple" to "house," and contradicting the final line. The Gospel of John appropriated or created its version at a time when that denial of physical resurrection was a threat to the doctrinal views of the author and his community, and employed this version in its wider defense of the physical nature of Jesus. The two communities are here in debate, each employing the saying in similar but opposing ways, distinct from the uses of the other Gospel writers; they are responding to each other.

# Chapter Five

# The Body and Resurrection in the Thomas Tradition
## *The Book of Thomas and the Acts of Thomas*

### *The Book of Thomas*

The *Book of Thomas* is the next surviving literary stage in the Thomas tradition; as Turner observes, it "occupies a median position in the stream of Syrian Thomas-tradition as we move from the *Gospel of Thomas* to the *Acts of Thomas*."[1] It purports to be a revelation dialogue of Jesus and his twin brother Thomas which takes place between Easter and the ascension, during which Thomas asks Jesus about the secrets of spiritual truth.[2] It is in many ways a continuation and development of the Thomas Christianity found in the *Gospel of Thomas*, displaying several parallels and dependencies of both theme and specific content.[3] Like the Gospel of John and sev-

---

1. John D. Turner, *The Book of Thomas the Contender*, 234. On the *Book of Thomas*, cf. John D. Turner, "A New Link in the Syrian Judas Thomas Tradition," in Martin Krause, ed., *Essays on the Nag Hammadi Texts in Honor of Alexander Böhlig* (NHS 3; Leiden: E. J. Brill, 1972) 109–119; idem, *The Book of Thomas the Contender*; D. Kirchner, "Das Buch des Thomas," in *TZ* 102 (1977) 793–804; P. Perkins, *The Gnostic Dialogue*, 100–107; Peter Nagel, "Thomas der Mitstreiter (zu NHC II, 7: p. 138,8)"; Raymond Kuntzmann, "L'identification dans le *livre de Thomas l'Athlète*"; J. Sell, *The Knowledge of the Truth — Two Doctrines: The Book of Thomas the Contender and the False Teachers in the Pastoral Epistles* (Frankfurt a. M.: Lang, 1982); Hans-Martin Schenke, "The Book of Thomas (NHC II.7): A Revision of a Pseudepigraphical Letter of Jacob the Contender"; idem, "Radikale sexuelle Enthaltsamkeit als hellenistisch-jüdisches Vollkommenheitsideal im Thomas-Buch (NHC II,7)," in Ugo Bianchi, ed., *La Tradizione dell'Enkrateia* (Roma: Edizione dell'Ateneo, 1985) 263–291; Raymond Kuntzmann, *Le Livre de Thomas: Texte établi et présenté* (Quebec: Laval, 1986); Bentley Layton, *The Gnostic Scriptures*, 400ff.

2. *BTh* 138.9: "It has been said that you [Thomas] are my [Jesus'] twin"; 138.23ff.: "Now Thomas said to the Lord, 'Tell me what I ask you before your ascension. . . .'"

3. For example, the opening two pages of the *Book of Thomas* follow the same subjects and themes in the same order as does the opening sayings of the *Gospel of Thomas*. Turner comments that "the author of . . . *Thomas the Contender* may

eral later works of developing orthodoxy, it is also concerned among other things with resurrection and the fate of the body after death. Yet it argues, in continuity with the *Gospel of Thomas*, the other side of the question, against the possibility of physical resurrection, as part of a larger discussion of ascetic spirituality and the perils of embodiment. In so doing, it again draws on Greek philosophical tradition much older than Christianity,[4] on the *Gospel of Thomas*, and the logic of its own religious worldview.

The *Book of Thomas* argues against those who are not, in the opinion of the author, sufficiently ascetic, who are yet attached to the body and its "fire" of lust. It pronounces woes upon all who engage in sexuality, beguiled by the body and the demonic forces which energize its passions (144.8–14):

> *Woe to you who love intercourse with women, and polluted*
>     *association with them!*
> *And woe to you in the grip of the powers of your body, for those*
>     *will afflict you!*
> *Woe to you in the grip of the workings of evil demons!*

One major goal of the instruction in the *Book of Thomas* is to persuade all the elect to abstain from sex. So momentous would this be that it would in fact alter the structure of the cosmos: the sun itself would return to its heavenly home. We read (139.28–30):

> But whenever all the chosen abandon beastly behavior [= sexuality], then this light [= the sun] will depart up to its essence.

The seat of sexual passion is of course the body. The Savior laments "the bitterness of the fire which blazes in the bodies of men"

---

have begun with the first few of the Logia of the *Gospel of Thomas* in mind": John D. Turner, *The Book of Thomas the Contender*, 136.

4. "It seems an inescapable conclusion that the author of *Thomas the Contender* is ultimately dependent on Plato . . . in his discussion of the fiery lust of the body which causes the soul so much grief": J. D. Turner, *The Book of Thomas the Contender*, 151.

which makes "their minds drunk and their souls deranged" (139.34ff.). Those who do not seek release from the body, both in this life and the next are in eternal danger. For example, 143.5–6 warns: "Woe to you who hope in the flesh and the prison which will perish." Here the philosophical commonplace of the body as the prison of the soul[5] is used as an argument against converse with the flesh. But not only is the body a prison, it is one which will perish, and therefore provides no basis for future hope; those who rely on it will be dragged downwards, "from heaven to the earth" (140.35), and perish along with it, their souls in the attempt to ascend to heaven weighed down by the material body.

The body for the *Book of Thomas* (and the philosophical tradition) is part of the visible, therefore impermanent and mutable, world. It is opposed to the invisible and unchangeable world of the eternal. One may also compare the similar view of the apostle Paul (2 Cor 4:18):

> We do not look at the visible things, but at the things which are not visible. For the visible things are temporal, but the invisible are eternal.

For the *Book of Thomas*, bodies arise from sexuality, feed on other bodies, engage in further sexuality, and perish in an unbroken cycle. Lust causes humans to act as though mere beasts, engaging in sex only to make more bodies, all of which will perish. Thus sexuality is a sign of impermanence, mutability, and mortality. The author compares the human body to that of beasts, and argues that if animal bodies perish, so will those of humans (139.2–10):

> For these bodies are things which are visible, devouring creatures similar to themselves. On this account, the bodies change. But whatever changes will decay and perish, and has no hope of life from then on, for this body is a beast. Indeed, just like

---

5. For example: Plato, *Cratylus* 400c, of the Orphics: σῶμα σῆμα; "the body is a tomb."

beasts, if their body perishes, so also these molded images will perish. Do they not derive from intercourse like that of the beasts?

Just as animal bodies do not survive death, so humans, whose bodies are of the same type, will face eternity bodiless. They will suffer punishment, imprisonment in Hades, fiery torments, and even torturers, all without bodies (142.30–143.7). This again is a common Greco-Roman viewpoint on the postmortem individual. The soul was by poetic convention impalpable, but once beyond the grave, substantial nonetheless. Plato's Myth of Er in *Republic* 10 describes wonderful rewards and terrible punishments for the souls of the just and unjust between incarnations. Tertullian had argued from these penalties the opposite position: if souls were to suffer these tortures in the afterlife, they would of necessity have bodies, for how could impalpable souls suffer such "physical" punishments? (*De Res. Mort.* 17). Yet he is pleading a case clearly at odds with his own culture: the "common opinion," he tells us, is that the soul is impalpable, and if it has substance without the body, as he and the Stoics argued, that substance will allow it to suffer without the flesh (ibid.).

In the *Book of Thomas*, the condemned soul of the unjust dead is described as attempting to flee ubiquitous fiery torments in Tartaros to three directions of the compass. However (143.5–7),

He does not find the way to the East, to flee there and be safe. For he did not find it in the day when he was in the body, in order that he might find it in the day of judgment.

In the East was the (entrance and) exit from the Underworld. Odysseus, after sailing to the edge of the earth and to the entrance of the house of Hades, returns in the extreme East, at "the island of Aiaia, where are the house of early-born Dawn and her dancing places and the risings of the Sun" (*Od.* 12.3–4). Thus by tradition, there is an eastern gateway to safety and the upper world; but it is unavailable to the one who does not find salvation while embodied.

Both the judgment and postmortem existence, as in Plato's Myth of Er, or Virgil's *Aeneid*, or Lucian's *True History*, and many other works, are experienced without the body.

One of the major arguments by the Church of the second century and later for the resurrection of the flesh was exactly this point: that the individual could be judged and experience reward or suffer torments only in the body for the deeds of the body. The very justice of God was at stake: how could the soul be held accountable for deeds the body committed? So we find in Athenagoras, *De Resurrectione* 21.4:[6]

> Where then is justice if the soul alone is judged, when it is the body which first experiences passions and then draws the soul to participate in them and share the deeds to which the body is driven? Where is justice if the desires and pleasures, as well as the fears and griefs, in which all that is immoderate deserves blame, arise from the body, and yet the sins which result and the punishments that follow are visited upon the soul alone, which as such needs or desires none of these things . . . ?

The soul is the innocent dupe of the body: why should it be judged for what the body caused? This sounds very much as though the argument used in the *Book of Thomas* is being answered directly. In fact, a related argument may be found countered within the *Book of Thomas* itself. The homily of Jesus against lust and the body is occasioned by a question of Thomas to the Savior (141.22–25):

> What teaching should we say to these pitiable mortals who say, "We came to do good, not for a curse." Yet on the other hand they s[ay], "If we not been begotten in the flesh, we would not have known [in]iquity."

6. The translation is that of William R. Schoedel, ed. and trans., *Athenagoras: Legatio and De Resurrectione* (Oxford: Clarendon Press, 1972). The authorship of this treatise has been challenged: Grant attributes it to a third or fourth century anti-Origenist. Cf. Robert M. Grant, "Athenagoras or Pseudo-Athenagoras," in *HTR* 47 (1954) 121–129.

These individuals assert their innocent intentions and purity of soul, and blame their iniquity on the fact of incarnation. Jesus in the *Book of Thomas* indicts them in any case, and tells Thomas: "Do not consider them as humans, but count them as beasts" (141.26). Their souls, just as in Greek philosophical tradition, are polluted by the lusts of the body. Again, as Paul had declared: "The mind-set of the flesh is death" (Rom 8:6).

Greco-Roman religious conception did not lack substantial afterlife; it was not in need of the idea of bodily resurrection to remedy a theological difficulty. The blessed dead could indeed enjoy reward in the Isles of the Blessed, or among the gods, or assimilated into the deity.[7] The unquiet dead, however, the unburied[8] and the souls of the unjust, were condemned to a less fortunate state, and were thought to wander among the tombs as ghosts. So Socrates tells his friend Cebes (Plato, *Phaedo* 81c-d):[9]

> And we must suppose, my friend, that this [the body] is heavy, oppressive, earthly and visible. And indeed, holding to it, such a soul is both weighted down and dragged back again into the visible realm, . . . and wanders around gravestones and tombs, around which indeed certain shadowy ghosts have been seen which are the images of such souls. . . . It is not likely, moreover, that these are the souls of the good, but those of the wicked, which are forced to wander about these places to pay penalty for their previous evil conduct. . . .

This passage describes the state of the unjust soul after death, without the body. Indeed, after wandering for sufficient time, the souls are again reincarnated into bodies of like character, into "donkeys

---

7. Cf. Franz Cumont, *Afterlife in Roman Paganism*, 190–213.

8. Cf. Pliny, *Epist.* 7.27; Lucian, *Philopseudes* 31 (both concern the ghost of an old man in chains haunting his house until properly buried); Suetonius, *Caligula* 59 (Caligula was improperly buried, and haunted the grave site until rites were performed); Franz Cumont, *Afterlife in Roman Paganism*, 134.

9. The passage is cited (in a different translation) by Turner, *The Book of Thomas the Contender*, 155–156.

and other perverse animals, . . . wolves, hawks, and kites" (81e-82a). So in the *Book of Thomas*, the souls of non-ascetics will suffer similar fate, but without possibility of reincarnation (141.5–19):

> Things visible among men will dissolve, for the vessel of their flesh will dissolve. . . . In a short time that which is visible will dissolve. Then shades will emerge without form, and in the midst of the tombs they will dwell upon the corpses forever, in pain and destruction of soul.

Christians like those of the Thomas tradition, who stood within the philosophical and religious tradition of their culture, divided the soul from the body, considering it an encumbrance to the soul. They were therefore able to envision, and look forward to, a disembodied eternity. The Great Church, however, in its defense of the bodily resurrection of Jesus, developed an argument over time for the embodied resurrection of all individuals, based on such "logic" as is visible in Athenagoras (quoted above). It is against these Christian proponents of physical resurrection that the *Book of Thomas* is written. That the author's opponents were other Christians is clear from several passages.[10] The seekers of true wisdom are said to have wings (140.1), yet "there are some who, although they have wings, rush to the visible things" (140.18–19), that is, they do not reject the body and engage in sexuality. These opponents once had "love for the faith" and "sight among the things that are not visible" (141.10, 12); they were baptized, but vainly: they "baptized their souls in the water of darkness" (144.1). These are clearly Christians, and it is this very group who will wander bodiless among the dead forever.

Not only did these opponents engage in sexuality (which must mean that they allowed marriage), they also believed in and espoused the doctrine of physical resurrection. The argument of the

10. Turner sees those addressed as "ascetic, syncretistic Christians . . . who evidently revered the figure of Thomas": J. D. Turner, *The Book of Thomas the Contender*, 216–217. Perkins sees these individuals "as other Christians who accepted esoteric Thomas tradition but rejected such radical asceticism": P. Perkins, *The Gnostic Dialogue*, 103; cf. also 106–107.

*Book of Thomas* is that the body is temporary and perishable, and an unworthy object of hope. The other side of that polemic was the "orthodox" position. The *Book of Thomas* closes with a series of woes and blessings. In the first two woes, the Savior decries their false hopes (143.9–14):

> Woe to you, godless ones, who do not have hope, who rely upon
>    things which will not come to pass!
> Woe to you who hope in the flesh [σάρξ], and the prison which
>    will perish!
> How long will you be asleep, and as for the things which perish,
>    (how long) will you think they will not perish?

Herein is described the hope of the opposing Christians. It is a hope which will not come to pass, and it is a hope for the flesh (the Greek σάρξ is transliterated in the Coptic text). The author, however, describes this flesh as the prison (of the soul) which will perish. In other words, the opponents hope for the future concerning the flesh, that it will *not* perish.

The underlined words in the translation are the rendering of an emendation of one letter in the Coptic text, from ⲁ to ⲉ, yielding the change from ⲛⲁⲧⲧⲉⲕⲟ (= "things which do not perish") to ⲛⲉⲧⲧⲉⲕⲟ (= "things which perish"). As the text stands, the sentence makes no sense in its context: "As for the things which do not perish, you think that they do not perish." This, as Turner points out, is a tautology;[11] the text clearly must be emended. Of the five possibilities for the meaning of the line which he discusses, he chooses to emend the text elsewhere and read the final word ⲁⲛ ("not") as Coptic ⲟⲛ ("too"; he is followed by Layton[12]). This eliminates the negative in the final clause and yields the following: "how long will you suppose that the imperishables will perish too?"[13] This change, however, produces a

---

11. J. D. Turner, *The Book of Thomas the Contender*, 173.

12. Bentley Layton, ed., *Nag Hammadi Codex II, 2–7* (Leiden: E. J. Brill, 1989) 2.196; also *The Gnostic Scriptures*, 407: "How long will you . . . suppose that the incorruptibles will perish?".

13. Turner's translation in Layton, *Nag Hammadi Codex II, 2–7*, 2.197. In *The Book of Thomas the Contender*, Turner renders the line: "And the imperishables, do

sense which is exactly the opposite of what is required by the context; the discussion is not about perishing imperishables, but the contrary: perishable bodies falsely thought to endure. The context of the immediately preceding sentences is that the opponents have future hope in the flesh, which the author says is vain. They believe in the resurrection of the flesh; they think that the perishable body is imperishable, that it will be raised, while the *Book of Thomas* argues throughout that it will dissolve with death. The emendation proposed here alleviates this difficulty, and gives excellent sense: the author asks his opponents how long they will continue to believe vainly in the resurrection of the body.[14]

Two closely related groups of Christians are here in disagreement over the resurrection of the body. If both these groups used and valued Thomas tradition, then conscious editorial activity may lie behind a difference in the text of the Greek and Coptic versions of one of the sayings in the *Gospel of Thomas*. *GTh* 5 according to the Coptic text reads:

> Jesus said: Know what is in front of your face, and what is hidden from you will become manifest to you. For there is nothing hidden which will not be revealed.

The Greek version, P. Oxy. 654.27–31, corresponds to this closely, but includes one further line: καὶ θεθαμμένον ὃ ο[ὐκ ἐγερθήσεται] ("and buried which will n[ot be raised]"). This final line seems to declare, among other possibilities, the resurrection of buried dead bodies. Thus two different texts existed: one group used a copy of

---

you think that they will also perish?" The five possibilities and choice of ⲟⲛ are found on pages 173–174.

14. Kuntzmann follows Turner's line of reasoning, but still finds the connection between "the imperishables" and the context unclear. He explains it as the perishable soul [!?], which is wrongly thought to be imperishable by the opponents of the *Book of Thomas*: Raymond Kuntzmann, *Le Livre de Thomas*, 135–137. This interpretation stretches the word "perishable" to cover punishment of a living but condemned soul, where it is used in the immediately preceding sentence to describe the literally perishable body. The simple emendation proposed alleviates this difficulty also.

the *Gospel of Thomas* with this line, represented by the Greek version, and another, represented by the Coptic version, used one without it.

A short version of this saying is preserved in each of the Synoptic Gospels (twice in Luke).[15] Excepting the introductory statement ("Know what is in front of your face, and what is hidden will be manifest to you"), it is each time similar to the Coptic version: "hidden / manifest; hidden / revealed." The first member of the comparison in each pair is the word "hidden" (or a synonym), while the second is some word of opposite meaning. There is no third member.

| MARK 4:22 | LUKE 8:17 | MATTHEW 10:26 | LUKE 12:2 |
|---|---|---|---|
| *For nothing is hidden except to be revealed, nor has anything been hidden away except to come to light.* | *For nothing is hidden which will not be revealed, nor hidden away which will not be known and come to light.* | *For there is nothing covered which will not be uncovered, and hidden which will not be known.* | *But there is nothing covered up which will not be uncovered and hidden which will not be known.* |

The third member in P. Oxy. 654 ("and buried which will not be raised") has clearly been added to the text. In reference to this supplement, Bultmann states correctly:[16]

the addition which has been made to the end of Matt 10:26 in Pap. Ox. 654 has to be described as dogmatically motivated; for the words (οὐ) τεθαμμένον ὃ οὐκ ἐγερθήσεται are obviously an expression of the doctrine of the resurrection.

The history of the text seems to have been that the original *Gospel of Thomas* did not contain this reference to resurrection. The oppo-

---

15. Mark 4:22; Matt 10:26; Luke 8:17 and 12:2.

16. R. Bultmann, *History of the Synoptic Tradition*, 94. Cf. also, J. A. Fitzmyer, "The Oxyrhynchus Logoi of Jesus," 526–527. Marcovich thinks "it looks like a late Christian marginal gloss or a secondary expansion. . . . Thus the probability is that it never belonged to the archetype of the *GTh*": M. Marcovich, "Textual Criticism on the Gospel of Thomas," 64. Quispel, on the other hand, takes the Coptic as primary: G. Quispel, *Makarius, das Thomasevangelium und das Lied von der Perle* (NovTSup 15; Leiden: E. J. Brill, 1967) 71.

nents of the author of the *Book of Thomas* "were probably orthodox Christians who also revered traditions that were said to have come from the risen Jesus through Thomas."[17] It may be that this group made the addition to the text of the *Gospel of Thomas*, and is the target of the *animus* of the author of the *Book of Thomas*.

The impossibility of physical resurrection in the *Book of Thomas* is part of a larger complex of ideas concerning the spiritual life. The visible and material world is destined to end, and along with it all flesh. The soul, which alone endures, must remain weightless and pure that it may "come forth out of the visible realm" into the "exalted height and the pleroma" (138.26, 33). But it may be influenced, deceived and entrapped by the body, whose main enticement is sexual lust. If caught, the soul is weighted down and polluted, identified with the material realm, and finally dragged down from its proper ethereal home into Tartaros to be tortured forever. In this venerable philosophical context, the reason for the impossibility of resurrection is clear.

## The Acts of Thomas

The *Acts of Thomas* presents a rather complicated situation with regard to Thomas tradition and its view of the body and physical resurrection. The *Acts* stems from a period when the controversy over the doctrine of physical resurrection was joined by some of the most influential Christian writers. The strict division between soul and body which had been developed in Greek philosophical and Eastern religious tradition was inherited by the Thomas tradition and a large part of the early Church. This division was attacked, especially in the West, as a means to substantiate claims for the necessity of bodily resurrection: the human being was not merely a soul imprisoned in a foreign and temporary body, but a totality, a "whole" composed of body and soul together. So Irenaeus, in the later second century, writes (*Adv. Haer.* 5.6.1):[18]

---

17. P. Perkins, *The Gnostic Dialogue*, 106.
18. Cf. also Tertullian, *De Res. Carnis* 32.8: *tam enim corpus homo quam et anima*; Athenagoras, *De Res.* 15. Cf. Lynn Boliek, *The Resurrection of the Flesh: A*

The soul and spirit can be considered a *part* of the human being, but in no way comprise the whole person; for the complete
"human" is a mixture and uniting of the soul receiving the
Spirit from the Father with that flesh which has been formed
according to the image of God.

The body, he goes on to say, is the "temple of God" (citing 1 Cor
3:16[19]), and therefore it is the "utmost blasphemy" to assert, as some
clearly were doing, that the body will not share in salvation, but simply be destroyed (5.6.2). Tertullian, a younger contemporary, asserts
that belief in the doctrine of the resurrection of the flesh had faltered
under the attacks of the "unbelief and perverseness" of heretics, but
that God had "now dispersed all the perplexities of the past," and
their "self-chosen allegories and parables,"[20] by the spiritual out-
pouring of the New Prophecy (i.e., Montanism; *De Res. Carnis* 63).
The "heresies" of the past, of course, predated by centuries any heresies encountered by Tertullian; the allegories and parables were old
hermeneutical strategies used by Greek philosophers to interpret
Homer and the poets, and by Hellenistic Judaism and "heretical"
Christianity to meld the Scriptures with Greco-Roman culture. The
waning of faith in physical resurrection to which Tertullian refers
was of course nothing of the sort: the doctrine which he and Irenaeus were advocating was being invented and developed in the late
first and second centuries by themselves and their fellows, like so
many other doctrines which eventually found their way into the
creeds. The *Acts of Thomas* displays features on both sides of this
discussion.

   As a Christian "romance," the *Acts of Thomas* was part of a genre
used and read by both "orthodox" and "heterodox" alike. The Apoc-

---

*Study of a Confessional Phrase* (Grand Rapids: Eerdmans, 1962) 25.

   19. 1 Cor 3:16: "Do you not know that you are a temple of God, and the spirit of
God dwells in you?"

   20. Meaning their two-level method of interpretation: literal meaning for Tertullian and his friends, and spiritual meaning reserved for the elite. Cf. James M.
Robinson, "From Jesus to Valentinus," 26–37.

ryphal Acts as a group may be said to stand between the beliefs and practices of their communities and the influences of genre and literary aspirations of their authors. There was, it seems, a "living link between the milieu wherein an apocryphal Acts originated and circles representing a traditional current" in an apostolic community.[21] So the *Acts of Thomas* contains Thomas tradition overlaid by the concerns of a burgeoning orthodoxy, and reflects not only tradition derived from the *Gospel of Thomas* and the Thomas community,[22] but that of the larger Church, its Scriptures and confessions.

The *Acts of Thomas* was not only written in a time of controversy, it also contains marks of that controversy in its very text. The nature of the text as "story" made it susceptible to elaboration and expansion: for example, the "Hymn of the Pearl" is not found in all manuscripts; several of the prayers, and even whole sections of text, are of quite different lengths in different manuscripts. In reference to the sacraments, the Greek and Syriac texts reflect different rites, apparently built over a core of earlier sectarian liturgy.[23] The text which has survived did so in the main through orthodox hands, and underwent revision and assimilation to the developing orthodoxy of the church.[24] Doctrinal features at home in circles on the edges of the Great Church stand side by side with thoroughly "orthodox" ideas.

21. Francois Bovon and Eric Junod, "Reading the Apocryphal Acts of the Apostles," in Dennis Ronald MacDonald, ed., *The Apocryphal Acts of Apostles* (Semeia 38; Decatur: Scholars Press, 1986) 163.

22. Cf. J. Michael LaFargue, *Language and Gnosis: The Opening Scenes of the Acts of Thomas* (HDR 18; Philadelphia: Fortress Press, 1985) 216.

23. Cf. According to Bornkamm, "The liturgical portions thus clearly point to a Gnostic sect which knew only the unction as a sacrament of initiation": G. Bornkamm, "The Acts of Thomas," in Hennecke-Schneemelcher, *New Testament Apocrypha*, 2. 438. This is probably saying too much; baptism was apparently part of the Thomas tradition, and other Jewish "baptismal sects" of early origin: cf. Jonathan Z. Smith, "Garments of Shame."

24. " . . . the scribes who transcribed these materials often shared with Eusebius and Photius an insistence on canonical orthodoxy, a desire for carefully crafted theological positions, and a scepticism of myth, legend of fanciful narrative": Dennis Ronald MacDonald, "Introduction: The Forgotten Novels of the Early Church," in idem, ed., *The Apocryphal Acts of Apostles* (Semeia 38; Decatur: Scholars Press, 1986) 5.

Genuine Thomas tradition has been both preserved and "corrected" in an effort to make it more palatable to the Church.[25]

Elements unique to the Thomas tradition are found in many passages of the *Acts of Thomas*.[26] He is expressly named "Judas" and "Judas Thomas" often, as in the *Gospel of Thomas* and the *Book of Thomas*, but not in the canon. Perhaps the single most striking example of Thomas tradition is the designation of Thomas as the twin of Jesus. He is so named by a demonic serpent (31), and a donkey's colt (39). In addition, the Holy Spirit is addressed as "the Holy Dove that bears the twin young" (50). Jesus appears more than once in the exact form of Thomas: he appears as Thomas to two different dead individuals in the realm of the dead (34 and 54–55); he leads two female disciples out of a locked room to the real Thomas (151–152), for which he earns the title, "Jesus of many forms" (153; cf. also 48); he appears to an affianced couple and must say that he is Thomas' brother (11). Likewise, before his death, Thomas declares, "I am not Jesus" (160). Thomas is the recipient of the "secret words" of Jesus, as in the incipit of both the *Gospel* and *Book of Thomas* (10 and 31). He is further the hearer of the "three words," which Jesus had spoken to him privately in *Gospel of Thomas* 13.

The influence of the canonical figure of Thomas in the Gospel of John is also present, as a correction of the Thomas tradition. In the *Gospel of Thomas*, Jesus states to Thomas directly that he is not Thomas' "Teacher" or "Master."[27] The figure of Thomas in the

25. This is particularly true in the Syriac versions, which reflect ". . . Syriac Christianity at a later stage in which special attention was paid to man's free will and the resurrection of the body": A. F. J. Klijn, *The Acts of Thomas*, 16. According to Bornkamm, the Syriac "displays numerous catholicizing revisions": G. Bornkamm, "The Acts of Thomas," in Hennecke-Schneemelcher, *New Testament Apocrypha*, 2. 428. Also, cf. Yves Tissot, "Les actes de Thomas, exemple de recueil composite," in F. Bovon, et al., eds., *Les Actes apocryphes de Apôtres: Christianisme et monde païen* (Publication de la faculté de théologie de l'Université de Genève 4; Geneva: Labor et Fides, 1981) 223.

26. Cf. the short list in G. Bornkamm, "The Acts of Thomas," in Hennecke-Schneemelcher, *New Testament Apocrypha*, 2. 427.

27. The salient part of *GTh* 13:
Thomas said to him: Master, my mouth will not at all be capable of saying whom you are like. Jesus said: I am not your master, because you have drunk and have become drunk from the bubbling spring which I measured out.

Gospel of John, however, is made to address Jesus as "my Lord and my God" (John 20:28). In the *Acts of Thomas*, all these titles are used of Jesus in his relationship with Thomas: a merchant asks Thomas if Jesus is his master, and Thomas replies that he is his Lord (2); the donkey's colt calls Jesus the "Lord and Teacher" of Thomas (40); a wild donkey calls Jesus all three, "Master, Teacher, and Lord" of Thomas (78). More significantly, Thomas himself prays to Jesus as "my Lord and my God" (10; 167), exactly as he addresses Jesus in John 20:28. In a prayer to raise two women from the dead, the formerly doubting Thomas says, "My Lord and my God, I do not doubt concerning you, nor do I call upon you in unbelief . . . " (81). The author of the *Acts* shows that Thomas has learned his Johannine lesson of submission and faith.

The other lesson of the Thomas pericope in the Gospel of John, however, that Jesus had a physical post-resurrection body, is nowhere in evidence. The Jesus of the *Acts* was crucified, and after three days raised from the dead (59; cf. also 80, 156, 158). But the post-resurrection body of Jesus is something other than the very same flesh in which he was crucified. He is the Jesus of "many forms" (48; cf. 80 Syr., 153), a phrase used elsewhere only of demons who have no bodies (44). Furthermore, he is seen not only as Thomas.[28] He appears to the new disciples, king Gundaphorus and his brother, with the same introduction he used to Thomas in John 20, saying "Peace be unto you." But the two men cannot see him, since they had not yet been sealed by the Holy Spirit. After the sealing, he is visible as a young man carrying a blazing torch, which outshines all other lights. This leads to the exclamation: "Beyond our comprehension, O Lord, is your light, . . . for it is greater than our sight."[29] Not only is the light of the Lord beyond sight, but so is the Lord himself. Thomas describes his appearing thus: "Jesus, who appears to us at all times, . . . you who are not seen with our bodily

---

28. Cf. David R. Cartlidge, "Transfigurations of Metamorphosis Traditions in the Acts of John, Thomas, and Peter," in Dennis Ronald MacDonald, ed., *The Apocryphal Acts of Apostles* (Semeia 38; Decatur: Scholars Press, 1986) 53–66.

29. Chapter 27. A similar appearance in "great light" is described of Thomas himself in chapter 118.

eyes, but are never hidden at all from those of our soul, and in your form are indeed hidden . . . " (53). In a remarkable reference to the transfiguration story of the Gospels, Thomas declares, "his appearance we saw transfigured with our eyes, but his heavenly form we could not see upon the mount" (143). When the captain of king Misdaeus asks the apostle to show him Jesus that he may believe, Thomas answers, "Stretch your mind upward as much as you can, for he does not appear to these bodily eyes, but is found with the eyes of the mind" (65). Jesus did appear to a dead young man beyond the grave, whom Thomas later raised, but his form is described as one of "beauty" and "radiant countenance," an "effulgence of light" (35).

The thought world of the *Acts of Thomas* is quite different from that which prompted the physical demonstrations of the body of the risen Jesus in the Gospels of John and Luke. It can only have been by conscious choice that this single aspect of the Doubting Thomas pericope, the touching of the body of the risen Jesus, was omitted. The author was clearly familiar with the canonical Gospels, and of the Thomas literature, with at least the *Gospel of Thomas*. Yet the Thomas tradition emphasized the division of soul from body, and the corrupting influences and perishability of the body, ideas found to a somewhat lesser extent in the canon itself. In spite of "orthodox" readership and revision, the *Acts of Thomas* preserves this emphasis.

The polemic against the body and its dangers which was present in the *Gospel of Thomas* and so much in evidence in the *Book of Thomas* is also found, in its own form, in the *Acts*. Sexuality is again one of the main targets of attack in both story and teaching. Such teaching is a constant message of the *Acts* (cf. for example, 28, 84, 96, 101), based in part on the doctrine that for God there is no sexual differentiation, "no male or female." But not only are the sexes not part of the divine world, sexuality is pollution. A newly married couple is persuaded on their wedding night to "abandon filthy intercourse," remain in chastity, and "marry" the eternal spouse in heaven, Jesus (11–15). Again, not only is the producing of children evil, but children themselves are the cause of evils, the majority of whom become evil (12; also 79, 126). Thomas fasts, and eats only sparingly (water, bread and salt: 104; fasting, 139); in fact he is described as not eating or drinking at all (96; cf. 5). He takes nothing from anyone, in payment for healing or otherwise (20). He recommends that all give away their possessions (100). This is in accord with the instruction that the believer must serve God "free from all bodily pleasures" (126).

There are important similarities with earlier Thomas tradition in the description of the body.[30] As in the *Gospel of Thomas* (*GTh* 71), the body is a dwelling of the soul and spirit, even the "temple" of God (94). But, as in the *Book of Thomas*, the body is set apart from the divine world by its mutability: it changes, grows old, and loses its beauty (88). The body is the storehouse of worthless deeds and desires, of money and possessions, clothing and beauty, all of which vanish; believers are to raise themselves out of "the whole body in which all these are stored and which growing old becomes dust, returning to its own nature" (37). It is a garment of the soul (147), in fact a dirty garment (126). So Thomas describes himself as "a man clothed with a body" (66). The Savior is the "nourisher, preserving and giving us rest in alien bodies, the Savior of our souls" (39).

This last point is emphasized often, that it is the soul which is saved; the body is not said to be raised or endure or be renewed in eternity.[31] Death is "not death, but deliverance and release from the body" (160; 163).[32] We are told that "Jesus alone abides forever, and

---

30. For other parallels, cf. Han J. W Drijvers, "Thomasakten," in Edgar Hennecke, *Neutestamentliche Apokryphen in deutscher Übersetzung*, ed. Wilhelm Schneemelcher (Tübingen: J. C. B. Mohr, 1989) 291.

31. Perhaps others will read the *Acts of Thomas* differently. There are a few passages which seem to be based on creedal formulations, and may stem from later redaction. But even these omit specific reference to resurrection of the body. One passage, however, in the Greek but not the Syriac, in a very "orthodox" account of the passion of Jesus, includes the words, "for the new grave and burial let us receive renewal of soul and body. Because you rose and came to life again, let us come to life again and live and stand before you in righteous judgment" (158). No other text in the *Acts* comes this close to physical resurrection.

32. Even those who are condemned to hell are released from the body. A young woman whom Thomas raises from the dead describes a tour of Hell, during which she sees souls being tormented in their offending "body" parts. Cf. Martha Him-

the souls which hope in him" (117). It is salvation of souls alone which is described (157), even though there is miraculous healing for the body. Jesus is the one who saves the soul, and "restores it to its own nature" (141). The restoration to its own nature finds explanation in the journey of the soul through the heavenly archons, the demonic "powers and dominions" of the regions between earth and heaven. Thomas prays that he might journey safely up to the judgment seat of God (148, 167), and thus that his soul might return to God. Likewise the bridegroom, describing the apostle's teaching, says that Thomas "showed me to seek myself and to recognize who I was and who and how I now am, that I may become again what I was" (15). So the "Hymn of the Pearl" describes the heavenly origin, descent, and reascent of the soul: it clothed itself in garments of Egypt on its arrival (= the body: 109.29), and then "took off and left in their land their dirty and unclean garment" (111.62–63) at its reascent. Thomas tells his disciples that "So long as we are in the body we cannot speak and declare what he is to give to our souls" (36); the gift, as in the Hymn, is clothing of the world above. Embodiment changes even the relationship of God to humans: God is Father to pure souls, but Judge of embodied souls. Thomas prays to God as "Lord of all and Father — but Father not of souls that are in bodies, but of those that are gone out; for of the souls that are in pollutions you are Lord and judge" (30).

The *Acts of Thomas* stands at a point between the growing confessional viewpoint of the Great Church and the Thomas tradition. One may observe conflicting passages in the *Acts* concerning the post-mortem fate of the individual, yet the eschatology of the resurrection is absent.[33] Jesus of the *Gospel of Thomas* declares that his body will not be raised. We are not told whether in the opinion of the community of the *Acts of Thomas* the tomb of Jesus was empty on Easter morning. Yet one analogy may be enlightening. When the

melfarb, *Tours of Hell: An Apocalyptic Form in Jewish and Christian Literature* (Philadelphia: Fortress Press, 1983) 11–13, 132–133.

33. Cf. Han J. W Drijvers, "Thomasakten," in Hennecke-Schneemelcher, 295.

women approached the tomb of Jesus in the Gospel of Mark, an angel told them, "He is risen; he is not here" (Mark 16:6). Likewise in the *Acts of Thomas*, while two disciples pass the night sitting next to the tomb of Judas, the twin brother of Jesus, he appears to them and says: "I am not here" (169). Yet his body remained in the grave.

# Summary and Conclusions

The Thomas tradition was heir to two important streams of tradition which helped form its view of the resurrection of Jesus. The long development in the eastern Mediterranean of Greek and Eastern philosophy and religion, with their emphasis on the supra-mundane nature of the soul and denigration of its "prison," the body, made the concept of physical resurrection not only unnecessary, but objectionable. The body was a negative accompaniment of earthly life, and death was release from its limitation, temptation to evil, and suffering. The soul was the substantial carrier of identity, with its recognizable form and functions, of which the body was a copy in physical material. In addition, popular Greco-Roman literature afforded ample precedent for the interpretation of the resurrection of Jesus in time-honored categories which excluded a physical body because of the substantive nature of the soul, and its ability postmortem to participate in all embodied human experiences. As Jesus had appeared to, spoken with, and even eaten with his disciples, so the souls of the dead were seen to do likewise and often. These ideas were strengthened in the culture at large by the ubiquitous cults of heroes and of the dead, and the stories of the heroic past, which for both Jew and Greek supported the concept of the substantial, yet disembodied, survival of the individual after death. Yet one aspect of the soul was relatively fixed in the ancient epic tradition: the postmortem soul was impalpable, and it was so from the time of Homer through Virgil and the rise of Christianity. Herein lay the motivation in Luke for physical demonstration of the body of Jesus, and in John for the Thomas pericope, in their attempts to counter ideas of a nonphysical post-Easter Jesus.

Such strategies were nevertheless unsuccessful in persuading the opponents of the idea of physical resurrection to abandon their traditional position, and adopt the new ideas of the developing Church. The controversy over physical resurrection grew in both sophistication and acrimony; neither side seemed able to let its opponent continue in "error." On one side, Luke's Paul asks, "Why is it considered incredible among you if God does raise the dead?" (Acts 26:8). On the other, the author of the *Book of Thomas* declares, "Woe to you who hope in the flesh, and in the prison which will perish!" (*BTh* 143.10f.). In like spirit, John portrays the figure of Doubting Thomas in stark and negative manner.

This portrayal of Thomas compares well with other characters in John, and consideration of John's method of characterization is an important means of deciphering the "message" of Doubting Thomas. Thomas is the final individual to appear in the Gospel (excluding chapter 21), and balances most favorably with the opening portrayal of John the Baptist. As the Baptist was the founder and spiritual father of a movement contemporaneous and in direct competition with the community of John, so Thomas was the same for the Thomas community. The portrayal of the Baptist is demonstrably drawn in ways designed to influence his community in favor of Jesus; the Baptist acts and speaks on Jesus' behalf, contrary to what is probable for the "historical" Baptist. So the figure of Thomas is likewise drawn to influence the Thomas community, especially away from its insistence, among other things, on the "spiritual", nonfleshly resurrection of Jesus.

The communities of John and Thomas were in close spiritual proximity to one another. Examination of the literature of each reveals large areas of agreement, and fundamental disagreements. These communities arose, according to the position taken here, "in conversation" with each other, that is, in a circumstance of reciprocal development and debate over, among other ideas, the issue of bodily resurrection. The creation of the Doubting Thomas pericope by the author of the Gospel of John is one side of this debate; the version of the Temple Saying ("Destroy this temple and in three days I will raise it up") in the *Gospel of Thomas* is another. But their knowledge of one another was hardly limited to this point. Close examination of the Doubting Thomas pericope itself reveals several other points of contact with signature features of the Thomas tradition countered creatively by the author of John. Not only did the Thomas tradition not accept physical resurrection, but also did not "believe in Jesus" in any Johannine sense, or consider Jesus as "Lord and God" as did the Johannine Christians. In addition, the rather obtuse nature of the character Thomas is an indication of the strident nature of the controversy between the two communities.

The Doubting Thomas pericope is evidence within the Gospel of John for the prior existence of the community of Thomas. The elements present and positions countered in the pericope cohere well with those in the *Gospel of Thomas*, and lead to the conclusion that the *Gospel of Thomas* itself was already at some stage of completion, either written or oral, and that its contents were known to the author of John, probably through verbal contact with members of this rival community. In addition, the *Gospel of Thomas* contains evidence of reciprocal debate with the community of John, although in a form which predates the Gospel. The Gospel of John is in no way the original source from which the Thomas tradition was formed, any more than it is the source of the tradition of John the Baptist. It was written in part as a reaction against, and a correction of, the earlier Thomas tradition, which held steadfastly to the "original," that is culturally prior, conception concerning the body and afterlife, and had its own independent and culturally prior mode of spirituality and relationship with the divine.

Finally, the picture of Doubting Thomas in John is shown to correspond well with the Thomas literature as a whole. All three of the major Thomas documents preserved, the *Gospel of Thomas*, the *Book of Thomas*, and the *Acts of Thomas*, are consistent in their denigration of the body, and their denial of physical resurrection. The *Gospel of Thomas*, among other passages, contradicts directly the tradition on which John drew for his use of the Temple Saying. The Jesus of the *Gospel of Thomas* declares that no one will be able to raise his body. The *Book of Thomas* pronounces woe upon, and assigns to eternal punishment, those who hold future hope for the body. The *Acts of Thomas*, while containing many "orthodox" interpolations and revisions, nevertheless presents a like picture, and closes with a scene similar to that in the Gospel Easter stories; yet in the scene of the *Acts*, the body of the twin brother of Jesus remains in the grave, while his soul ascends to heaven. This is supported, among other passages, by one of the most famous poems in Gnostic Christian literature, the Hymn of the Pearl, which describes the archetypical journey of the soul for the Thomas disciple: the soul descends into a body, and abandons it upon return to the heavenly realms.

Early Christianity proclaimed the resurrection of Jesus, yet it inherited a variety of conceptions of the afterlife, few of which included the doctrine of the resurrection of the flesh. The early views of the afterlife were in the main of a spiritual nature, that the soul survived death and enjoyed its reward or suffered its punishment apart from the body. So it was that the early idea of the resurrection of Jesus and the postmortem state of his followers was spiritual, represented in various ways by Paul, the Hellenistic Church to a large extent, and Thomas Christianity. In the controversies over the resurrection in the later first and second centuries there developed the doctrine of the resurrection of the flesh in defense of the real humanity of Jesus, that Jesus was a man of flesh not only before the crucifixion, but always, even after rising from the dead. Such a doctrine was new to the Greco-Roman world and stridently argued by the second and third century apologists against critics both pagan and Christian. Yet many Christians held for centuries to the earlier conception, that Jesus had risen alive as a spiritual being, in a spiritual body of light. So they too hoped in the promise of a heavenly afterlife, to be free from the body and its sufferings as spiritual beings, or to be like the angels and themselves to wear the "body of his glory." So they too doubted the truth of the new proclamation, as had their spiritual predecessor among Jesus' own disciples, Doubting Thomas.

# Bibliography

Abel, Ernest L. *Ancient Views on the Origins of Life.* Rutherford: Far-leigh Dickenson Univ. Press, 1973.

Akagi, Tai. *The Literary Development of the Coptic Gospel of Thomas.* Ph. D. Diss. Western Reserve University, 1965. Ann Arbor: University Microfilms, 1965.

Albertz, M. "Zur Formgeschichte der Auferstehungsberichte." In *ZNW* 21 (1922) 259–269.

Allen, Thomas W. *Homeri Opera.* Oxford: Clarendon Press, 1978.

Alsup, John E. *The Post-Resurrection Appearance Stories of the Gospel Tradition.* Calwer Theologische Monographien. Stuttgart: Calwer Verlag, 1975.

Arthur, Richard L. *The Gospel of Thomas and the Coptic New Testament.* Th. D. Dissertation, Graduate Theological Union. Ann Arbor: University Microfilms, 1976.

Attridge, Harold W. "The Gospel According to Thomas. Appendix: The Greek Fragments." In *Nag Hammadi Codex II*, 2–7, 1.96–128. Edited by Bentley Layton. Leiden: E. J. Brill, 1989.

Aune, David E. *Prophecy in Early Christianity and the Ancient Mediterranean World.* Grand Rapids: Eerdmans, 1983.

Bacon, Benjamin W. *The Gospel of the Hellenists.* Edited by Carl H. Kraeling. New York: Henry Holt and Company, 1933.

Bader, Robert. *Der ΑΛΗΘΗΣ ΛΟΓΟΣ des Kelsos.* Stuttgart-Berlin: Verlag von W. Kohlhammer, 1940.

Badham, Paul. *Christian Beliefs about Life after Death.* London: Macmillan, 1976.

Baker, Aelred. "Pseudo-Macarius and the Gospel of Thomas." In *VC* 18 (1964) 215–225.

Bammel, Ernst. "The Poor and the Zealots." In *Jesus and the Politics of his Day*, 109–128. Edited by idem and C. F. D. Moule. Cambridge: Cambridge Univ. Press, 1984.

———. "The *titulus*." In *Jesus and the Politics of his Day*, 353–364.

Edited by idem and C. F. D. Moule. Cambridge: Cambridge Univ. Press, 1984.

Barnard, L. W. "The Origins and Emergence of the Church in Edessa during the First Two Centuries A.D." In *VC* 22 (1968) 161–175.

Barrett, C. K. *The Gospel of John and Judaism.* Translated from the German by D. M. Smith. Philadelphia: Fortress Press, 1975.

———. *The Gospel according to St. John.* Second edition. Philadelphia: Westminster, 1978.

———. "Immortality and Resurrection." In *Resurrection and Immortality: A Selection from the Drew Lectures on Immortality,* 68–88. Edited by Charles S. Duthie. London: Samuel Bagster and Sons, 1979.

Barth, Marcus. *Der Augenzeuge: Eine Untersuchung über die Wahrnehmung des Menschensones durch die Apostle.* Zürich: Evangelischer Verlag, 1946.

Bassler, Jouette M. "Mixed Signals: Nicodemus in the Fourth Gospel." In *JBL* 108 (1989) 635–646.

Bauer, Walter. *Orthodoxy and Heresy in Earliest Christianity.* Edited by Robert Kraft and Gerhard Krodel. Translated by members of the Philadelphia Seminar on Christian Origins. Philadelphia: Fortress Press, 1971.

Beare, F. W. "Sayings of the Risen Jesus in the Synoptic Tradition: An Inquiry into their Origin and Significance." In *Christian History and Interpretation: Studies Presented to John Knox,* 161–181. Edited by W. R. Farmer, C. F. D. Moule and R. R. Niebuhr. Cambridge: Cambridge Univ. Press, 1967.

———. *The Gospel According to Matthew.* San Francisco: Harper and Row, 1981.

Beasley-Murray, G. R. *A Commentary on Mark Thirteen.* London: Macmillan, 1957.

Bernard, J. H. *A Critical and Exegetical Commentary on the Gospel according to John.* Edited by A. H. McNeille. 2 volumes. International Critical Commentary Series. New York: Charles Scribner's Sons, 1929.

Bickerman, Elias J. *The Jews in the Greek Age.* Cambridge, Mass.: Harvard Univ. Press, 1988.

Black, Matthew. "The Essenes in Hippolytus and Josephus." In *The Background of the New Testament and Its Eschatology,* 172–175. Edited by W. D. Davies and D. Daube. Cambridge: Cambridge Univ. Press, 1964.

————. "The Dead Sea Scrolls and Christian Origins." In *The Scrolls and Christianity,* 97–106. Edited by Matthew Black. SPCK Theological Collection, 11. London: SPCK, 1969.

Blair, E. P. "Thomas" In *The Interpreter's Dictionary of the Bible,* 4.631–632. Edited by G. A. Buttrick, et al. Nashville: Abingdon, 1962.

Blass, F.; and Debrunner, A. *A Greek Grammar of the New Testament and Other Early Christian Literature.* Translated by Robert W. Funk. Chicago and London: Univ. of Chicago Press, 1961.

Boliek, Lynn. *The Resurrection of the Flesh: A Study of a Confessional Phrase.* Grand Rapids: Eerdmans, 1962.

Borgen, Peder. *Bread from Heaven: An Exegetical Study of the Concept of Manna in the Gospel of John and the Writings of Philo.* Supplements to *Novum Testamentum,* 10. Leiden: E. J. Brill, 1981.

Borleffs, J. G. Ph. *Q. S. Fl. Tertulliani. De Resurrectione Mortuorum. Corpus Christianorum: Series Latina II. Tertulliani Opera: Pars II.* Turnholti: Typographi Brepolis, 1954.

Bornkamm, Gunther. "The Acts of Thomas." In Edgar Hennecke, *New Testament Apocrypha,* 2. 425–531. Edited by Wilhelm Schneemelcher. Translated by R. McL. Wilson. 2 volumes. Philadelphia: Westminster Press, 1964.

Bousset, Wilhelm. *Kyrios Christos: A History of the Belief in Christ from the Beginnings of Christianity to Irenaeus.* Translated by John E. Steely. Nashville: Abingdon, 1970.

Bovon, Francois; and Junod, Eric. "Reading the Apocryphal Acts of the Apostles." In *The Apocryphal Acts of Apostles,* 161–171. Edited by Dennis Ronald MacDonald. Semeia, 38. Decatur: Scholars Press, 1986.

Brandon, S.G.F. *Jesus and the Zealots.* Manchester: Manchester Univ. Press, 1967.

———. *The Trial of Jesus of Nazareth.* New York: Dorset Press, 1968.

———. *The Fall of Jerusalem and the Christian Church.* Second edition. London: SPCK, 1978.

Bream, Howard N. "Life without Resurrection: Two Perspectives from Qoheleth." In *A Light unto My Path: Old Testament Studies in Honor of Jacob M. Myers,* 49–65. Edited by H. N. Bream, R. D. Heim, C. A. Moore. Philadelphia: Temple Univ. Press, 1974.

Bremmer, Jan. *The Early Greek Concept of the Soul.* Princeton: Princeton Univ. Press, 1983.

Brown, Raymond E. "The Gospel of Thomas and St John's Gospel." In *NTS* 9 (1962) 155–177.

———. "John the Baptist in the Gospel of John." In idem, *New Testament Essays,* 132–140. New York: Paulist Press, 1965.

———. "The Problem of Historicity in John." In idem, *New Testament Essays,* 143–167. New York: Paulist Press, 1965.

———. *The Gospel according to John.* Anchor Bible, 29 and 29A. New York: Doubleday, 1966 (volume 29) and 1970 (volume 29A).

———, Karl P. Donfried, and John Reumann, editors. *Peter in the New Testament.* Minneapolis: Augsburg and New York: Paulist Press, 1973.

———. "'Other Sheep Not of This Fold': The Johannine Perspective on Christian Diversity in the Late First Century." In *JBL* 97 (1978) 5–22.

Brownlee, William H. "Whence the Gospel according to John?" In *John and Qumran,* 166–194. Edited by James H. Charlesworth. London: Geoffrey Chapman, 1972.

Bruce, F. F. "Paul on Immortality." In *SJT* 24 (1971) 457–472.

Brun, L. *Die Auferstehung Christi in der urchristlichen Überlieferung.* Oslo, 1925.

Bultmann, Rudolf. *The Gospel of John: A Commentary.* Edited by R. W. N. Hoare and J. K. Riches. Translated by G. R. Beasley-Murray. Philadelphia: Westminster Press, 1971.

————. *History of the Synoptic Tradition.* Translated by John Marsh. Revised edition. New York: Harper and Row, 1976.

Burkert, Walter. *Ancient Mystery Cults.* Cambridge, Mass.: Harvard Univ. Press, 1987.

Bury, R. G. *The Symposium of Plato: Edited, with Introduction, Critical Notes and Commentary.* Second edition. Cambridge: W. Heffer and Sons, 1973.

Byrne, Brendan. "The Faith of the Beloved Disciple and the Community in John 20." In *JSNT* 23 (1985) 83–97.

Cameron, Ron, editor. *The Other Gospels: Non-Canonical Gospel Texts.* Philadelphia: Westminster, 1982.

Carnley, Peter. *The Structure of Resurrection Belief.* Oxford: Clarendon Press, 1987.

Cartlidge, David R. "Transfigurations of Metamorphosis Traditions in the Acts of John, Thomas, and Peter." In *The Apocryphal Acts of Apostles*, 53–66. Edited by Dennis Ronald MacDonald. Semeia, 38. Decatur: Scholars Press, 1986.

Cavallin, Hans Clemens Caesarius. *Life After Death: Paul's Argument for the Resurrection of the Dead in 1 Cor 15. Part I: An Enquiry into the Jewish Background.* Lund, Sweden: CWK Gleerup, 1974.

Chadwick, Henry. *Origen: Contra Celsum. Translated with an Introduction and Notes.* Cambridge: Cambridge Univ. Press, 1965.

Charles, R. H. *Eschatology: The Doctrine of a Future Life in Israel, Judaism, and Christianity. A Critical History.* New York: Schocken, 1970.

Charlesworth, J. H. *The Old Testament Pseudepigrapha.* Two Volumes. Garden City, N.Y.: Doubleday, 1985.

Charlesworth, Martin Percival. "Some Observations on Ruler-Cult Especially in Rome." In *HTR* 38 (1935) 5–44.

Chase, George H. *Greek, Etruscan, and Roman Art: The Classical Collection of the Museum of Fine Arts, Boston.* Revised by Cornelius C. Vermeule III and Mary B. Comstock. Meriden, Conn.: Meriden Gravure Co., 1972.

Chronis, Harry L. "The Torn Veil: Cultus and Christology in Mark 15:37–39." In *JBL* 101 (1982) 97–114.

Clavier, H. "Brèves remarques sur la notion de σῶμα πνευματικόν." In *The Background of the New Testament and Its Eschatology*, 342–362. Edited by W. D. Davies and D. Daube. Cambridge: Cambridge Univ. Press, 1964.

Cobb, John B., Jr. "The Resurrection of the Soul." In *HTR* 80 (1987) 213–227.

Coldstream, J. N. "Hero Cults in the Age of Homer." In *JHS* 96 (1976) 8–17.

Conzelmann, H. *1 Corinthians*. Translated by James W. Leach. Hermeneia Series. Philadelphia: Fortress Press, 1975.

Corrigan, K. "Body and Soul in Ancient Religious Experience." In *Classical Mediterranean Spirituality: Egyptian, Greek, Roman*, 360–383. Edited by A. H. Armstrong. New York: Crossroad, 1986.

Craig, W. L. "The Historicity of the Empty Tomb of Jesus." In *NTS* 31 (1985) 39–67.

Crossan, John Dominic. *In Fragments: The Aphorisms of Jesus*. San Francisco: Harper and Row, 1983.

———. *The Cross That Spoke: The Origins of the Passion Narrative*. San Francisco: Harper and Row, 1988.

Crum, W. *A Coptic Dictionary*. Oxford: Clarendon Press, 1939; reprinted, 1972.

Cullmann, Oscar. *Jesus and the Revolutionaries*. Translated by Gareth Putnam. New York: Harper and Row, 1970.

Cumont, Franz. *After Life in Roman Paganism*. New York: Dover Publications, 1959.

Cunliff, Richard John. *A Lexicon of the Homeric Dialect*. Norman: Univ. of Oklahoma Press, 1963.

Dahl, M. E. *The Resurrection of the Body*. Studies in Biblical Theology 36. London: SCM Press, 1962.

Dahl, Nils Alstrup. "The Passion Narrative in Matthew." In *The Interpretation of Matthew*, 42–55. Edited by Graham Stanton. IRT, 3. London: SPCK and Philadelphia: Fortress Press, 1983.

Dauer, Anton. "Zur Herkunft der Thomas-Perikope Joh 20,24–29." In *Biblische Randbemerkungen: Schülerfestschrift für Rudolph*

*Schnackenburg zum 60. Geburtstag*, 56–76. Edited by Helmut Merklein and Joachim Lange. Würzberg: Echter-Verlag, 1974.

———. *Johannes und Lukas*. FB, 50. Würzberg: Echter-Verlag, 1984.

Davies, Stevan L. *The Gospel of Thomas and Christian Wisdom*. New York: Seabury Press, 1982.

De Jonge, M. "Nicodemus and Jesus: Some Observations on Misunderstanding and Understanding." In *BJRL* 53 (1971) 338–358.

———. "Jewish Expectations About the 'Messiah' According to the Fourth Gospel." In *NTS* 19 (1973) 246–270.

———. "Matthew 27:51 in Early Christian Exegesis." In *Christians among Jews and Gentiles: Essays in Honor of Krister Stendahl on His Sixty-Fifth Birthday*, 67–79. Edited by George W. E. Nickelsburg with George W. MacRae, S. J. Philadelphia: Fortress Press, 1986.

De la Potterie, I. "Parole et Espirit dans S. Jean." In *L'Évangile de Jean: Sources, rédaction, théologie*, 177–201. Edited by M. De Jonge. Louvain: J. Duculot, 1977.

Delling, Gerhard. "The Significance of the Resurrection of Jesus for Faith in Jesus Christ." In *The Significance of the Message of the Resurrection for Faith in Jesus Christ*, 77–104. Studies in Biblical Theology, Second Series, 8. Edited by C. F. D. Moule. Translated by R. A. Wilson. London: SCM, 1968.

Den Boer, W. "Aspects of Religion in Classical Greece." In *HSCP* 77 (1973) 1–21.

De Vaux, Roland. *Ancient Israel*. Two volumes. New York: McGraw-Hill, 1965.

De Vogel, C. J. *Greek Philosophy: A Collection of texts with Notes and Explanations*. Third edition. Leiden: E. J. Brill, 1973.

Diels, Hermann. *Die Fragmente der Vorsokratiker: Griechisch und Deutsch*. Seventh edition. Edited by Walther Kranz. Berlin: Weidmannsche Verlagsbuchhandlung, 1954.

Dodd, C. H. *The Interpretation of the Fourth Gospel*. Cambridge: Cambridge Univ. Press, 1953.

———. *The Parables of the Kingdom*. Revised edition. New York: Charles Scribner's Sons, 1961.

————. *Historical Tradition in the Fourth Gospel*. Cambridge: Cambridge Univ. Press, 1963.

Dodds, E. R. *The Greeks and the Irrational*. Berkeley: Univ. of California Press, 1951.

————. *Plato: Gorgias. A Revised Text with Introduction and Notes*. Oxford: Clarendon Press, 1959.

Donahue, John R. *Are You the Christ? The Trial Narrative in the Gospel of Mark*. Society of Biblical Literature Dissertation Series, 10. Missoula: Univ. of Montana, 1973.

————. "Temple, Trial, and Royal Christology." In *The Passion in Mark: Studies on Mark 14-16*, 61–79. Edited by Werner H. Kelber. Philadelphia: Fortress Press, 1976.

————. *The Theology and Setting of Discipleship in the Gospel of Mark*. Milwaukee: Marquette Univ. Press, 1983.

Doresse, J. *L'Évangile selon Thomas, ou les paroles secrètes de Jésus*. Paris: Librairie Plon, 1959.

Dow, Sterling and Gill, David H., S. J. "The Greek Cult Table." In *AJA* 69 (1965) 103–114.

Drijvers, Han J. W. "Facts and Problems in Early Syriac Speaking Christianity." In *SecCent* 2 (1982) 157–175.

————. "Thomasakten." In Edgar Hennecke, *Neutestamentliche Apokryphen in deutscher Übersetzung*, 289–303. Edited by Wilhelm Schneemelcher. Tübingen: J.C.B. Mohr, 1989.

Dubarle, André-Marie. "Belief in Immortality in the Old Testament and Judaism." In *Immortality and Resurrection*, 34–45. Edited by Pierre Benoit and Roland Murphy. Herder and Herder, 1970.

Edelstein, Ludwig. *The Meaning of Stoicism*. Cambridge, Mass.: Harvard Univ. Press, 1966.

Ehlers, Barbara. "Kann das Thomasevangelium aus Edessa stammen?" In *NovT* 12 (1970) 284–317.

Eichrodt, Walther. *Theology of the Old Testament*. Translated by J. A. Baker. 2 volumes. Philadelphia: Westminster Press, 1967.

Ellis, I. P. "'But Some Doubted.'" In *NTS* 14 (1967–68) 574–580.

Ellis, Peter F. *The Genius of John: A Composition-Critical Commentary on the Fourth Gospel*. Collegeville: Liturgical Press, 1984.

Evans, C. F. *Resurrection and the New Testament*. Studies in Biblical Theology, Second Series, 12. London: SCM Press, 1970.

Ferguson, John. *Plato: Republic Book X*. London: Methuen, 1957.

Filson, F. V. "Who Was the Beloved Disciple?" In *JBL* 63 (1949) 83–88.

Finkelstein, Louis. *The Pharisees: The Sociological Background of Their Faith*. Philadelphia: Jewish Publication Society, 1938.

Fitzmyer, J. A. "The Oxyrhynchus Logoi of Jesus and the Coptic Gospel According to Thomas." In *TS* 20 (1959) 505–560.

Flückiger, F. "Die Redaktion der Zukunftsrede in Markus 13," in *TZ* 26 (1970) 395–409.

Flusser, D. "Two Notes on the Midrash on 2 Sam. vii." In *IEJ* 9 (1959) 99–109.

Foerster, W. "κύριος." In *Theological Dictionary of the New Testament*, 3.1039–1095. Edited by Gerhard Kittel. Translated and edited by Geoffrey W. Bromiley. Grand Rapids: Eerdmans, 1964.

Fortna, Robert T. *The Gospel of Signs*. Society for New Testament Studies Monograph Series, 11. Cambridge: Cambridge Univ. Press, 1970.

Freed, Edwin D. "Did John Write His Gospel Partly to Win Samaritan Converts?" In *NovT* 12 (1970) 241–256.

Frymer-Kensky, Tikva. "Biblical Cosmology." In *Backgrounds for the Bible*, 231–240. Edited by Michael Patrick O'Connor and David Noel Freedman. Winona Lake, Ind.: Eisenbrauns, 1987.

Fuller, Reginald H. *The Formation of the Resurrection Narratives*. Philadelphia: Fortress Press, 1980.

Gardner-Smith, P. *The Narratives of the Resurrection: A Critical Study*. London: Methuen and Co., 1926.

———. *Saint John and the Synoptic Gospels*. Cambridge: Cambridge Univ. Press, 1938.

Garland, Robert. *The Greek Way of Death*. Ithaca, N.Y.: Cornell Univ. Press, 1985.

Gärtner, Bertil. *The Theology of the Gospel According to Thomas*. Translated by Eric J. Sharpe. New York: Harper and Row, 1961.

Gaston, Lloyd. *No Stone on Another: Studies in the Significance of the Fall of Jerusalem in the Synoptic Gospels.* NovTSup, 23. Leiden: E. J. Brill, 1970.

Gill, David, S. J. "*Trapezomata*: A Neglected Aspect of Greek Sacrifice." In *HTR* 67 (1974) 117–137.

Gillabert, Émile; Bourgeois, Pierre; and Haas, Yves. *Évangile selon Thomas.* Paris: Dervy-Livres, 1985.

Gilmore, S. M. "The Christophany to More Than Five Hundred Brethren." In *JBL* 80 (1961) 248–252.

———. "Easter and Pentecost." In *JBL* (1962) 62–66.

Giverson, S. *Thomas Evangeliet.* Copenhagen: Gads, 1959.

Gnilka, Joachim. *Johannesevangelium.* Würzberg: Echter-Verlag, 1983.

Goguel, Maurice. *La foi a la résurrection de Jésus dans le Christianisme primitif.* Paris: Librairie Ernest Leroux, 1933.

Goodenough, Erwin R. "Philo on Immortality." In *HTR* 39 (1946) 85–108.

———. *By Light, Light: The Mystic Gospel of Hellenistic Judaism.* Amsterdam: Philo Press, 1969.

Gordon, Cyrus H. *The Common Background of Greek and Hebrew Civilizations.* New York: W. W. Norton, 1965.

Grant, Robert M. "Athenagoras or Pseudo-Athenagoras." In *HTR* 47 (1954) 121–129.

———; and Freedman, David Noel. *The Secret Sayings of Jesus.* Garden City, N.Y.: Doubleday, 1960.

Grass, H. *Ostergeschehen und Osterberichte.* Göttingen: Vandenhoeck and Ruprecht, 1962.

Grundmann, W. "Das Problem des hellenistischen Christentums innerhalb der Jerusalemer Urgemeinde." In *ZNW* 38 (1939) 45–73.

Guillaume, Jean-Marie. *Luc interprète des anciennes traditions sur la résurrection de Jésus.* Paris: Librairie Lecoffre, 1979.

Guillaumont, A. *et al. The Gospel according to Thomas: Coptic Text Established and Translated.* New York: Harper and Row, 1959.

Gunther, John J. "The Meaning and Origin of the Name 'Judas Thomas.'" In *Mus* 93 (1980) 113–148.

Guthrie, W. K. C. *Orpheus and Greek Religion*. Revised edition. New York: W. W. Norton, 1966.

———. *The Greeks and Their Gods*. Boston: Beacon Press, 1955.

Haenchen, Ernst. *John*. Hermeneia Series. Translated by Robert W. Funk. 2 volumes. Philadelphia: Fortress Press, 1984.

Harnack, Adolf. *Militia Christi: The Christian Religion and the Military in the First Three Centuries*. Translated by David McInnes Gracie. Philadelphia: Fortress Press, 1981.

Harris, Murray J. *Raised Immortal: Resurrection and Immortality in the New Testament*. Grand Rapids: Eerdmans, 1983.

Harrison, Jane. *Prolegomena to the Study of Greek Religion*. Cleveland and New York: World Publishing, 1959.

Hartmann, G. "Die Vorlage der Osterberichte in Joh 20." In *ZNW* 55 (1964) 197–220.

Hauck, Robert J. "'They Saw What They Said They Saw': Sense Knowledge in Early Christian Polemic." In *HTR* 81 (1988) 239–249.

Hauerwas, Stanley. "The Politics of Charity." In *Int* 31 (1977) 251–262.

Hawkin, David J. "The Incomprehension of the Disciples in the Markan Redaction." In *JBL* 91 (1972) 491–500.

Hendrickx, Herman. *The Resurrection Narratives of the Synoptic Gospels*. Revised edition. London: Geoffrey Chapman, 1984.

Hengel, Martin. *Christ and Power*. Translated by Everett R. Kalin. Philadelphia: Fortress Press, 1977.

———. *Judaism and Hellenism*. Translated by John Bowden. Philadelphia: Fortress Press, 1981.

Henrichs, Albert. "The 'Sobriety' of Oedipus: Sophocles *OC* 100 Misunderstood," in *HSCP* 87 (1983) 87–100.

Herford, R. Travers. *The Pharisees*. Boston: Beacon Press, 1962.

Himmelfarb, Martha. *Tours of Hell: An Apocalyptic Form in Jewish and Christian Literature*. Philadelphia: Fortress Press, 1983.

Hinnells, John R. "Zoroastrian Savior Imagery and its Influence on the New Testament." In *Numen* 16 (1969) 161–185.

Hoffmann, R. Joseph. *Marcion: On the Restitution of Christianity. An Essay on the Development of Radical Paulinist Theology in the*

*Second Century.* American Academy of Religion Academy Series, 46. Chico: Scholars Press, 1984.

Hooke, S. H. *The Resurrection of Christ as History and Experience.* London: Darton, Longman and Todd, 1967.

Horbury, William. "The Benediction of the *Minim* and Early Jewish-Christian Controversy." In *JTS* 33 (1982) 19–61.

Horsley, Richard A. *Jesus and the Spiral of Violence: Popular Jewish Resistance in Roman Palestine.* San Francisco: Harper and Row, 1987.

How, W. W. and Wells, J. *A Commentary on Herodotus.* Two Volumes. Oxford: Clarendon Press, 1936.

Hubbard, Benjamin J. *The Matthean Redaction of a Primitive Apostolic Commissioning: An Exegesis of Matthew 28:16–20.* Society of Biblical Literature Dissertation Series, 19. Missoula: SBL and Scholars Press, 1974.

Hunter, A. M. *The Gospel according to John.* Cambridge: Cambridge Univ. Press, 1965.

Hurd, Jr., John C. *The Origin of 1 Corinthians.* Macon: Mercer Univ. Press, 1983.

Hussey, Edward. *The Pre-Socratics.* New York: Charles Scribner's Sons, 1972.

Jaeger, Werner. *Paideia: The Ideals of Greek Culture.* Translated by Gilbert Highet. 3 volumes. Oxford: Oxford Univ. Press, 1943.

———. *The Theology of the Early Greek Philosophers.* Translated by Edward S. Robinson. Oxford: Clarendon Press, 1947.

Jaubert, A. "The Calendar of Qumran and the Passion Narrative in John." In *John and Qumran,* 62–75. Edited by James H. Charlesworth. London: Geoffrey Chapman, 1972.

Jensen, Ellis E. "The First Century Controversy over Jesus as a Revolutionary Figure." In *JBL* 60 (1941) 261–272.

Jeremias, Joachim. *Heiligengräber in Jesu Umwelt* (Göttingen: 1958)

———. *Jerusalem in the Time of Jesus: An Investigation into Economic and Social Conditions during the New Testament Period.* Translated by F. H. and C. H. Cave. Philadelphia: Fortress Press, 1969.

Jonas, Hans. *The Gnostic Religion: The Message of the Alien God and the Beginnings of Christianity.* Second edition, revised. Boston: Beacon Press, 1963.

Kahn, Charles H. "Pythagorean Philosophy Before Plato." In *The Pre-Socratics: A Collection of Critical Essays*, 161–185. Edited by A.P.D. Mourelatos. Garden City, N.Y.: Doubleday, 1974.

Kaiser, Otto, and Lohse, Eduard. *Death and Life.* Translated by John E. Steely. Nashville: Abingdon, 1981.

Karris, Robert J. "Luke 23:47 and the Lukan View of Jesus' Death." In *JBL* 105 (1986) 65–74.

Käsemann, Ernst. "The Disciples of John the Baptist in Ephesus." In idem, *Essays on New Testament Themes*, 136–148. Translated by W.J. Montague. Philadelphia: Fortress Press, 1982.

Kaufmann, Yehezkel. *The Religion of Israel.* Abridged and translated by M. Greenberg. Chicago: Univ. of Chicago Press, 1960.

Kearney, Peter J. "He Appeared to 500 Brothers (1 Cor 15:6)." In *NovT* 22 (1980) 264–284.

Kee, Howard C. "The Testaments of the Twelve Patriarchs." In *The Old Testament Pseudepigrapha*, 1.777–828. Edited by J.H. Charlesworth. Garden City, N.Y.: Doubleday, 1985.

Kelly, J.N.D. *Early Christian Creeds.* Third edition. New York: Longman, 1972.

———. *Early Christian Doctrines.* Revised edition. San Francisco: Harper, 1978.

Kennedy, Charles A. "Early Christians and the Anchor." In *BA* 38 (1975) 115–124.

Kim, Seyoon. *The Origin of Paul's Gospel.* Grand Rapids: Eerdmans, 1981.

Kimelman, Reuven. "*Birkat Ha-Minim* and the Lack of Evidence for an Anti-Christian Jewish Prayer in Late Antiquity." In *Jewish and Christian Self-Definition. Vol. 2: Aspects of Judaism in the Greco-Roman Period*, 226–244. Edited by E.P. Sanders with A.I. Baumgarten and Alan Mendelson. Philadelphia: Fortress Press, 1981.

Kingsbury, Jack Dean. "The Figure of Peter in Matthew's Gospel as a Theological Problem." In *JBL* 98 (1979) 67–83.

Kirchner, D. "Das Buch des Thomas." In *TZ* 102 (1977) 793–804.

Kirk, G. S., Raven, J. E., and Schofield, M. *The Presocratic Philosophers.* Second edition. Cambridge: Cambridge Univ. Press, 1983.

Klijn, A. F. J. *The Acts of Thomas: Introduction, Text and Commentary.* NovTSup, 5. Leiden: E. J. Brill, 1962.

———. "Christianity in Edessa and the Gospel of Thomas." In *NovT* 14 (1972) 70–77.

Koester, Helmut. *Synoptische Überlieferung bei den Apostolischen Vätern.* TU 65. Berlin: Akademie-Verlag, 1957.

———. "*GNOMAI DIAPHORAI*: The Origin and Nature of Diversification in the History of Early Christianity." In James M. Robinson and Helmut Koester, *Trajectories through Early Christianity*, 114–157. Philadelphia: Fortress Press, 1971.

———. *Introduction to the New Testament. Vol. 2: History and Literature of Early Christianity.* Philadelphia: Fortress Press, 1982.

———. "La tradition apostolique et les origines du gnosticisme." In *RTP* 119 (1987) 1–16.

———. "Introduction: The Gospel according to Thomas." In *Nag Hammadi Codex II, 2–7,* 1. 38–49. Nag Hammadi Studies, 20. Edited by Bentley Layton. Leiden: E. J. Brill, 1989.

———. "Les discours d'adieu de l'évangile de Jean: Leur trajectoire au premier et deuxième siècle." In *La Communauté johannique et son histoire: La trajectoire de l'évangile de Jean aux deux premiers siècles,* 269–280. Edited by Jean-Daniel Kaestli et al. Genève: Labor et Fides, 1990.

Kremer, Jacob. *Lazarus: Die Geschichte einer Auferstehung.* Stuttgart: Katholisches Bibelwerk, 1985.

Kroymann, Aem. *Q. S. Fl. Tertulliani. Adversus Marcionem. Corpus Christianorum: Series Latina. Tertulliani Opera: Pars I.* Turnholti: Typographi Brepolis, 1954.

Kuntzmann, Raymond. "L'identification dans le *livre de Thomas l'Athlète*." In *Colloque International sur les textes de Nag Ham-*

*madi: Quebec, 22–25 Aout* 1978, 279–287. Edited by Bernard Barc. Quebec: Laval, 1981.

———. *Le Livre de Thomas: Texte établi et présenté.* Quebec: Laval, 1986.

Kwik, Robert J. "Some Doubted." In *ET* 77 (1966) 181.

LaFargue, J. Michael. *Language and Gnosis: The Opening Scenes of the Acts of Thomas.* Harvard Dissertations in Religion 18. Philadelphia: Fortress Press, 1985.

Lake, Kirsopp. *The Apostolic Fathers.* Loeb Classical Library, 24. Cambridge, Mass.: Harvard Univ. Press, 1975.

Lambdin, Thomas O. "The Gospel according to Thomas." English Translation. In *Nag Hammadi Codex II,* 2–7, 1.53–93. Edited by Bentley Layton. Leiden: E. J. Brill, 1989.

Layton, Bentley. *The Gnostic Scriptures.* Garden City, N.Y.: Doubleday, 1987.

Layton, Bentley, editor. *Nag Hammadi Codex II,* 2–7. 2 volumes. Leiden: E. J. Brill, 1989.

Leaney, A. R. C. "Why There Were Forty Days Between the Resurrection and the Ascension in Acts 1:3." In *SE,* 6.417–419. Edited by F. L. Cross. Berlin: Akademie, 1968.

Leonard, W. E. and Smith, S. B., eds. *T. Lucreti Cari: De Rerum Natura.* Madison: Univ. of Wisconsin Press, 1968.

Lewis, Theodore J. *Cults of the Dead in Ancient Israel and Ugarit.* Harvard Semitic Monographs, 39. Atlanta: Scholars Press, 1989.

Lightstone, Jack N. *The Commerce of the Sacred: Mediation of the Divine Among Jews in the Greco-Roman Diaspora.* BJS, 59. Chico: Scholars Press, 1984.

Lincoln, Andrew T. "The Promise and the Failure — Mark 16:7, 8." In *JBL* 108 (1989) 283–300.

Lincoln, Bruce. "Thomas-Gospel and Thomas Community: A New Approach to a Familiar Text." In *NovT* 19 (1977) 65–76.

Lindars, Barnabas. *The Gospel of John.* New Century Bible. London: Oliphants, 1971.

Lloyd, G. E. R. *Early Greek Science: Thales to Aristotle.* New York and London: W. W. Norton, 1970.

Lloyd-Jones, Hugh. *The Justice of Zeus*. Revised Edition. Berkeley: Univ. of California Press, 1983.

Lohse, Eduard. *History of the Suffering and Death of Jesus Christ*. Translated by Martin O. Dietrich. Philadelphia: Fortress Press, 1967.

———. *Die Texte aus Qumran*. München: Kösel-Verlag, 1971.

Long, A. A. *Hellenistic Philosophy: Stoics, Epicureans, Sceptics*. Second edition. Berkeley: Univ. of California Press, 1986.

Lord, Albert B. *The Singer of Tales*. New York: Atheneum, 1978.

Luz, Ulrich. "The Disciples in the Gospel According to Matthew." In *The Interpretation of Matthew*, 98–128. Edited by Graham Stanton. IRT, 3. London: SPCK and Philadelphia: Fortress Press, 1983.

MacDonald, Dennis Ronald. "Introduction: The Forgotten Novels of the Early Church." In *The Apocryphal Acts of Apostles*, 1–6. Edited by idem. Semeia, 38. Decatur: Scholars Press, 1986.

———. *There is No Male and Female: The Fate of a Dominical Saying in Paul and Gnosticism*. HDR 20. Philadelphia: Fortress Press, 1987.

MacLeod, M. D. *Luciani Opera*. Oxford Classical Texts. Oxford: Clarendon Press, 1972.

MacMullen, Ramsay. *Paganism in the Roman Empire*. New Haven and London: Yale Univ. Press, 1981.

———. *Christianizing the Roman Empire*. New Haven and London: Yale Univ. Press, 1984.

Mahoney, Robert. *Two Disciples at the Tomb: The Background and Message of John 20.1–10*. Theologie und Wirklichkeit, 6. Frankfort am Main and Bern: Peter D. Lang, 1974.

Marchadour, Alain. *Lazare: Histoire d'un récit, Récits d'une histoire*. Paris: Les éditions du Cerf, 1988.

Marcovich, M. "Textual Criticism on the Gospel of Thomas." In *JTS* 20 (1969) 53–74.

Marcus, Ralph. *Philo: Questions and Answers on Genesis*. Supplement 1. Loeb Classical Library, 380. Cambridge, Mass.: Harvard Univ. Press, 1979.

Martin, James P. "History and Eschatology in the Lazarus Narrative: John 11.1–44," in *SJT* 17 (1964) 332–343.

Martin, Luther H. *Hellenistic Religions: An Introduction*. Oxford: Oxford Univ. Press, 1987.

Martin, Ralph P. *Carmen Christi: Philippians 2:5–11 in Recent Interpretation and in the Setting of Early Christian Worship*. Revised edition. Grand Rapids: Eerdmans, 1983

Martin-Achard, Robert. *From Death to Life: A Study of the Development of the Doctrine of the Resurrection in the Old Testament*. Translated by John Penney Smith. Edinburgh and London: Oliver and Boyd, 1960.

Martyn, J. L. "We Have Found Elijah." In *Jews, Greeks and Christians: Religious Cultures in Late Antiquity. Essays in Honor of William David Davies*, 181–219. Edited by Robert Hammerton-Kelly and Robin Scroggs. Leiden: E. J. Brill, 1976.

———. "Glimpses into the History of the Johannine Community." In idem, *The Gospel of John in Christian History*, 90–121. New York: Paulist Press, 1978.

———. *History and Theology in the Fourth Gospel*. Revised and enlarged edition. Nashville: Abingdon, 1979.

Matill, Jr., A. J. "Johannine Communities Behind the Fourth Gospel: Georg Richter's Analysis." In *TS* 38 (1977) 294–315.

Mauer, Chr. "The Gospel of Peter." In Edgar Hennecke, *New Testament Apocrypha*, 1.179–187. Edited by Wilhelm Schneemelcher. English translation by R. McL. Wilson. Philadelphia: Westminster Press, 1963.

McArthur, Harvey K. "'On the Third Day.'" In *NTS* 18 (1971–72) 81–86.

McGehee, Michael. "A Less Theological Reading of John 20:17." In *JBL* 105 (1986) 299–302.

McPolin, James. *John*. Wilmington: Michael Glazier, 1979.

Meeks, Wayne A. "The Man from Heaven in Johannine Sectarianism." In *JBL* 91 (1972) 44–72. Reprinted in *The Interpretation of John*, 141–173. IRT, 9. Edited by John Ashton. Philadelphia: Fortress Press and SPCK: London, 1986.

Ménard, Jacques-É. *L'Évangile selon Thomas*. NHS 5. Leiden: E. J. Brill, 1975.

Metzger, Bruce M. "The Meaning of Christ's Ascension." In *Search the Scriptures: Studies in Honor of R. T. Stamm*, 118–128. Edited by J. M. Meyers, O. Reimherr, and H. N. Bream. Leiden: E. J. Brill, 1969.

————. *A Textual Commentary on the Greek New Testament: A Companion Volume to the United Bible Societies' Greek New Testament (third edition)*. United Bible Societies, 1971.

Meyer, E. *Ursprung und Anfänge des Christentums*. 3 volumes. Stuttgart, 1921.

Meyers, Eric M. "Secondary Burials in Palestine." In *BA* 33 (1970) 91–114.

————. *Jewish Ossuaries: Reburial and Rebirth*. BibOr, 24. Rome: Biblical Institute Press, 1971.

Michel, Otto. "ναός." In *Theological Dictionary of the New Testament*, 4.880–890. Edited by Gerhard Kittel. Translated and edited by Geoffrey W. Bromiley. Grand Rapids: Eerdmans, 1964.

————. "οἶκος, οἰκία." In *Theological Dictionary of the New Testament*, 5.119–134. Edited by Gerhard Kittel. Translated and edited by Geoffrey W. Bromiley. Grand Rapids: Eerdmans, 1964.

————. "The Conclusion of Matthew's Gospel." In *The Interpretation of Matthew*, 30–41. Translated by Robert Morgan. Edited by Graham Stanton. IRT, 3. London: SPCK and Philadelphia: Fortress Press, 1983.

Millar, Fergus. "The Imperial Cult and the Persecutions." In *Le Culte des Soverains dans l'Empire Romain*, 145–175. Edited by Willem den Boer. Geneva: Fondation Hardt, 1973.

Minear, P. "The Beloved Disciple in the Gospel of John." In *NovT* 19 (1977) 105–123.

Monroe, D. B. and Allen, T. W. *Homeri Opera*. Oxford Classical Texts. London: Oxford Univ. Press, 1976.

Morris, Leon. *The Gospel according to John*. Grand Rapids: Eerdmans, 1971.

Mosley, A.W. "Historical Reporting in the Ancient World." In *NTS* 12 (1965–66)10–26.

Moulton, James Hope; and Milligan, George. *The Vocabulary of the Greek Testament Illustrated from the Papyri and Other Non-literary Sources.* Grand Rapids: Eerdmans, 1930. Reprinted 1972.

Murphy-O'Connor, Jerome. "Tradition and Redaction in 1 Cor 15:3–7." In *CBQ* 43 (1981) 582–589.

Mynors, R.A.B. *P. Vergili Maronis Opera.* Oxford Classical Texts. Oxford: Clarendon Press, 1976.

Nagel, Peter. "Thomas der Mitstreiter (zu NHC II, 7: p. 138,8)." In *Mélanges offerts à M. Werner Vycichl. Société d'Égyptologie Genève, Bulletin* 4 (1980) 65–71.

Nagy, Gregory. *The Best of the Achaians: Concepts of the Hero in Archaic Greek Poetry.* Baltimore: Johns Hopkins Univ. Press, 1979.

Nations, Archie Lee. *A Critical Study of the Coptic Gospel according to Thomas.* Ph.D. Dissertation. Vanderbilt University, 1960. Ann Arbor: University Microfilms, 1960.

Nickelsburg, George. *Resurrection, Immortality and Eternal Life in Intertestamental Judaism.* HTS, XXVI. Cambridge, Mass.: Harvard Univ. Press, 1972.

Nikolainen, Aimo T. *Der Auferstehungsglauben in der Bibel und ihrer Umwelt. I: Religionsgeschichtlicher Teil.* Helsinki: Druckerei — A. G. der finnischen Literatur-gesellschaft, 1944.

Nisetich, Frank J. *Pindar's Victory Songs.* Baltimore: Johns Hopkins Univ. Press, 1980.

Nock, A.D. "The Cult of Heroes." In *HTR* 37 (1944) 141–174.

Obach, Robert E. and Kirk, Albert. *A Commentary on the Gospel of John.* New York: Paulist Press, 1981.

Oepke, Albrecht. "ἀνίστημι." In *Theological Dictionary of the New Testament*, 1.368–371. Edited by Gerhard Kittel. Translated and edited by Geoffrey W. Bromiley. Grand Rapids: Eerdmans, 1964.

O'Grady, John F. "Johannine Ecclesiology: A Critical Evaluation." In *BTB* 7 (1977) 36–44.

Onians, Richard Broxton. *The Origins of European Thought.* New York: Arno Press, 1973.

Osborne, Grant R. *The Resurrection Narratives: A Redactional Study.* Grand Rapids: Baker Book House, 1984.

Otto, Ioann. Carol. Theod. *Corpus Apologetarum Christianorum Saeculi Secundi.* Vol. 1: *Iustinus Philosophus et Martyr.* Second edition. Jena, 1847.

Page, Denys. *The Homeric Odyssey.* Westport, Conn.: Greenwood Press, 1976.

Patte, Daniel. *The Gospel According to Matthew: A Structural Commentary on Matthew's Faith.* Philadelphia: Fortress Press, 1987.

Patterson, Stephen J. *The Gospel of Thomas within the Development of Early Christianity.* Doctoral Diss. Claremont Graduate School, 1988.

Pearson, A. C. *Sophoclis Fabulae.* Oxford Classical Texts. London: Oxford Univ. Press, 1975.

Perkins, Pheme. *The Gnostic Dialogue: The Early Church and the Crisis of Gnosticism.* New York: Paulist Press, 1980.

———. *Resurrection: New Testament Witness and Contemporary Reflection.* Garden City, N.Y.: Doubleday, 1984.

Perrin, Norman. "The High Priest's Question and Jesus' Answer (Mark 14:61-62)." In *The Passion in Mark: Studies on Mark 14-16,* 80-95. Edited by Werner H. Kelber. Philadelphia: Fortress Press, 1976.

———. *The Resurrection according to Matthew, Mark, and Luke.* Philadelphia: Fortress Press, 1977.

———. "The Christology of Mark: A Study in Methodology." In *The Interpretation of Mark,* 95-108. Edited by William Telford. IRT, 7. London: SPCK and Philadelphia: Fortress Press, 1985.

Pesch, R. *Die Vision des Stephanus: Apg. 7,55-56 im Rahmen der Apostelgeschichte.* Stuttgarter Bibelstudien, 12. Stuttgart: Katholisches Bibelwerk, 1966.

———. *Naherwartungen: Tradition und Redaktion in Mk 13.* Düsseldorf: Patmosverlag, 1968.

Peterson, Norman R. "Pauline Baptism and 'Secondary Burial.'" In *Christians Among Jews and Gentiles*, 217–226. Edited by George W. E. Nickelsburg and George W. MacRae, S. J. Philadelphia: Fortress Press, 1986.

Peuch, H.-Ch. "Une collection de paroles de Jésus récemment retrouvé: L'Évangile selon Thomas." In *Comptes rendus de l'Académie des Inscriptions et Belles Lettres* (Paris, 1957) 146–166.

————. "The Gospel of Thomas." In Edgar Hennecke, *New Testament Apocrypha*, 1.278–223. Edited by Wilhelm Schneemelcher; English translation by R. McL. Wilson. Philadelphia: Westminster Press, 1963.

Pichler, Karl. *Streit um das Christentum: Der Angriff des Kelsos und die Antwort des Origenes*. Regensburger Studien zur Theologie, 23. Frankfort am Main and Bern: Peter D. Lang, 1980.

Podipara, P. J. *The Thomas Christians*. Bombay: St. Paul Publications, 1970.

Price, S. R. F. "Gods and Emperors: The Greek Language of the Roman Imperial Cult." In *JHS* 104 (1984) 79–95.

Pryke, John. "Eschatology in the Dead Sea Scrolls." In *The Scrolls and Christianity*, 45–57. Edited by Matthew Black. SPCK Theological Collection, 11. London: SPCK, 1969.

Purvis, James D. "The Fourth Gospel and the Samaritans." In *NovT* 17 (1975) 161–198.

Quispel, G. *Makarius, das Thomasevangelium und das Lied von der Perle*. Supplements to *NT*, 15. Leiden: E. J. Brill, 1967.

Renehan, Robert. "The Meaning of ΣΩΜΑ in Homer: A Study in Methodology." In *CSCA* 12 (1979) 269–282.

————. "On the Origins of the Concepts Incorporeality and Immateriality." In *GRBS* 21 (1980) 105–138.

Rengstorf, Karl Heinrich. "δώδεκα." In *Theological Dictionary of the New Testament*, 2.321–328. Edited by Gerhard Kittel. Translated and edited by Geoffrey W. Bromiley. Grand Rapids: Eerdmans, 1964.

Richter, G. "Die Fleischwerdung des Logos im Johannesevangelium." Sections 1–3 in *NovT* 13 (1971) 81–126; sections 4–5 in *NovT* 14 (1972) 257–276.

————. "Präsentische und futurische Eschatologie im 4. Evangelium." In *Gegenwart und kommendes Reich: Schülergabe Anton Vögtle*. Edited by Peter Fiedler and Dieter Zeller. Stuttgart: Katholisches Bibelwerk, 1975.

Ringgren, Helmer. *Israelite Religion*. Translated by D. Green. Philadelphia: Fortress Press, 1966.

Rivkin, Ellis. *A Hidden Revolution*. Nashville: Abingdon, 1978.

Robertson, A. T. *A Grammar of the Greek New Testament in the Light of Historical Research*. Nashville: Broadman, 1934.

Robinson, James M. "Basic Shifts in German Theology." In *Int* 16 (1962) 76–97.

————. "From Jesus to Valentinus (or to the Apostles Creed)." In *JBL* 101 (1982) 5–37.

Robinson, J. A. T. "Elijah, John and Jesus." In *NTS* 4 (1957–58) 263–281.

————. "The Baptism of John and the Qumran Community." In idem, *Twelve New Testament Studies*, 11–27. SBT, 34. London: SCM, 1962.

Rudolph, Kurt. "Zum gegenwärtigen Stand der mandäischen Religionsgeschichte." In *Gnosis und Neues Testament*, 121–148. Edited by Karl-Wolfgang Tröger. Berlin: Gütersloher Verlagshaus, 1973.

————. "Probleme einer Entwicklungsgeschichte der mandäischen Religion." In *Le Origini dello Gnosticismo*, 583–596. Edited by U. Bianchi. Leiden: E. J. Brill, 1967.

————. *Gnosis*. Translation edited by Robert McLaughlin Wilson. San Francisco: Harper and Row, 1983.

Rusten, Jeffrey S. "ΓΕΙΤΩΝ ΗΡΩΣ: Pindar's Prayer to Heracles (N. 7.86–101) and Greek Popular Religion." In *HSCP* 87 (1983) 289–297.

Samburcky, S. *The Physical World of the Greeks*. Princeton: Princeton Univ. Press, 1956.

————. *Physics of the Stoics*. Princeton: Princeton Univ. Press, 1959.

Sanders, E. P. "The Covenant as a Soteriological Category and the Nature of Salvation in Palestinian and Hellenistic Judaism." In

*Jews, Greeks and Christians: Religious Cultures in Late Antiquity,* 11–44. Edited by Robert Hamerton-Kelly and Robin Scroggs. Leiden: E. J. Brill, 1976.

―――. *Jesus and Judaism.* Philadelphia: Fortress Press, 1985.

Sanders, J. N. "Who Was the Disciple Whom Jesus Loved?." In *Studies in the Fourth Gospel,* 72–82. Edited by F. L. Cross. London: A. R. Mowbray, 1957.

Sandmel, Samuel. *Philo of Alexandria: An Introduction.* New York and Oxford: Oxford Univ. Press, 1979.

Säve-Söderbergh, Torgny. "Gnostic and Canonical Gospel Traditions (with Special Reference to the Gospel of Thomas)." In *The Origins of Gnosticism: Colloquium of Messina,* 13–18 *April* 1966, 552–562. Edited by U. Bianchi. Leiden: E. J. Brill, 1970.

Schenke, Hans-Martin. "The Book of Thomas (NHC II.7): A Revision of a Pseudepigraphical Letter of Jacob the Contender." In *The New Testament and Gnosis: Essays in Honor of R. McL. Wilson,* 213–228. Edited by A. H. B. Logan and A. J. M. Wedderburn. Edinburgh: T. and T. Clark, 1983.

―――. "Radikale sexuelle Enthaltsamkeit als hellenistisch-jüdisches Vollkommenheitsideal im Thomas-Buch (NHC II,7)." In *La Tradizione dell' Enkrateia,* 263–291. Edited by Ugo Bianchi. Roma: Edizione dell' Ateneo, 1985.

Schnackenburg, Rudolph. *The Gospel according to St John.* Translated by David Smith and G. A. Kon. 3 volumes. New York: Crossroad, 1987

Schneider, Gerhard. "The political charge against Jesus (Luke 23:2)." In *Jesus and the Politics of his Day,* 403–414. Edited by E. Bammel and C. F. D. Moule. Cambridge: Cambridge Univ. Press, 1984.

Schoedel, William R., editor and translator. *Athenagoras: Legatio and De Resurrectione.* Oxford: Clarendon Press, 1972.

―――. *Ignatius of Antioch.* Hermeneia. Edited by H. Koester. Philadelphia: Fortress Press, 1985.

Schoeps, H. J. *Theologie und Geschichte des Judenchristentums.* Tübingen: J. C. B. Mohr, 1949.

Schou-Pedersen, V. "Überlieferungen über Johannes den Täufer." In *Der Mandäismus*, 206–226. Edited by Geo Widengren. Translated by Almut und Rüdiger Schmitt. *Wege der Forschung*, 167. Darmstadt: Wissenschaftliche Buchgesellschaft, 1982.

Schubert, K. "Biblical criticism criticised: with reference to the Markan report of Jesus' examination before the Sanhedrin." In *Jesus and the Politics of his Day*, 385–402. Edited by E. Bammel and C. F. D. Moule. Cambridge: Cambridge Univ. Press, 1984.

Schürer, Emil. *The History of the Jewish People in the Age of Jesus Christ.* New English edition. Revised and edited by G. Vermes, Fergus Millar and Matthew Black. Edinburgh: T. and T. Clark, 1979.

Schweizer, Eduard. *The Good News According to Matthew.* Translated by David E. Green. Atlanta: John Knox Press, 1975.

––––––. "Matthew's Church." In *The Interpretation of Matthew*, 129–155. Translated by Robert Morgan. Edited by Graham Stanton. IRT, 3. London: SPCK and Philadelphia: Fortress Press, 1983.

Scobie, Charles H. H. "John the Baptist." In *The Scrolls and Christianity*, 58–69. Edited by Matthew Black. SPCK Theological Collection, 11. London: SPCK, 1969.

Segal, J. B. *Edessa 'The Blessed City.* Oxford: Clarendon Press, 1970.

Seidensticker, P. *Die Auferstehung Jesu in der Botschaft der Evangelisten.* BS, 26. Stuttgart: Katholisches Bibelwerk, 1967.

––––––. "Das Antiochenische Glaubensbekenntnis I Kor. 15, 3–7 im Lichte seiner Traditionsgeschichte." In *TGl* 57 (1967) 286–323.

Sell, J. *The Knowledge of the Truth—Two Doctrines: The Book of Thomas the Contender and the False Teachers in the Pastoral Epistles.* Frankfurt a. M.: Lang, 1982.

Simon, Marcel. *Jewish Sects at the Time of Jesus.* Translated by James H. Farley. Philadelphia: Fortress Press, 1967.

Sjöberg, Eric. "πνεῦμα, πνευματικός: C. III. רוח in Palestinian Judaism." In *Theological Dictionary of the New Testament*, 6.375–389. Edited by Gerhard Friedrich. Translated and edited by Geoffrey W. Bromiley. Grand Rapids: Eerdmans, 1968.

Smith, D. Moody. "The Milieu of the Johannine Miracle Source: A Proposal." In *Jews, Greeks and Christians: Religious Cultures in Late Antiquity: Essays in Honor of William David Davies,* 164–180. Edited by Robert Hamerton-Kelly and Robin Scroggs. Leiden: E. J. Brill, 1976.

Smith, Jonathan Z. "The Garments of Shame." In *HR* 5 (1966) 217–238.

Smith, Mark S. *The Early History of God.* San Francisco: Harper and Row, 1990.

Smith, Robert Houston. "The Tomb of Jesus." In *BA* 30 (1967) 74–90.

Smith, Terence V. *Petrine Controversies in Early Christianity.* Tübingen: J. C. B. Mohr, 1985.

Smyth, Herbert W. *Greek Grammar.* Revised by Gordon M. Messing. Cambridge, Mass.: Harvard Univ. Press, 1956.

Snell, Bruno. *The Discovery of the Mind in Greek Philosophy and Literature.* Translated by T. G. Rosenmeyer. New York: Dover, 1982.

Snyder, Graydon F. *Ante Pacem: Archaeological Evidence of Church Life Before Constantine.* Mercer: Mercer Univ. Press, 1985.

Stemberger, Günter. *Der Leib der Auferstehung: Studien zur Anthropologie und Eschatologie des palästinischen Judentums im neutestamentlichen Zeitalter (ca. 170 v. Cr. − 100 n. Chr.).* Rome: Biblical Institute Press, 1972.

Sylva, Dennis D. "The Temple Curtain and Jesus' Death in the Gospel of Luke." In *JBL* 105 (1986) 239–250.

Tabor, James D. "'Returning to the Divinity': Josephus' Portrayal of the Disappearances of Enoch, Elijah, and Moses." In *JBL* 108 (1989) 225–238.

Tannehill, Robert C. "The Disciples in Mark: The Function of a Narrative Role." In *JR* 57 (1977) 386–405.

Taylor, Vincent. *The Gospel according to St. Mark.* London: Macmillan, 1952.

Teeple, Howard M. "The Historical Beginnings of the Resurrection Faith." In *Studies in New Testament and Early Christian Literature: Essays in Honor of Allen P. Wikgren,* 107–120. NovTSup, 33. Edited by David Edward Aune. Leiden: E.J.Brill, 1972.

Thackeray, H. St. J. *Josephus*. Loeb Classical Library, vol. 203. Cambridge, Mass.: Harvard Univ. Press, 1926.

Theissen, Gerd. *Sociology of Early Palestinian Christianity*. Translated by John Bowden. Philadelphia: Fortress Press, 1978.

Thyen, Hartwig. "Entwicklungen innerhalb der johannischen Theologie und Kirche im Spiegel von Joh. 21 und der Lieblingsjüngertexte des Evangeliums." In *L'Évangile de Jean: Sources, rédaction, théologie*, 259–299. Edited by M. De Jonge. Louvain: J. Duculot, 1977.

Tissot, Yves. "Les actes de Thomas, exemple de recueil composite." In *Les Actes apocryphes de Apôtres: Christianisme et monde païen*, 223–232. Edited by F. Bovon, *et al.* Publication de la faculté de théologie de l'Université de Genève, 4. Geneva: Labor et Fides, 1981.

Titus, E. L. "The Identity of the Beloved Disciple." In *JBL* 69 (1950) 323–328.

Toynbee, J. M. C. *Death and Burial in the Roman World*. Ithaca: Cornell University Press, 1971.

Turner, John D. "A New Link in the Syrian Judas Thomas Tradition." In *Essays on the Nag Hammadi Texts in Honor of Alexander Böhlig*, 109–119. Edited by Martin Krause. Nag Hammadi Studies, 3. Leiden: E. J. Brill, 1972.

———. *The Book of Thomas the Contender*. SBLDS, 23. Missoula: Scholars Press, 1975.

———. "The Book of Thomas the Contender Writing to the Perfect: Introduction." In *Nag Hammadi Codex II, 2–7*, 2.173–178. Edited by Bentley Layton. Leiden: E. J. Brill, 1989.

Turner, Nigel. *A Grammar of New Testament Greek*. Edited by J. H. Moulton. Edinburgh: T. and T. Clark, 1963.

Tyson, J.B. "The Blindness of the Disciples in Mark." In *JBL* 80 (1961) 261–268.

Ussishkin, David. "The Necropolis from the Time of the Kingdom of Judah at Silwan, Jerusalem." In *BA* 33 (1970) 34–46.

Van Iersel, Bas. "The Resurrection of Jesus — Information or Interpretation?" Translated by Theo Westow. In *Immortality and*

*Resurrection*, 54–67. Edited by Pierre Benoit and Roland Murphy. Herder and Herder, 1970.

Vawter, Bruce. "Intimations of Immortality and the Old Testament." In *JBL* 91 (1972) 145–157.

Vermes, Geza. *The Dead Sea Scrolls: Qumran in Perspective*. Revised edition. Philadelphia: Fortress Press, 1981.

Vermeule, Emily. *Aspects of Death in Early Greek Art and Poetry*. Berkeley: Univ. of California Press, 1979.

Vielhauer, P. "Jewish-Christian Gospels." In Edgar Henneke, *New Testament Apocrypha*, 1.117–165. Edited by Wilhelm Schneemelcher. Translated by R. McL. Wilson. Philadelphia: Westminster Press, 1964.

Visser, Margaret. "Worship Your Enemy: Aspects of the Cult of Heroes in Ancient Greece." In *HTR* 75 (1982) 403–28.

Walls, A. F. "The References to Apostles in the Gospel of Thomas." In *NTS* 7 (1960–61) 266–270.

Weeden, Sr., Theodore J. "The Heresy that Necessitated Mark's Gospel." In *ZNW* 59 (1968) 145–158.

———. "The Cross as Power in Weakness (Mark 15:20b-41)." In *The Passion in Mark: Studies on Mark* 14–16, 115–134. Edited by Werner H. Kelber. Philadelphia: Fortress Press, 1976.

Weltin, E. G. *Athens and Jerusalem: An Interpretive Essay on Christianity and Classical Culture*. American Academy of Religion Studies in Religion, 49. Atlanta: Scholars Press, 1987.

Westcott, B. F.; and Hort, J. F. A. *The New Testament in the Original Greek. Vol. 1: Text. Vol. 2: Introduction [and] Appendix*. Cambridge and London: Macmillan and Company, 1881. Second edition of volume 2, 1896.

Westcott, B. F. *The Gospel according to St. John*. New impression. London: John Murray, 1908.

Widengren, Geo. "Iran and Israel in Parthian Times with Special Regard to the Ethiopic *Book of Enoch*." In *Religious Syncretism in Antiquity: Essays in Conversation with Geo Widengren*, 85–129. Edited by Birger A. Pearson. Missoula: Scholars Press, 1975.

Wilckens, Ulrich. *Resurrection. Biblical Testimony to the Resurrec-*

*tion: An Historical Examination and Explanation.* Translated by A. M. Stewart. Atlanta: John Knox Press, 1978.

Wilkins, Michael J. *The Concept of Disciple in Matthew's Gospel as Reflected in the Use of the Term Μαθητής.* Leiden: E. J. Brill, 1988.

Williams, David Salter. "Reconsidering Marcion's Gospel." In *JBL* 108 (1989) 477–496.

Wilson, R. McL. *Studies in the Gospel of Thomas.* London: A. R. Mowbray, 1960.

Wilson, Thomas. *St. Paul and Paganism.* Edinburgh: T. and T. Clark, 1927.

Wolfson, Harry Austryn. *Philo: Foundations of Religious Philosophy in Judaism, Christianity, and Islam.* 2 volumes. Second printing, revised. Cambridge, Mass.: Harvard Univ. Press, 1948.

Wright, R. B. "Psalms of Solomon." In *The Old Testament Pseudepigrapha*, 2.639–670. Edited by J. H. Charlesworth. Garden City, N.Y.: Doubleday, 1985.

Yoder, John Howard. *The Politics of Jesus.* Grand Rapids: Eerdmans, 1972.

# Index of Ancient Sources

## Early Jewish Literature

## Early Christian Literature

## Nag Hammadi Tractates

# Index of Modern Authors